ENGLISH CREWEL DESIGNS

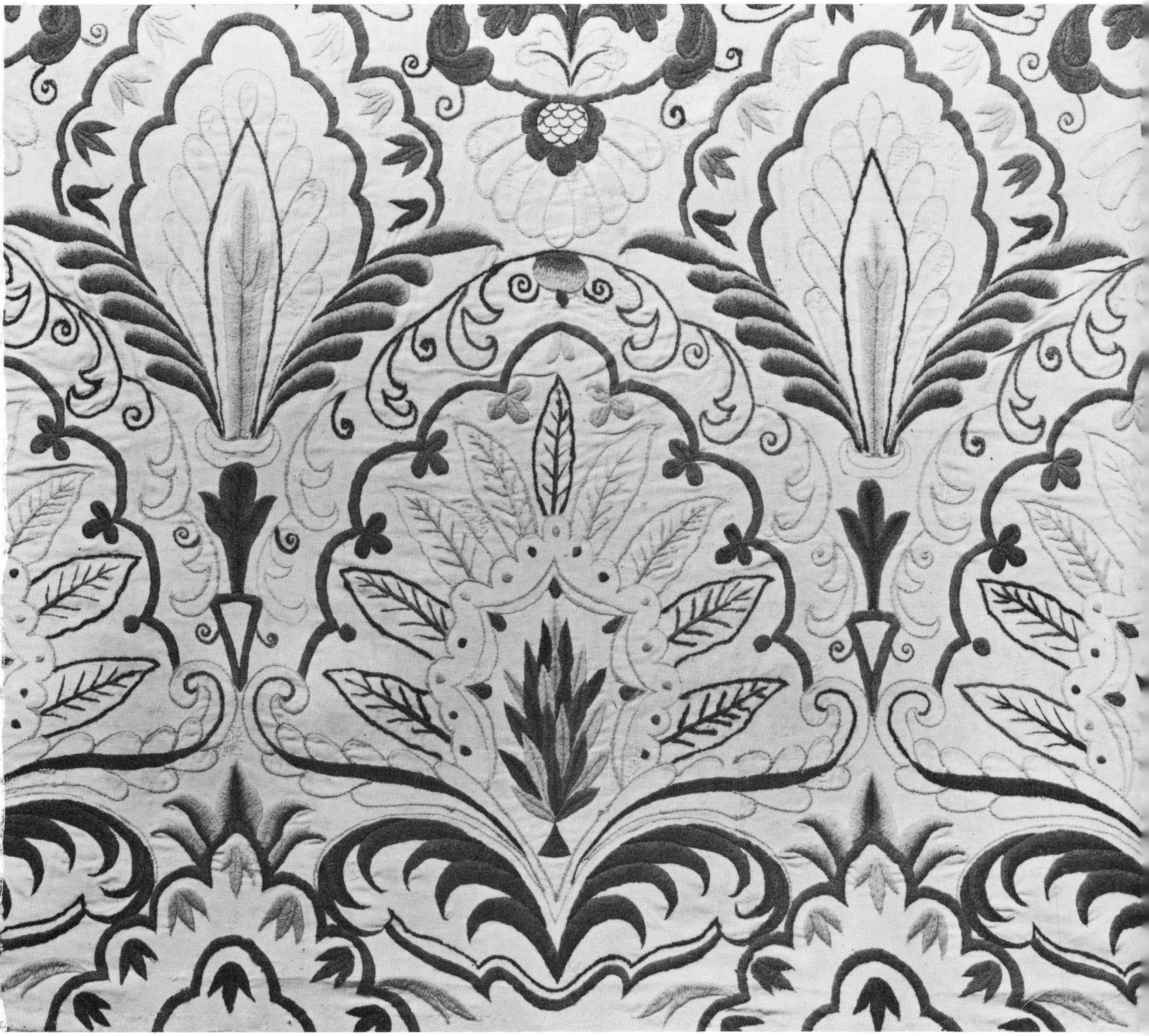

ENGLISH CREWEL DESIGNS

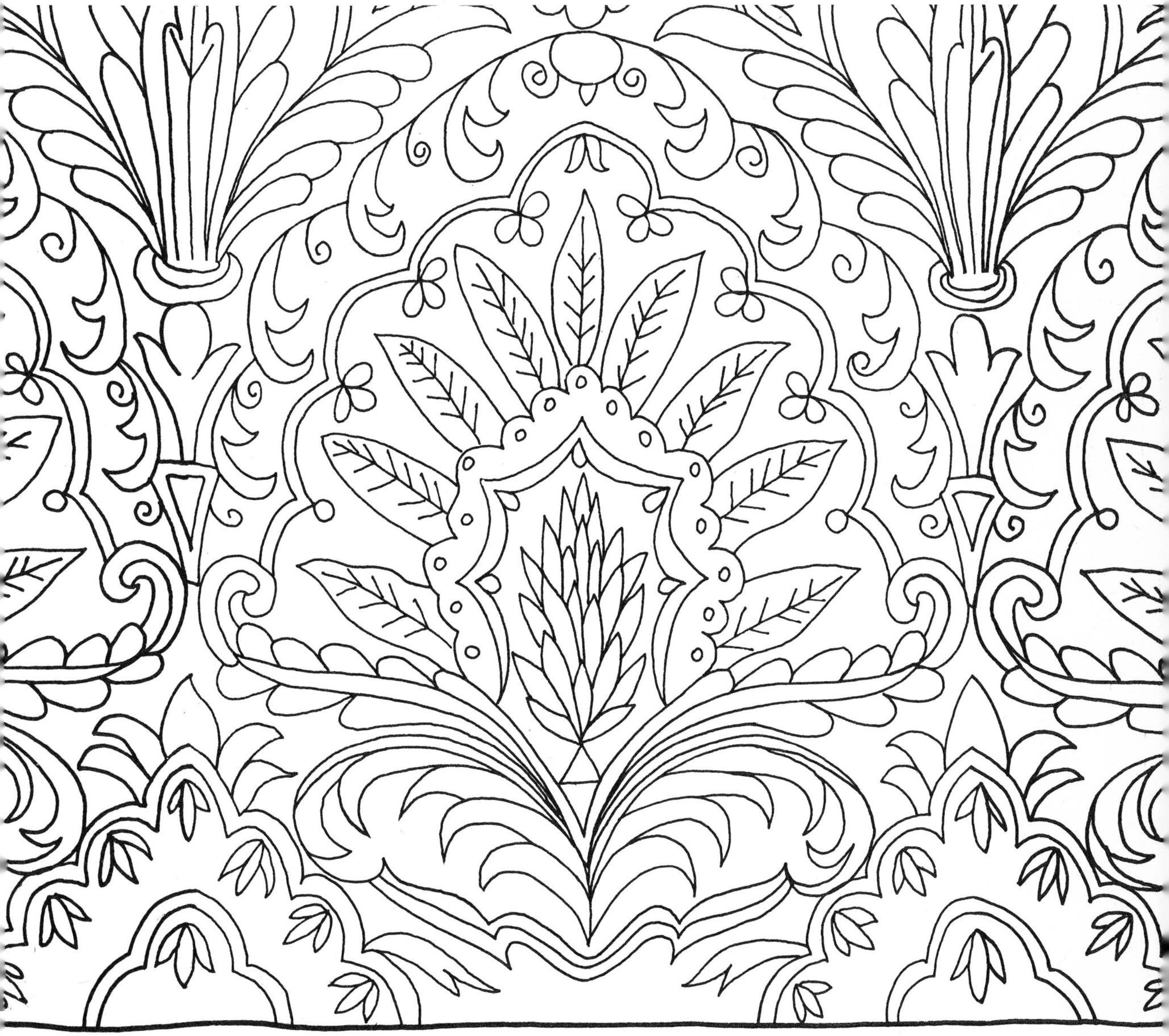

Mary Eirwen Jones

William Morrow & Company, Inc. New York

ISBN 0–688–00288–9

Produced by Walter Parrish International Limited, London

Printed in Great Britain

Designed and drawn by Judy A Tuke

Library of Congress Catalog Card Number 74–7633

Contents

Introduction 7

History 8

Using the designs 14

STITCHES 18

Outline stitches
Outline and stem 18
Running 18
Back 18
Split 18
Lacing 18

Flat stitches
Satin 19
Long and short 19
Roumanian 19
Herringbone 19
Cross 20
Blanket and buttonhole 20
Feather 20

Looped stitches
Cretan 20

Chain stitches
Chain 21
Detached chain 21

Knotted stitches
French knot 21
Bullion 21
Coral 22

Couching and filling stitches
Couching 22
Jacobean couching 22
Seeding 22
Brick 22
Laid work 22

DESIGNS 23

Panels 25

Motifs 42

Foliage 58

Birds and animals 76

Flowers 92

Tree of Life 122

Borders 148

List of illustrations 157

Acknowledgements 159

Further reading 160

Preface

This book is a unique and beautiful collection of historic English crewel designs selected from museums and private collections throughout England. Crewel work has been a practical and decorative art for many hundreds of years, and remains today one of the most popular of the needlecrafts on both sides of the Atlantic.

Yet there has been little to show even the English embroiderer the varied work of her country. Until now, books have concentrated on general techniques, and in the United States the emphasis has been almost entirely on the less elaborate and less sophisticated American crewel, with only brief mention of the fact that English crewel is its prototype and inspiration. An abundance of English pieces dating as far back as the 16th century still exist today, and many of the most interesting of these are presented here.

The introductory text gives a concise history of the subject, followed by an explanation of how to use the designs, some useful hints, and short descriptions of the basic stitches.

It is hoped that with the help of this book the crewel worker of today can use this marvellously rich heritage to create with her needle the heirlooms of tomorrow.

Introduction

Crewel work is a form of embroidery (ornamental needlework) that is done in wool on a coarse-grained material. The word 'crewel' refers to the type of wool used—a special worsted yarn of two twisted strands. In the very early days it seems that crewels were also used for making tapestries and even lace. Their characteristic soft, muted colours were derived from home-made dyes, most of which can be duplicated today.

Old specimens of crewel embroidery show much originality in design. Many were inspired by nature—by flowers, fruits, insects, birds, and animals. Patterns were sometimes used but, even then, individual flourishes gave a free and graceful effect. Sometimes an element of humour was introduced by figures and symbols that were totally out of perspective. Eventually, designs became more stylized, and with the establishment of trading routes came an injection of eastern culture.

Crewel embroidery decorated upholstery, dress, and personal accessories. Although large frames were used, most embroiderers worked on small sections that could be sewn together later. Original Tudor and Stuart specimens are greatly treasured, for much wool stitchery has been lost through time and hard wear. Fortunately, old crewel designs are often found in silk embroidery that has been preserved with care.

The background materials changed with time. Some of the earlier ones were velvets and brocades; then linen, weft with a cotton twill, and wool, were used; and later a preference was shown for fairly stiff materials such as crash or oatmeal cloth. Crewel embroidery is always most effective on pliable yet reasonably solid material that resists puckering.

To the modern crewel worker stitches fall into four basic groups that are derived from back, knot or coral, running, and loop stitches. Some of the early ones cannot be identified without unpicking them, but this method is not permissible to the research worker.

With such a long history, it is not surprising that designs, stitchery, and colours have become largely traditional. Like all embroidery, crewel work has been subject to the vagaries of fashion, but interest in it has never been wholly eclipsed. Its wide variety of stitches, subtle colour harmonies, and scope for individual creativity have ensured its continued wide and ever increasing appeal.

History

There is some evidence of stitchery in wool dating back to the ancient Egyptians and Greeks, and several biblical references imply that the valuable curtains in the Jewish tabernacles were embroidered in wool, but, due to its perishable nature, the exact origin of wool embroidery is lost in antiquity.

Women at all times and in all spheres of life are known to have recorded in embroidery the exploits of their kindred and the outstanding events of their time. Although the Bayeux Tapestry is certainly not an isolated example of such work, it must surely be one of the most famous. In seventy-two lively and interesting scenes this wall hanging gives a pictorial account of the Norman Conquest of England (1066). It measures over 230 feet long and almost 20 inches wide, and was worked in six sections, the joins being covered by stitchery. Eight shades of wool are used: three greens, two blues, red, yellow, and buff. (When it was restored in 1842 some new colours were introduced.) The legend that runs under the pictures, the outlines, and some details are worked in outline and stem stitch; and the laid and couched work used for the solid embroidery is both effective and economical. In his *Short History of the English People* J. H. Green pays tribute to the Bayeux Tapestry: 'Stitch work must tell its own tale simply and straightforwardly; it cannot lose itself in the rhetoric of Eadward's biographer or in the invective of William of Poitiers [the chronicler of the Norman court], and the tale the Tapestry tells comes infinitely nearer the genuine English story than it does even to the narrative of the Conqueror's laureate.' In short, it is a diary written with the needle.

The English ecclesiastical embroideries (*Opus Anglicanum*) of the 10th century onwards were rich in gold and jewels and held pride of place in Europe. They doubtless had secular counterparts that used wool instead of silk and metallic threads —liberal use had long been made in Europe of worsted yarns for ornamentation, and weaver's clippings of long-staple worsted, called crewels, were reasonably cheap and easily obtained. By the beginning of the 14th century a great variety of fabrics had been introduced into Europe. Among the most popular was fustian, first made in Fustat (Cairo); it had the warp of linen and weft of cotton twill.

When the terrible plagues swept across the western world, not only England's culture but also her economy, including the wool trade, suffered very badly. However, in the climate of great cultural revival of the Renaissance, attention was again turned to embroidery. Crewel work as a specific form began to flourish in England in the 16th and early 17th centuries. The modern needle was probably introduced into England from China, and although the exact date is not known, steel needles were being manufactured in the country by 1545.

During Elizabeth I's reign (1558–1603) life became in many ways kinder and more luxurious. The manor house had replaced the draughty fortress castle, and the growing middle classes built comfortable town and country houses. More women turned their hand to the creative arts, including embroidery. They made carpets for floors and tables; cushions and coverlets for the somewhat uncomfortable and massive Tudor chairs, benches, and window seats; wall hangings designed to warm and brighten the dark rooms; and bed hangings comprised of curtains, valance, and canopy. Their jackets, waistcoats, bodices, and smocks, as well as bags, purses, and book covers, were lavishly embroidered with floral designs. Silk for needlework was expensive and had to be imported from the Levant, but wool was readily obtained at home and was often spun by the needlewoman herself. Crewel work done on a large scale had a well-recognized intrinsic worth: embroidered curtains, cushions, costumes, and accessories represented the labour and skill of many years and their value is mentioned in old inventories and wills.

Linen hanging embroidered with coloured wools from the burying ground at Shuik Shata, Lower Egypt, 4th to 5th century AD. Of interest is the scroll or projecting border. The work is done mainly in satin, outline, and chain stitches.

Crown copyright, Victoria and Albert Museum, London

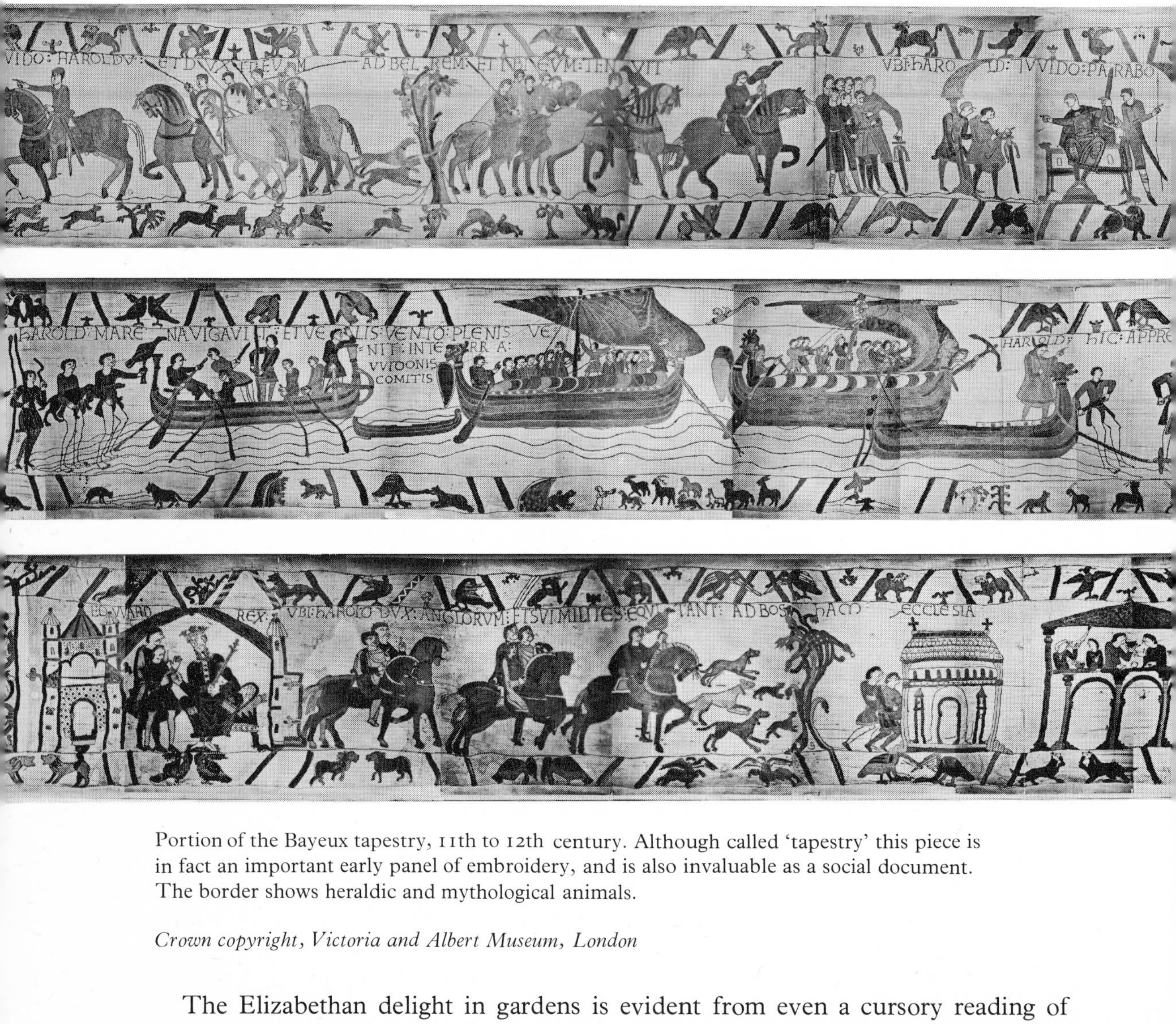
REX
ECCLESIA

Portion of the Bayeux tapestry, 11th to 12th century. Although called 'tapestry' this piece is in fact an important early panel of embroidery, and is also invaluable as a social document. The border shows heraldic and mythological animals.

Crown copyright, Victoria and Albert Museum, London

The Elizabethan delight in gardens is evident from even a cursory reading of Shakespeare. The flora of the neighbouring countryside—the carnation, daffodil, narcissus, marigold, pansy, and tulip—all inspired designs and were treated naturistically by the needlewoman. The humbler flowers of the field and hedgerow were also depicted, such as the cornflower, primrose, violet, cowslip, daisy, and forget-me-not. Herbs were greatly valued by the Elizabethans as Tusser's *Book on Husbandrie* testifies, and embroidery designs of the time incorporated rosemary and rue, lavender, germander, and thyme. Fruits had their place too: nuts and acorns, currants, the more exotic pomegranate, and the newly acclaimed potato plant and strawberry. At times, imaginative flowers, herbs and fruit were shown that no botanist could ever identify!

With the invention of printing, patterns became available to everyone. The new herbals and bestiaries that circulated all over Europe contained clear, clean-cut illustrations that needlewomen were swift to copy. Foreign and legendary animals were pictured, along with the more familiar creatures of field and fen: the rabbit, fox, squirrel, stag, raven, falcon, and owl, and smaller creatures and insects, such as the moth, dragonfly, caterpillar, and beetle.

The renowned East India Company was founded in 1600 and trade with the Orient became a direct and, in many ways, a powerful influence. Rich imported fabrics brought a cornucopia of exotic images. Taoist and Buddhist emblems introduced a galaxy of strange new flowers, most of which were depicted with strong realism, but some were treated symbolically: spring was symbolized by the magnolia and the peony, summer by the lotus flower, autumn by the chrysanthemum, and winter by the rose and prunus.

During the Stuart period that followed, the East India Company's trade increased. Shiploads of painted cottons called palampores were imported into England from India and their polychrome designs greatly inspired crewel workers. Oriental motifs became familiar in the West, such as the Tree of Life in its various forms, the scroll, the wave, the hillock, and leaves and flowers, both natural and fantastic, but in the main they had lost their traditional significance.

There were also other influences that affected embroidery. Curtains for various purposes were now made out of light-coloured, washable materials. These proved more acceptable than the heavy velvets and brocades of earlier times, and were worked chiefly in coloured worsteds, although there were some monochrome designs. The popularity of flower motifs continued, in particular the tulip, tulip rose, harebell, Canterbury bell, foxglove, carnation, and pansy. Honeysuckle was a useful and adaptable subject with its trailing stem, and peacocks and birds of paradise were welcomed for their colour and lustre.

In 1624 a pattern book was published—Richard Shoreleyker's *A Schole-House for the Needle*—which proved to be extremely popular, for by 1640 it was in its twelfth edition. In the prefatory poem to his book *The Needle's Excellency*, John Taylor, the Water Poet, gives an illuminating list of stitches in use at the time:

> For tent worke, raised worke, first worke, laid worke, net worke,
> Most curious purl or rare Italian cut worke,
> Fire, ferne stitch, finny stitch, new stitch, chain stitch,
> Brave bred stitch, fisher stitch, Irish stitch and Queen stitch.
> The Spanish stitch, Rosemary stitch and mowle stitch.
> The smarting whip stitch, back stitch and cross stitch;
> All these are good, and this we must allow
> And they are everywhere in practice now.

The Stuart era was temporarily interrupted by the Puritan austerity of the Commonwealth; although embroidery was still regarded as an admirable feminine pursuit, its use and motifs were much restrained. During the Restoration, when the monarchy was re-established, the acorn and the oak, symbols of Charles I, were often used. Upholstered furniture became fashionable so crewel work concentrated on curtains, bed hangings, and valances. Lace and ribbon were used extravagantly on costume, but crewel work, particularly scroll designs, was still greatly valued. In general it became lighter and more delicate: with the greater skills now acquired, effective use could be made of fewer stitches, and this was particularly so in large pieces. Outline (or stem) stitches, herringbone, coral, and knot stitches all remained very popular, and subtle shading was introduced by long and short stitch. Intelligent use of colour involved fewer shades being used; in fact much work was monochromatic.

Around this time the first English settlers were arriving in America. Over the generations the English patterns they had taken with them developed their own characteristic appearance. The lighter, more open designs used less wool (still scarce in the colonies) and the dyes were home-made. Indigenous plants and animals were depicted, and also scenes of the new way of life in a young and unknown country. However, even in the 18th and 19th centuries the traditions of English crewel design still formed the basis of American needlework.

Royal patronage and practice continued under Queen Anne, but gradually gros point and petit point became more popular for upholstery because the solidly covered canvas wore better than surface work. Delight in embroidering flowers persisted. An old pamphlet, *Wild Flowers and Birds as Seen on 18th Century Needlework*, states:

When Dame Flora
In die Aurora
Had covered the meadow with flowers
And all the fylde
Was over dystylde
With lucky Aprill showers
For my disporte
Me to comforte
Whan the day began to springe
Foorth I went
With a great intent
To hear the byrdes sing.

The poem goes on to speak of the 'birds praising Our Lord without discord, the popyngay, the mavys, partryge, pecocke, thrushe, nyghtyngale, larke, egle, dove, phenix, wren, the tyrtle trew, the hawke, the pelly cane, the swalowe, all singing in quaint blending of Latin and English the praises of God.' The value of such an inventory is not only in its reference to contemporary embroidery but in its direct inspiration to designers of later centuries.

In the 19th century, novelties such as Berlin wool work, bead work, and embroidered pictures became fashionable. Somehow crewel survived this Victorian enthusiasm for what was called 'fancy art needlework', and with the beginning of the Arts and Craft movement at the close of the century, traditional and modern designs were worked again, not on linen but on grounds of wool, silk, or velvet. To meet this unexpected demand several books were produced: Miss Turner's *Practical Hints on the Revived Art of Crewel and Silk Embroidery* (1877); Zeta's *Crewel Work: Fifteen Designs in Bold and Conventional Character* (1879); and Hatchards published a series on the subject. Design was influenced by William Morris and Lewis F. Day. Morris revived the best traditions of crewel work: his large flowing designs were often based on Elizabethan and Jacobean originals, and they used soft, natural colours based on the old vegetable dyes.

Earlier this century crewel and other handcrafts lost their popular appeal. However, in recent years, there has been the most tremendous upsurge of interest and enthusiasm. English and American needlewomen are rediscovering the satisfaction and pleasure gained from creating beautiful yet useful objects with a piece of material, a needle, and a 'handful of cruell'.

Using the designs

This book has been planned so that beginners as well as experts can create their own crewel designs using traditional patterns that can be adapted to almost any requirement.

The fifty photographs show some fine examples of English crewel work; they are arranged in sections and illustrate over one hundred designs that have been in use at different times. The drawings give details of the designs, which can be used alone or linked with other motifs to make up a larger pattern. Individual stitches are shown clearly so that traditional techniques may be followed as accurately as possible, but of course the outlines could be filled in any way one chooses. The designs can be reproduced in the same size as the drawings or they can be enlarged or reduced by means of the grey background grid (alternatively a local photocopying firm will do this).

Transferring the Designs

To transfer a design onto the working material, a tracing of it has first to be made on paper, and this in turn is transferred onto the material (see below). If it is to be the same size as the drawing, it can be traced directly onto the paper, but if the size is to be changed, the grid (or, if available, photocopiers) must be used.

The half-inch grid is a very easy way to enlarge or reduce a design. First decide on the exact size required. On a separate piece of paper draw a second grid to this size, but with the same number of squares as the printed grid. For example, if the design is to be reduced to half its size, when the second grid is drawn the lines will be found to be a $\frac{1}{4}$ inch apart; similarly if the design is enlarged to twice its size the lines will be one inch apart.

With a fairly soft pencil, copy the design and stitches from within each square of the original onto the corresponding square of the second grid. Reducing to a very small scale will leave room only for outlines, while a very much enlarged drawing may need additional filling stitches to add detail.

Once a paper trace of the design is obtained it can then be transferred onto the material in one of three ways.

The first and simplest method is to use dressmaker's carbon paper. Pin the tracing on top of the material along two adjacent sides. Slip a sheet of carbon between them, carbon side down, and pin the tracing, carbon, and material along the remaining two sides. (Use dark carbon for a light ground and white carbon for a dark ground.)

Make sure they are all perfectly flat and, working on a firm surface, trace the design onto the material. For a large piece that has no closely spaced lines or details use a tracing wheel; for more detailed work use a sharp medium-hard pencil, knitting needle, or similar pointed instrument, but be careful not to tear the pattern if it is to be used again.

In the second method, pin the tracing paper to the material and loosely baste along all the main outlines with a coloured silk thread. Snip the stitches and pull off the paper, leaving the design marked by the silk thread (which is removed after the embroidery is finished). With a complicated design this method can be a little tedious, especially if the stitches are to be followed as well.

The third method is the oldest but is still useful when the fabric will not take carbon easily. Trace the design onto art paper and lay it flat on a pin-up board made of cork or similar material (or a thick piece of felt may be used but it must be stretched over a flat surface). Prick the paper along the design lines with the point of a needle whose blunt end is held in a cork. Work as evenly as possible, keeping the holes close together, but not so close that the paper tears. Then rub the back of the drawing very lightly with fine sandpaper or glass paper to smooth away any pieces that have been pushed through the holes. Pin the pricked drawing to the material and use a black-board eraser or a folded piece of felt to rub powdered charcoal through the holes (for dark grounds use powdered chalk). Lift off the pattern carefully, and an outline of tiny dots will be seen on the material. The dots will disappear as soon as they are touched, so go over them with Indian ink, Chinese white, or acrylic paint, and blow off any remaining chalk or charcoal. (Felt-tip pens are not recommended as they can cause smudging.)

Some useful hints

1 An embroidery frame is a good investment, as well-stretched material is easier to handle. Frames come in different kinds and sizes, but a medium-sized one is best for a beginner.

2 Any fabric that will not pucker may be used, but a neutral ground of unbleached linen or twill is traditional, especially for 17th- and 18th-century designs. Remember that the better the fabric the longer it will last.

3 Hands should always be kept clean and the embroidery protected between workings with cotton or plastic.

4 A pair of sharp scissors is essential; when threading a needle or finishing off always *cut* the wool.

5 Special cases are available for keeping the skeins separate and untangled but, alternatively, they can be placed between the pages of a notebook held together by a rubber band.

6 Crewel needles come in various sizes, so choose one with an eye large enough for the wool to pass through without strain: a large one will be needed for double threads, a fine one for working minute details. Blunt tapestry needles are useful for interlacing, laid work, and couching.

7 Thread the needle with the end of the wool just cut off from the skein. To prevent fraying and reduce handling avoid cutting too long a thread (a good idea is to keep a supply of needles threaded in advance).

8 It is very important not to draw the stitches too tightly as this will cause puckering.

9 When starting or finishing off a thread, make a few running stitches at the back (knots cause bumps).

10 Colour harmony is important and, traditionally, brilliant and harsh tones should be avoided. Early crewel work is rich in well-blended shades and has an even distribution of colour over the whole work (these colours are available today in the crewel wool ranges of Paterson and Appleton). Often, colour is interchangeable, but, if this is done, the relative tones values in the design should be closely followed.

11 Shading is a matter of individual taste but a sound rule is not to employ too many shades in one piece. Light and dark effects can be achieved with variations in stitches (for example, satin stitch on one half of a leaf and back stitch or seeding on the other) or by using light and dark wool. 'Painting' with two closely related shades gives a more delicate appearance, and long and short stitch is ideal for blending the stitches into each other imperceptibly.

12 Padding stitches can be used to give a raised effect that will add variety to a work. Coarse cotton or wool is best for outlining flowers and leaves before they are sewn (usually in satin or buttonhole stitch), and loose, short running stitches can fill vacant spaces.

13 Stitch direction is important and has a pronounced effect. The shape of petals or leaves usually suggests the way for the stitches to run—across, diagonally, in two directions forming a V, and so on.

14 Do not crowd the design into one part of the material and always leave a good margin. Try to balance a central motif with an attractive border in a complementary colour and style.

15 Bedspreads and curtains do not have to be worked in one piece. Narrow strips, oblongs, or squares can be joined after embroidering, and the seams covered with decorative outlining. For upholstery, cut out and hem the material before transferring the design.

16 Crewel embroidery should be kept simple. Use bold and definite lines, and do not overlap, bunch, or foreshorten flowers and leaves.

17 When the piece is completed it has to be blocked and finished off, and this varies according to the background material and the purpose of the finished article. Further information, including a catalogue of stitches, can be obtained from any good, basic instruction book. (The following section has been limited to only those stitches that are used in pieces that appear in this book.)

The drawings

The drawings of the motifs serve two purposes. The first is to show the individual stitches (left-hand shape in the example below) by means of a stitch code, which is explained in the stitch section. The second is to indicate where the colour zones fall (right-hand shape in the example below). Beginners should follow the stitches and zones carefully, but advanced workers could if they wished be more ambitious and make their own choice of stitches.

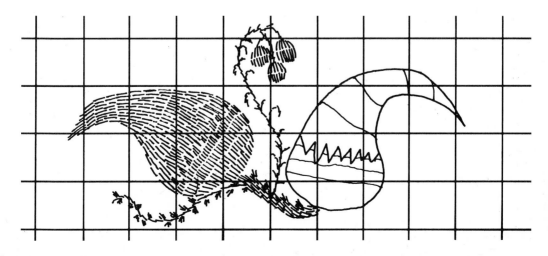

Stitches

Examples of how the stitches are represented on the design drawings are given alongside the relevant stitch diagrams.

Outline stitch and stem stitch

Make small, regular, slightly slanting stitches along the line of the design to give a rope-like effect. Outline stitch is very small, while stem stitch is slightly longer. They are used for flower stems, outlines, etc., and, when worked closely in rows, stem stitch can be used as a filling. In old reference books this is often called crewel stitch.

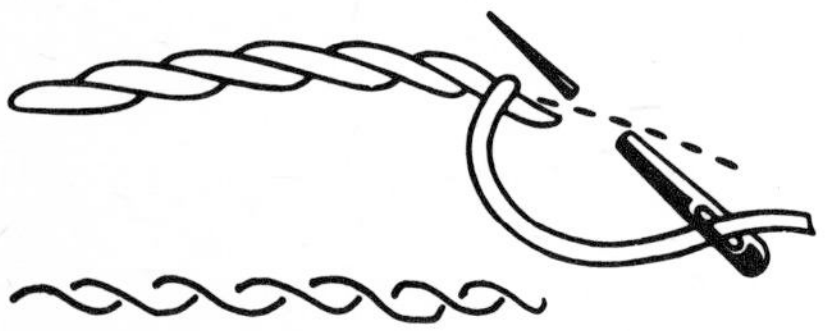

Running stitch

Pass the needle in and out of the material, making sure that the stitches are of equal length and that the spaces are also even, but of half the size or less of the stitches.

Back stitch

Working from right to left, make a small stitch from left to right; bring the needle through on the line of the design, but to the left of the

starting point. Repeat the process, inserting the needle where the previous stitch began so that the stitches make up a continuous line (or if preferred a small space can be left between each stitch). Ensure that the stitches (and the spaces) are even.

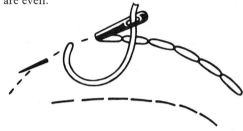

Split stitch

Working from left to right, pick up a small back stitch along the line of the design, bringing the needle out just short of the starting point in order to pierce the working thread. Pull the thread through the split, and repeat to the right. This is a filling stitch and gives a fine, flat surface.

Lacing

Running stitch, back stitch, and others can be attractively decorated by lacing, that is, weaving a thread or threads of contrasting colour in and out of the stitches already made. Use a round-pointed needle (a blunt tapestry needle is best), and be careful not to pick up any of the fabric. Pull through to the back and finish off in the usual way (by making a few running stitches).

Satin stitch

Make closely worked stitches across the shape, ensuring that the edges are neat and that the stitches are parallel and not too long (or they could be pulled out of position or easily caught on buttons or snags). For leaves, satin stitch can be done either side of the central line to form a series of Vs. To give a raised effect, running stitch or chain stitch can be worked first to form a padding underneath.

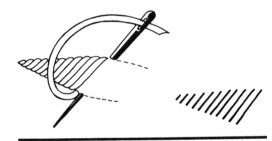

Long and short stitch

This is a type of satin stitch, but here stagger the stitches in rows until the shape is filled, keeping the stitches and rows close together. The stitches in the first and last rows are alternately long and short, while those in between are usually long. It can fill a shape too large or irregular for satin stitch and, by using threads of different colours or tones, can achieve an attractive shaded effect.

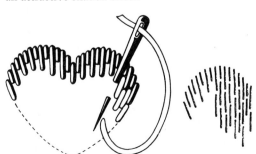

Roumanian stitch

Working down the material, make a stitch from left to right across the width of the shape. Bring the needle through near the centre of the stitch, just above the thread. Then make a small cross-over stitch (whose size and obliqueness can be varied) to pin down the first stitch, bringing the needle out on the left side of the shape. Keep the stitches close together.

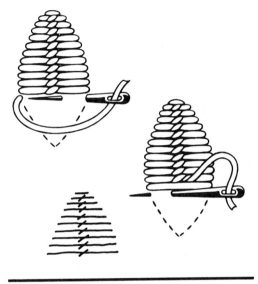

Herringbone stitch

Work this from left to right between two parallel lines. Starting from the bottom line, pick up a small back stitch (right to left) above and to the right of the starting point. Then bring the needle down level with the starting point and pick up a second back stitch below and to the right of the first. Repeat with a third above and to the right of the second, and so on, keeping the stitches even. This is a useful filling stitch for a small space, and can be laced with a matching or contrasting thread.

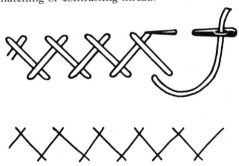

Cross stitch

Starting from the right, sew a row of even, diagonal stitches, spaced out so that the top of one does not overlap with the bottom of the next. Then, from the left, complete each cross by sewing its other diagonal. The crosses can be a continuous row or can be slightly separate.

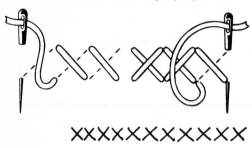

XXXXXXXXXXX

Blanket stitch and buttonhole stitch

Work this from left to right. Bring the thread out on the line of the design and insert the needle to the right of and above the starting point. Take a short downward stitch to the line, leaving a loop of thread below the needle. Hold this loop down with the left thumb and pull the needle through with the loop under the needle point. While making the next stitch, hold the emerging thread down with the left thumb. In buttonhole stitch the stitches are close together, while those in blanket stitch are more widely spaced.

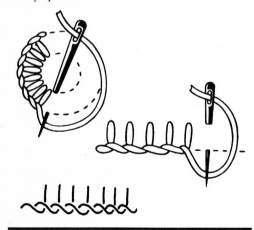

Feather stitch

This is similar to blanket stitch. Make a small stitch from left to right, leaving a loop of thread below the needle. Hold this loop down with the

left thumb and bring the needle out below and centred between the two ends of the loop. Pull through, keeping the loop under the needle point. Form a second stitch to the left of the first one, and a third to the right of the second, and so on. For double feather stitch, work two to the right, two to the left, etc.

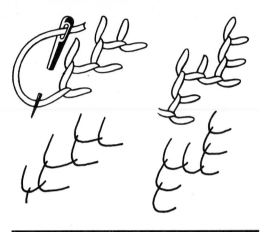

Cretan stitch

Working from left to right, always keep the thread to the right of and underneath the needle. With the thread emerging from the top half of the shape take an upward stitch from the lower edge of the shape, pointing the needle slightly to the right and keeping the thread under the needle point. Then from the top edge of the shape take a downward stitch, needle again pointing slightly to the right and thread again under the needle. This stitch is usually used for fairly solid filling. In open Cretan stitch, which is used for borders, the stitches are evenly spaced out.

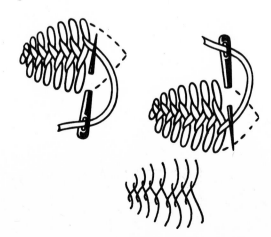

Chain stitch

From left to right, make as small a stitch as possible across the line of the design, leaving a loop of thread below the needle. Hold the loop down with the left thumb and bring the point of the needle out below the first stitch and just to the left of the line of the design. Pull through, keeping the loop under the needle point. Ensure that the loops are even. Chain can be used instead of outline stitch, and also, if worked closely together, as a filling stitch. In open chain stitch the tops of the loops are wider apart. Another variation is the fly stitch, which is V-shaped.

the thread twice or more round the needle (depending on how big the knot is to be). Holding the thread firmly, manipulate the needle so that it can be inserted in the material where it first emerged. Pull through and secure the thread at the back for a single French knot, or bring the needle out at the position of the next one. French knots make attractive outline variation for leaves and petals; they should be well spaced and in a darker shade than the rest of the design. They are also used for the centres of flowers and as filling stitches.

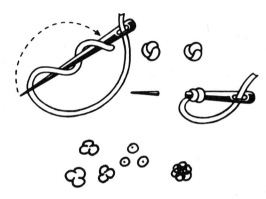

Detached chain (daisy) stitch

Form one chain stitch and fasten the bottom of the loop to the material with a small, downward, cross-over stitch. It can be worked singly or in groups to form flower petals.

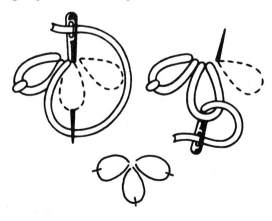

French knot

Bring the thread out at the required position. With the right hand hold the needle next to the emerging thread and with the left hand wind

Bullion stitch

Pick up a back stitch, the size of the bullion stitch required, and bring the needle out at the starting point, but do not pull it through yet. With the left hand wind the thread round the needle as many times as necessary to equal the length of the back stitch. With the left thumb firmly on the coiled thread, pull the needle through and insert it again at the other end of the back stitch. Pull the thread through until the bullion stitch lies flat. (Use a needle with a small eye to allow it to pass through the coils easily.)

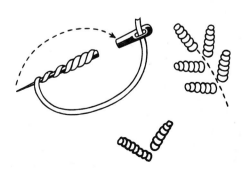

Coral stitch

Lay a short length of emerging thread along the line of the design from right to left, and hold it down with the left thumb. Letting the rest hang in a loop below, insert the needle just to the right of the thumb, and take a tiny downward stitch under the line and tautly held thread. Pull through with the loop under the needle point. Keep the stitches fairly close together.

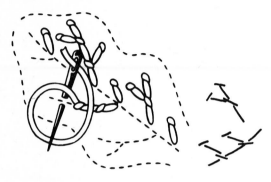

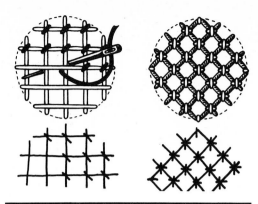

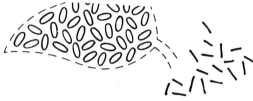

Couching

Bring a needle holding one or more threads through to the front, and lay the thread or threads along the line of the design (it may be easier to remove the needle). With another thread, which can be a different shade or colour, tie the laid thread or threads down at regular intervals with a small cross-over stitch. Finish off the threads as usual. (See laid work.)

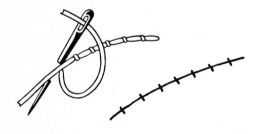

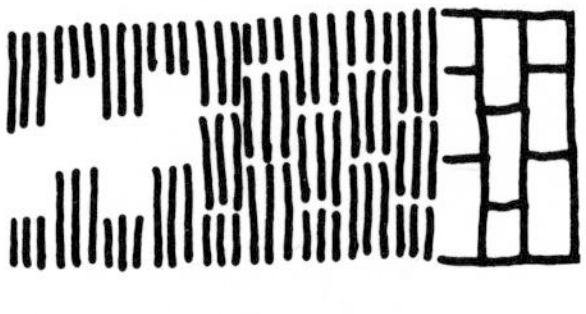

Jacobean couching or trellis

Lay evenly spaced threads (vertical and horizontal, or diagonal) across the design shape, and tie down all intersections with a different thread. The tiny tie or couching stitches can be slanting stitches or small crosses. Trellis work is a delightful filling for open leaf or flower shapes. It has a very light and delicate effect, and can cover large areas very quickly.

Seeding

Place small, even back stitches over the shape at random. It is a light filling stitch.

Brick stitch

Arrange small, rectangular blocks of horizontal or vertical satin stitches in staggered columns, to give a brick-wall effect. The blocks of stitches can be of different shades or colours. It is used for filling large spaces.

Laid work

Lay a series of parallel threads close together, and tie them down at regular intervals with seeding, couching, fly stitch, or open chain stitch. For fairly simple spaces, fix both ends of the laid threads to the material before adding the tying stitches; for more complicated shapes, especially curves, only fix the starting end (the other end is done later). It can be used to fill a variety of spaces and has the advantage of being quickly worked.

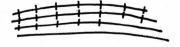

Designs

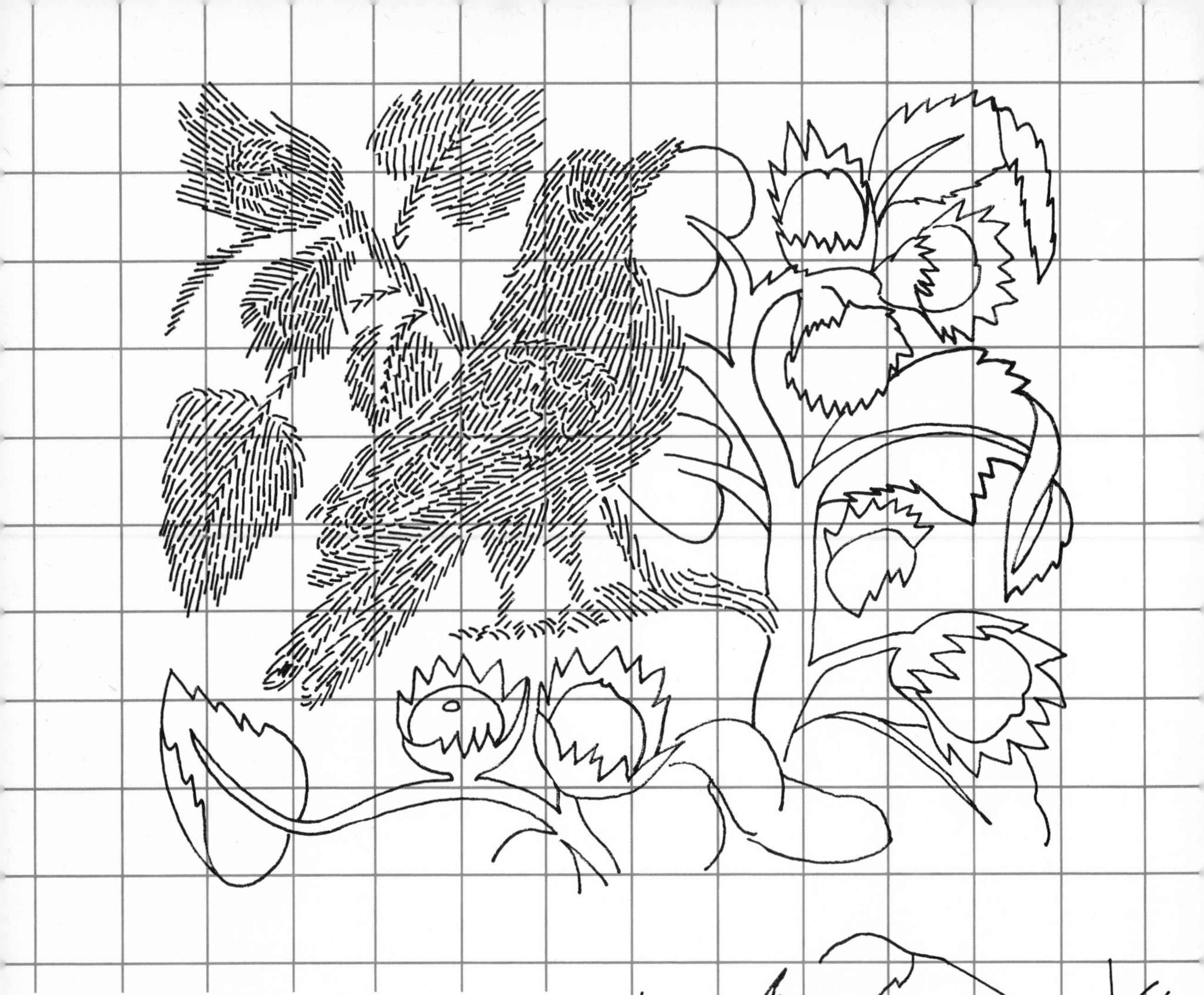

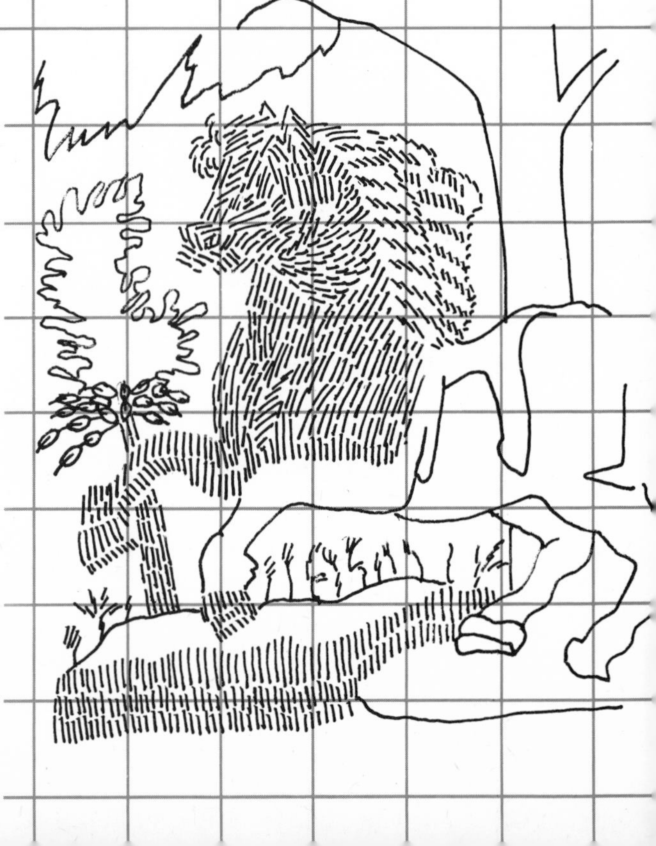

Wall hanging; about 1675 (overleaf)

Rectangles containing bunches of flowers alternate with rectangles showing trees and animals, which have symbolic or emblematic significance. The designs are derived from embroidery pattern books and also works on natural history and emblems. Long and short stitch is worked in red, green, yellow, blue, and brown colours.

Courtesy Institut für angewandte Kunst, Berne

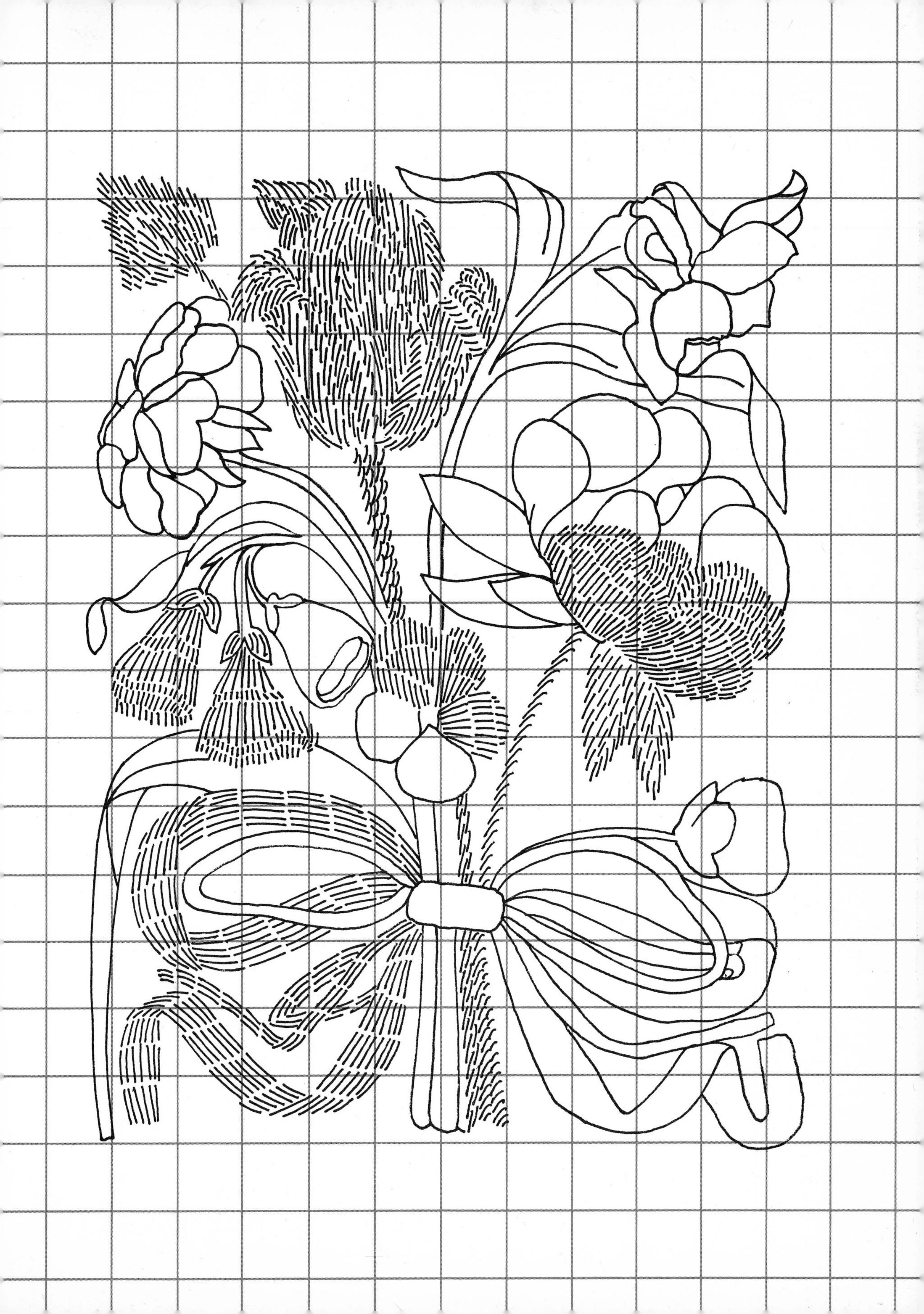

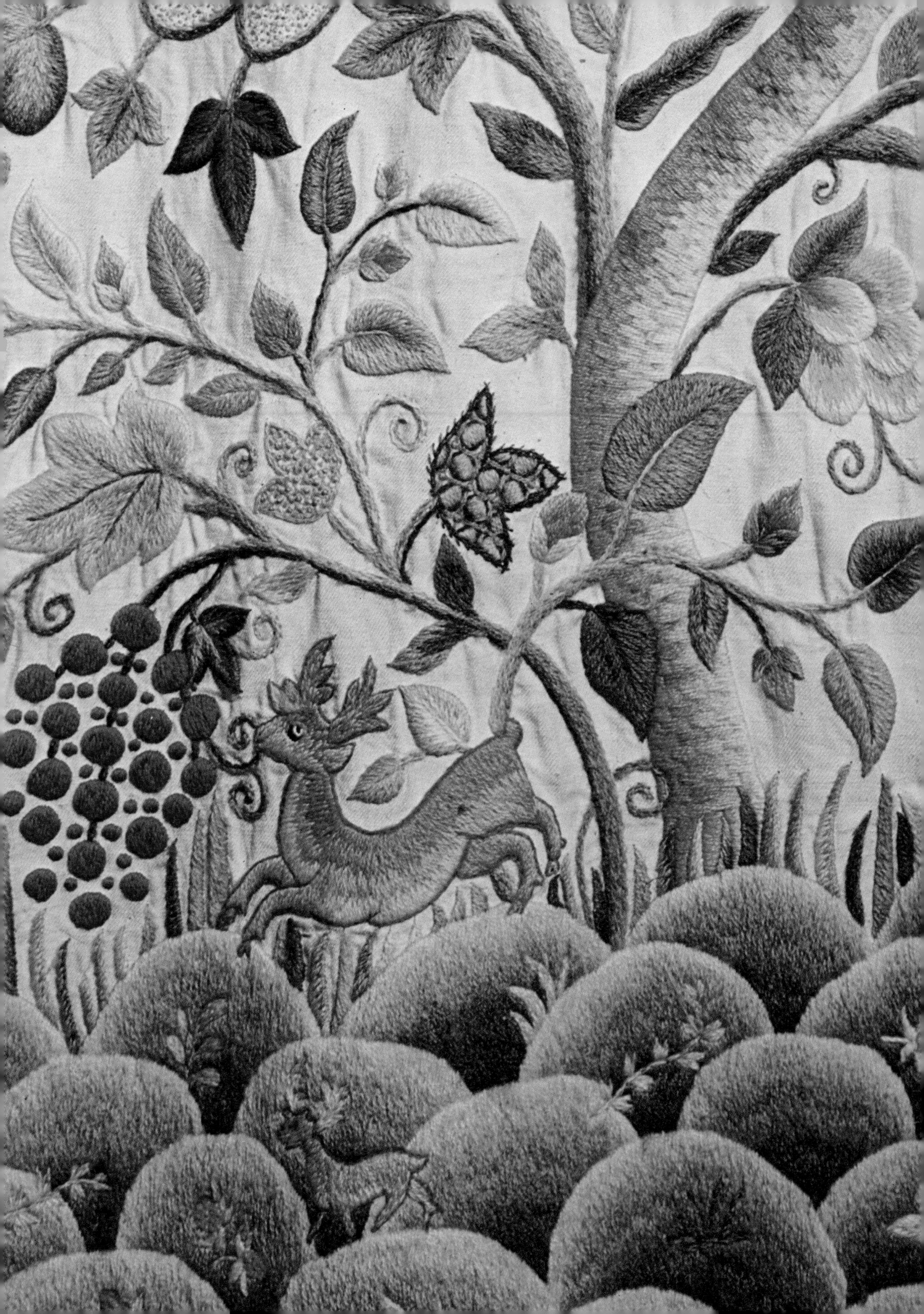

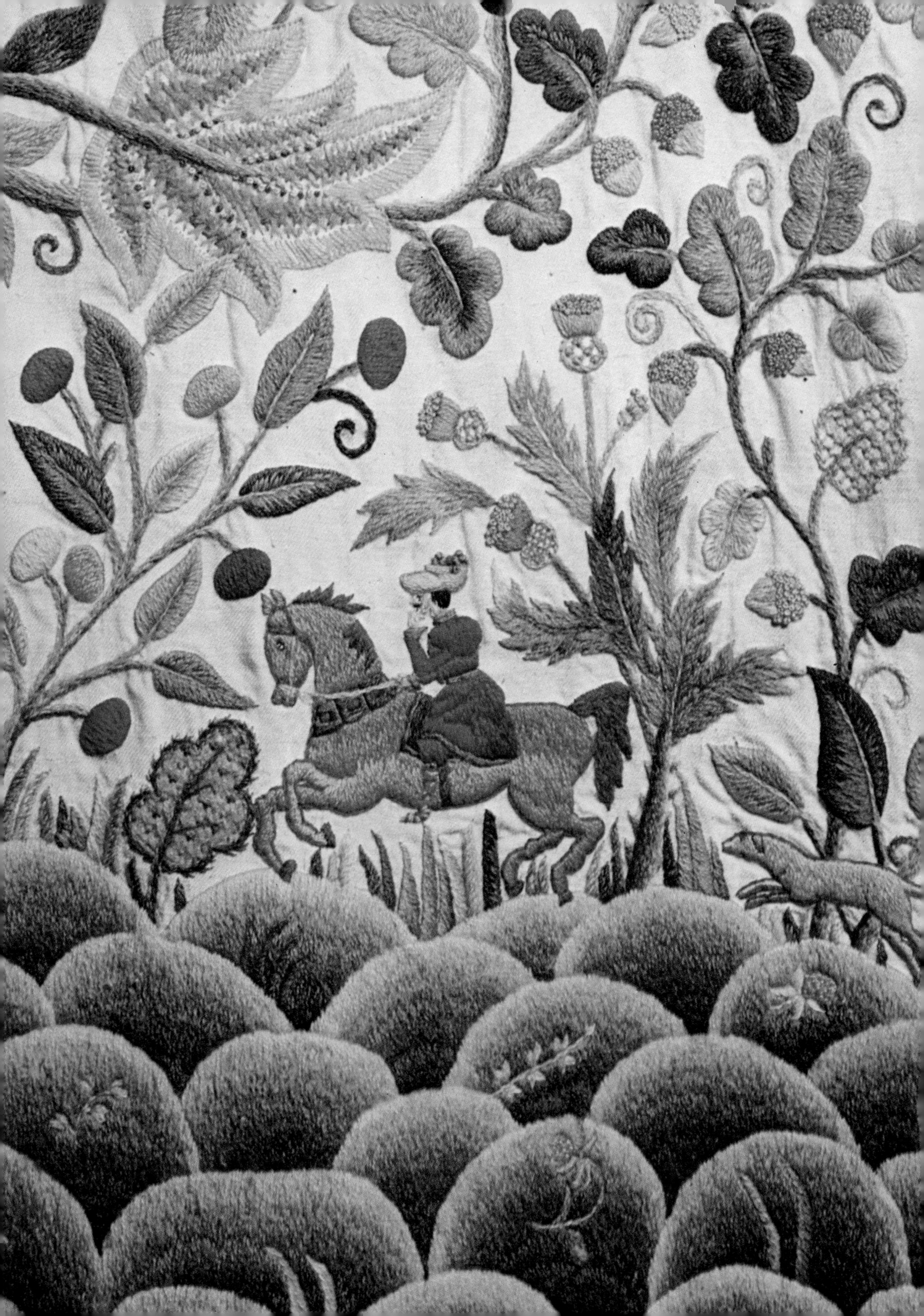

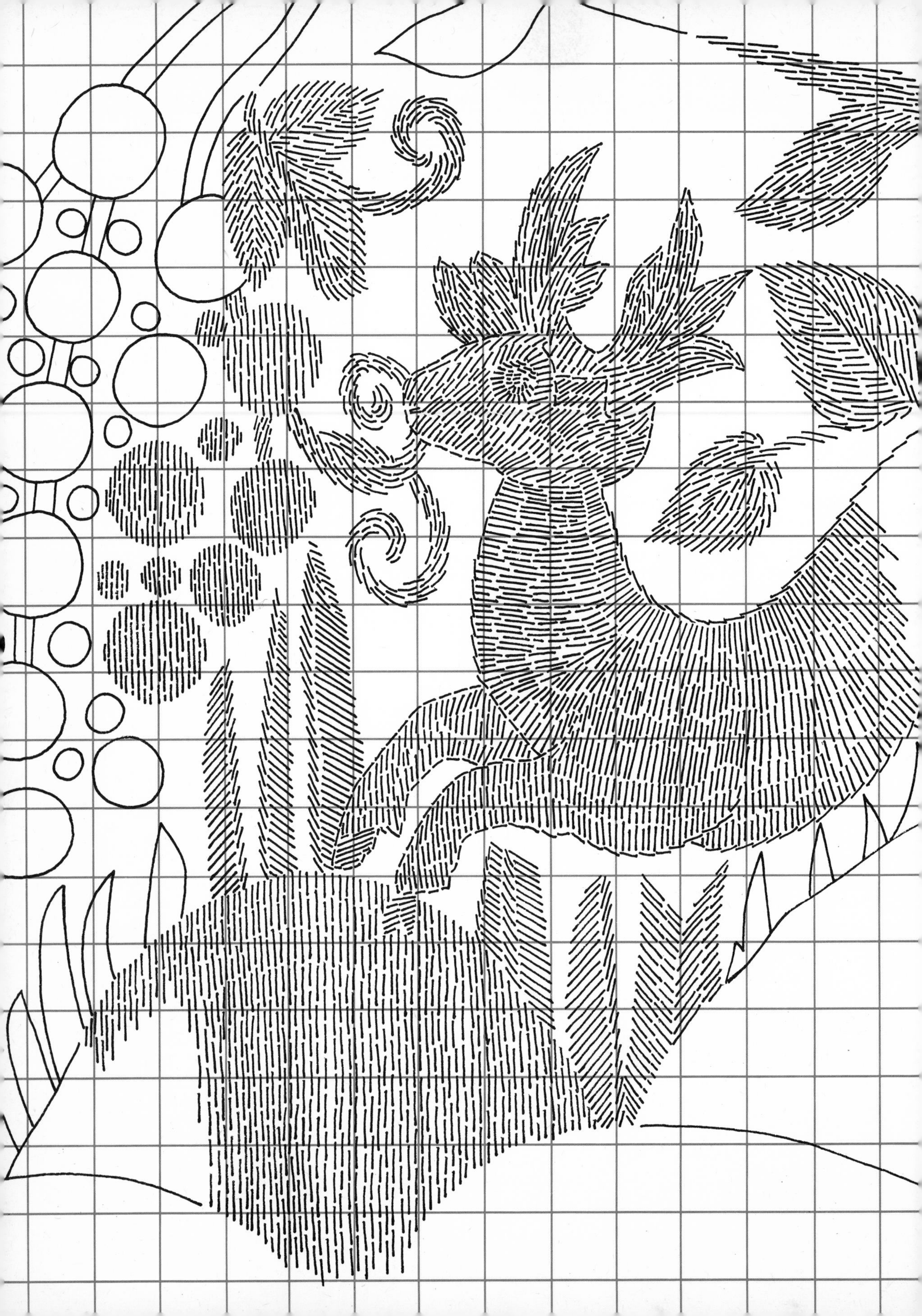

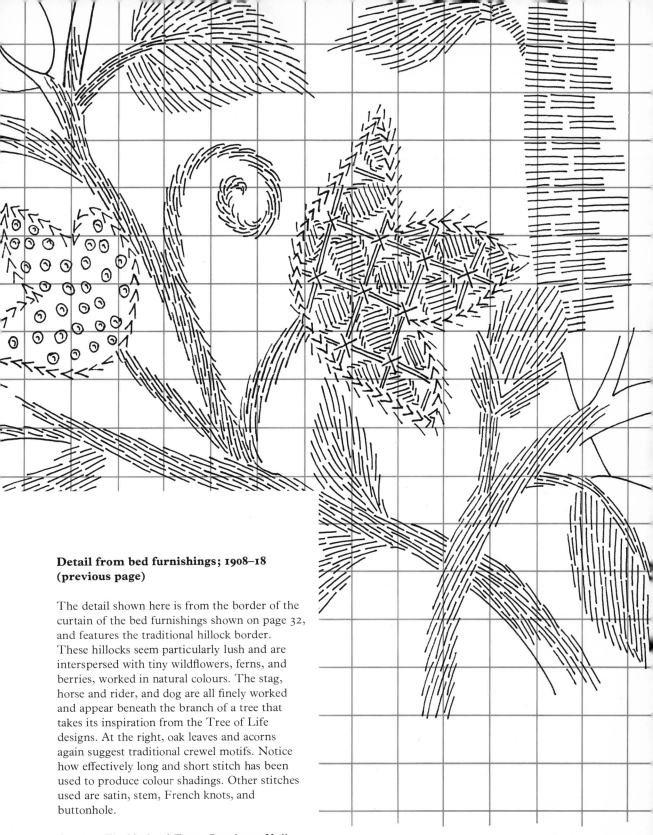

**Detail from bed furnishings; 1908–18
(previous page)**

The detail shown here is from the border of the
curtain of the bed furnishings shown on page 32,
and features the traditional hillock border.
These hillocks seem particularly lush and are
interspersed with tiny wildflowers, ferns, and
berries, worked in natural colours. The stag,
horse and rider, and dog are all finely worked
and appear beneath the branch of a tree that
takes its inspiration from the Tree of Life
designs. At the right, oak leaves and acorns
again suggest traditional crewel motifs. Notice
how effectively long and short stitch has been
used to produce colour shadings. Other stitches
used are satin, stem, French knots, and
buttonhole.

*Courtesy The National Trust, Gawthorpe Hall,
Lancashire*

A set of bed furnishings comprising curtain, valance, and cover for a four-poster; 1908–18

Designed and embroidered by the Hon. Rachel Kay-Shuttleworth at Gawthorpe Hall, Lancashire, these beautiful hangings were finished on Armistice Day, 1918. Family coats of arms appear on the borders. The ground is a natural twill weave linen, and stitches include satin, long and short, stem, French knots, and buttonhole.

Courtesy The Rachel Kay-Shuttleworth Collection, Gawthorpe Hall, Lancashire

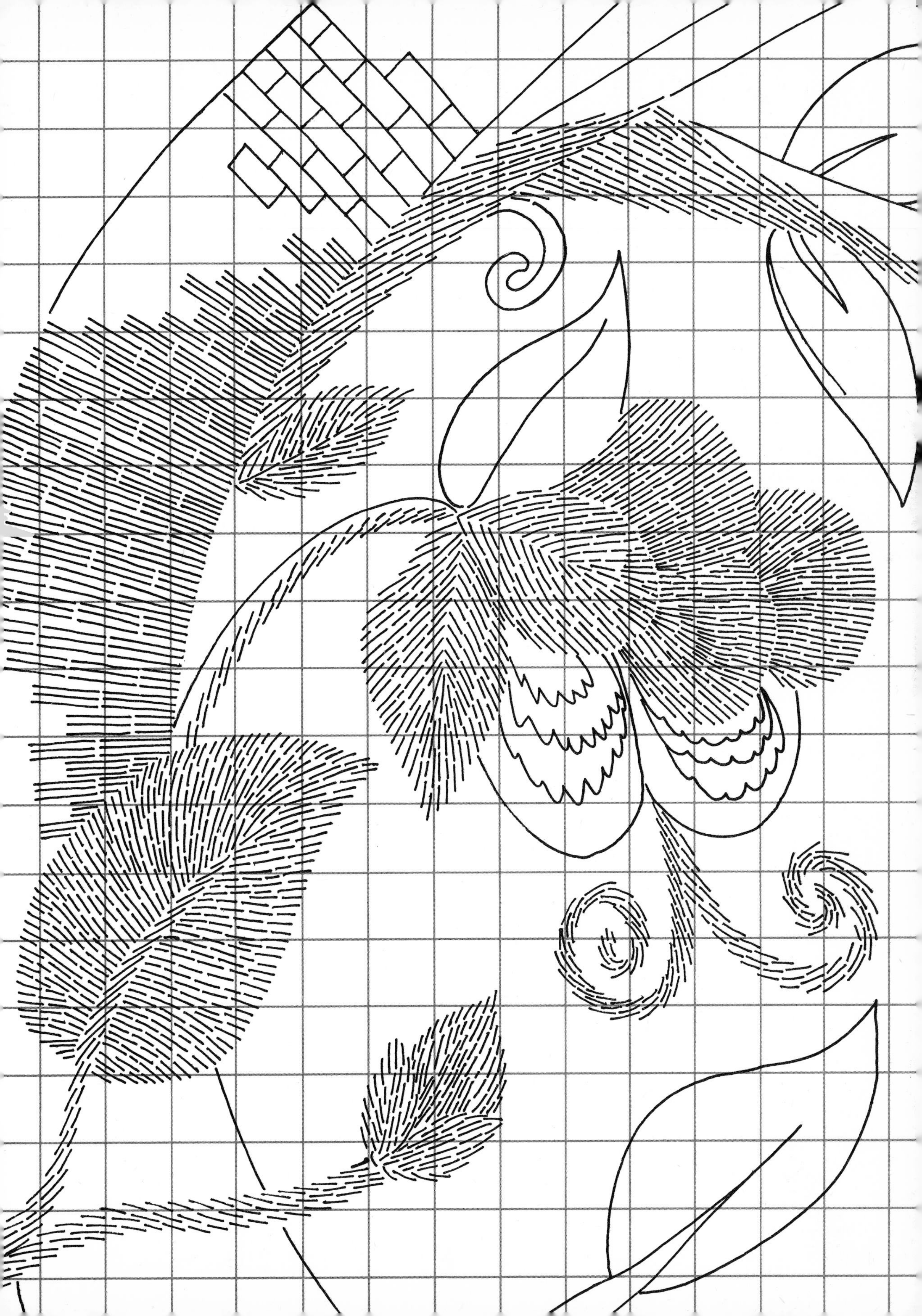

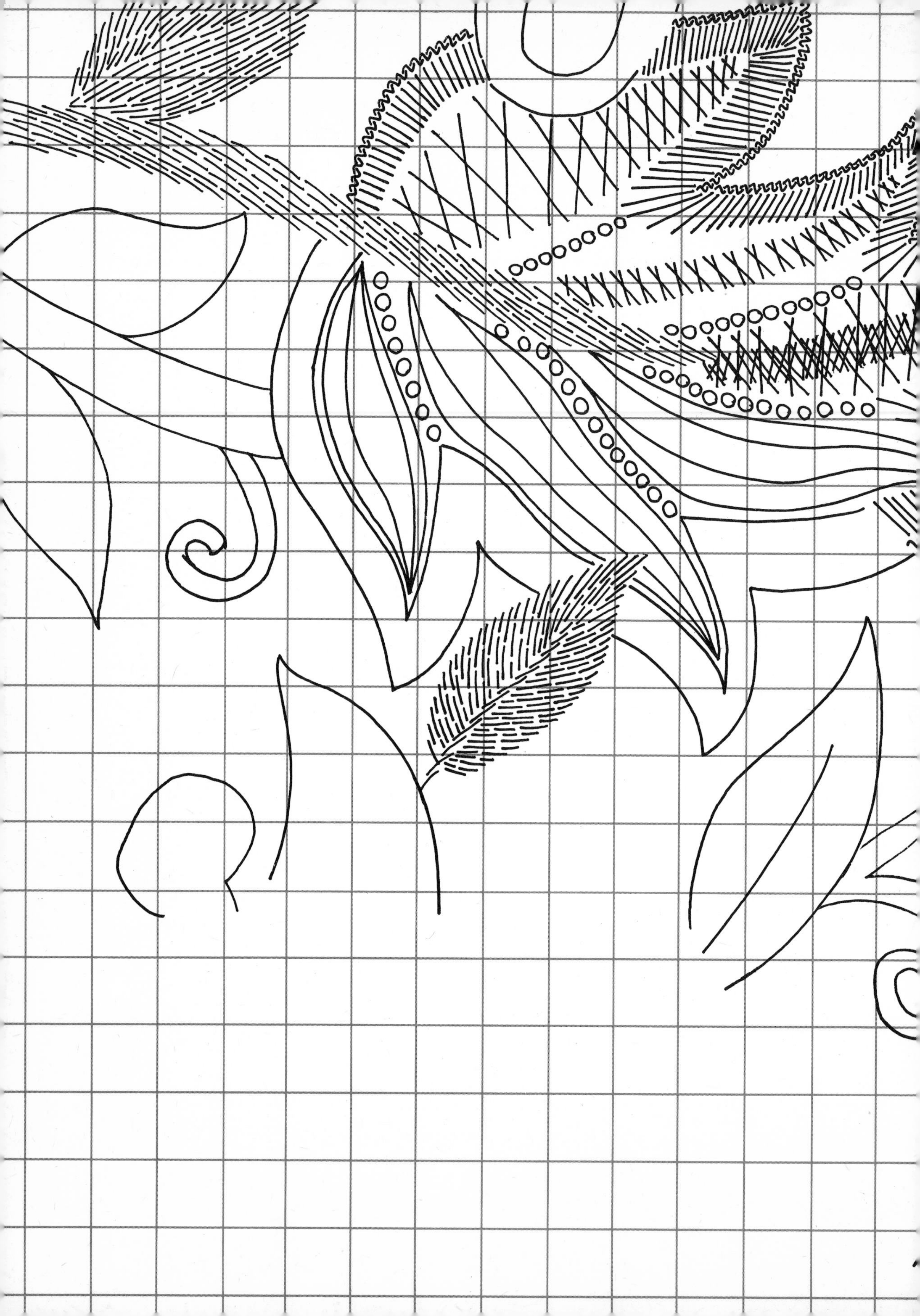

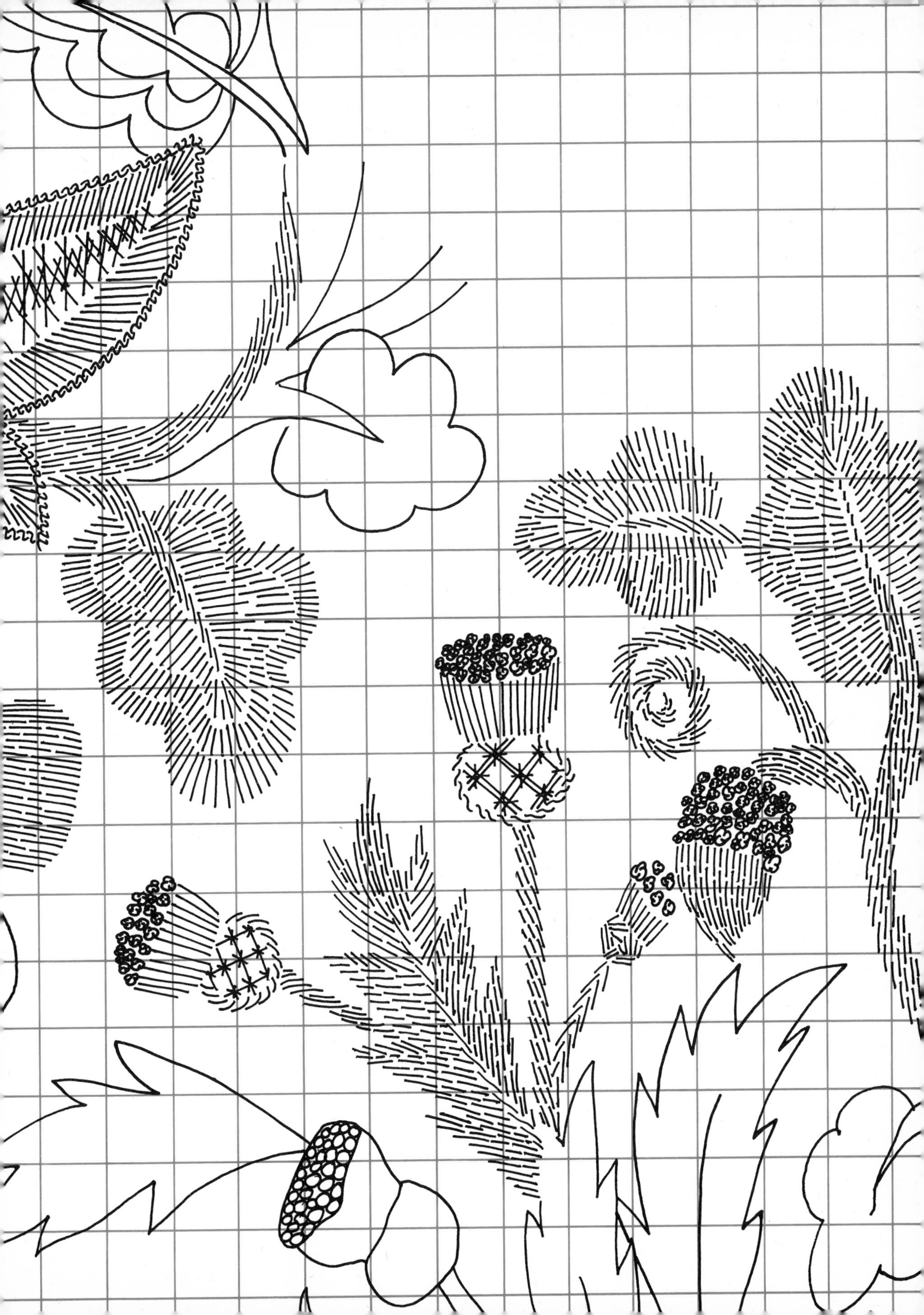

**Panel worked in crewel wools, called
The Travellers**

There has been intense pleasure in pictorial
story-telling in embroidery since early times
despite the fact that the needle is more limited
than the brush in depicting scenes.

Here there is a discreet use of landscape with
hills, trees, and animals contributing to
perspective. Human figures, always difficult to
illustrate with the needle, are introduced with
remarkable pictorial effect. Clear lines and
simplicity of composition achieve a lively
result, and fine needlework mainly in satin
and outline stitch produces an effect of
movement. Borders of trailing leaves and
heraldic shields enclose the scene.

*Courtesy Mrs Joyce Knowles;
photograph lent by H. E. Kiewe*

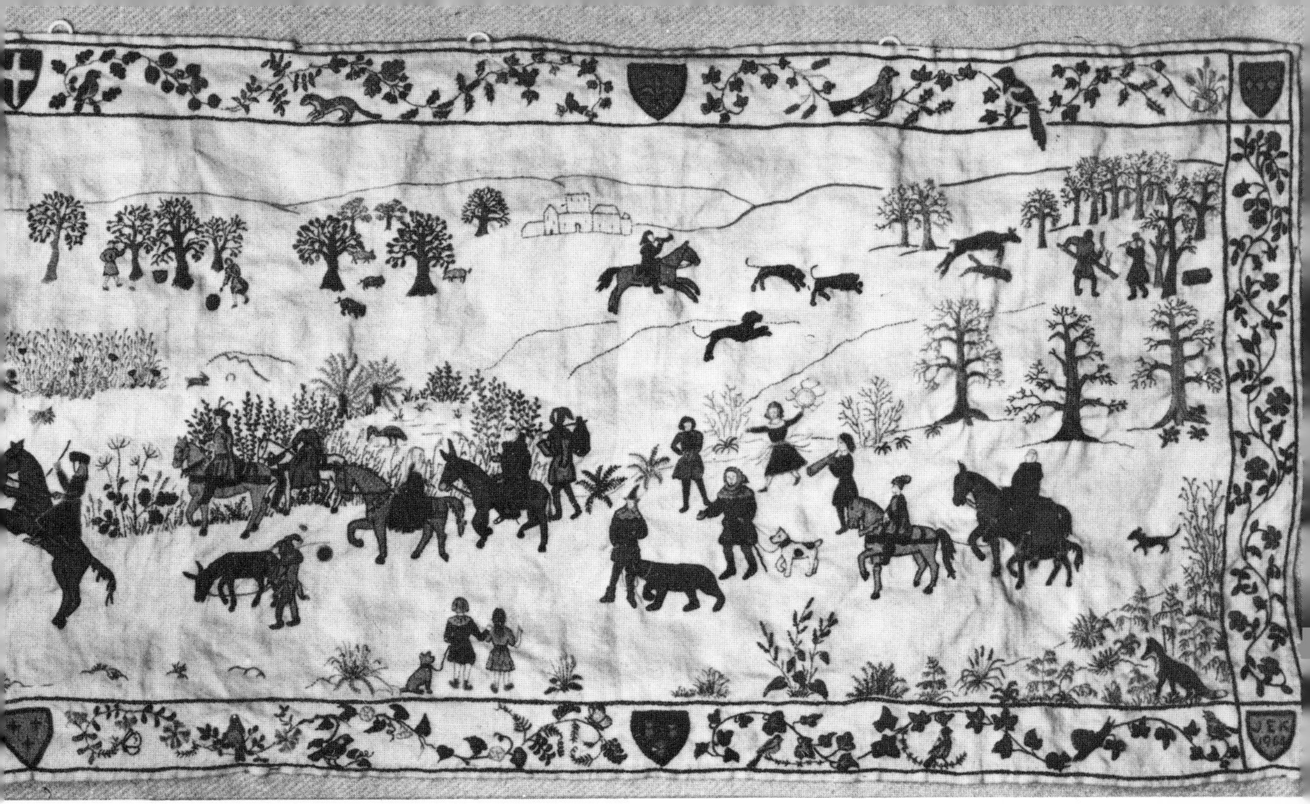

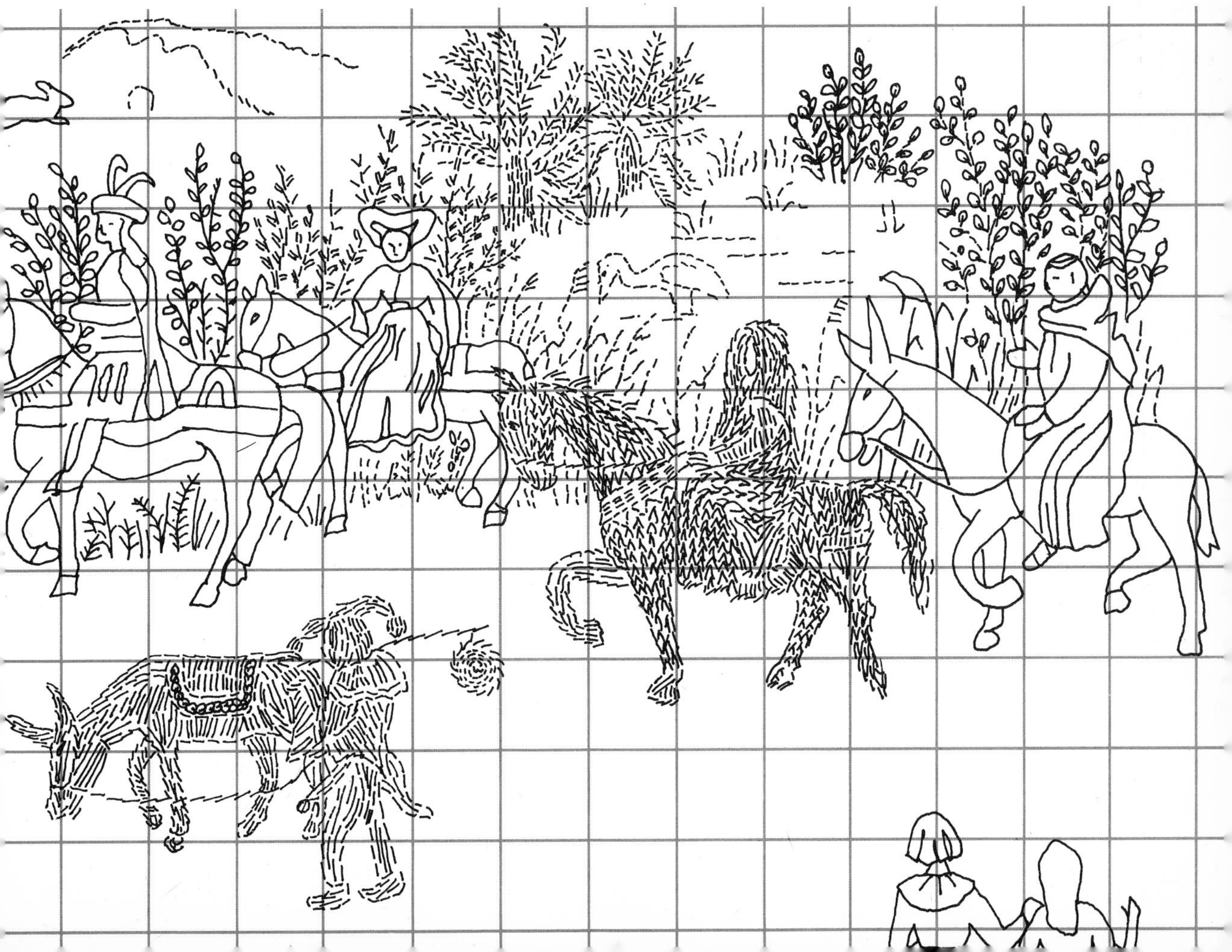

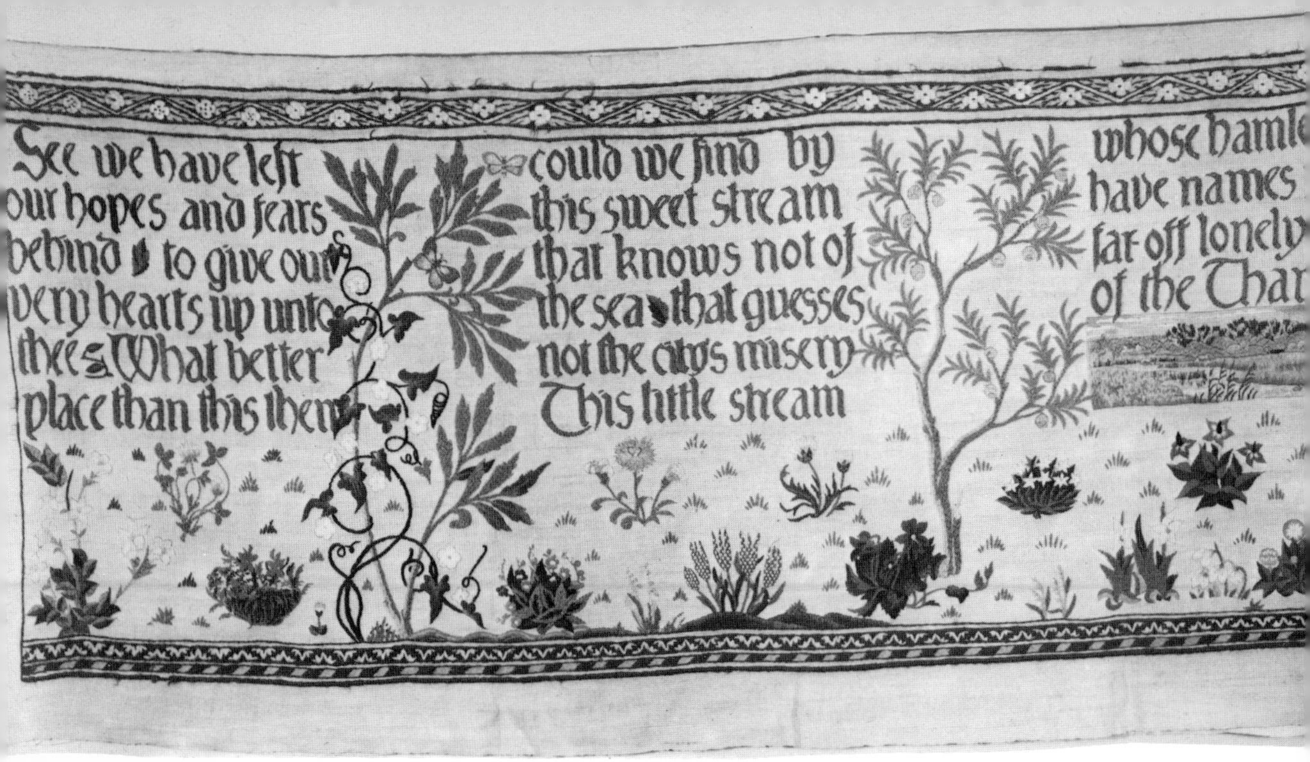
See we have left
our hopes and fears
behind to give our
very hearts up unto
thee What better
place than this then
could we find by
this sweet stream
that knows not of
the sea that guesses
not the citys misery
This little stream
whose hamle
have names
far-off lonely
of the Thar

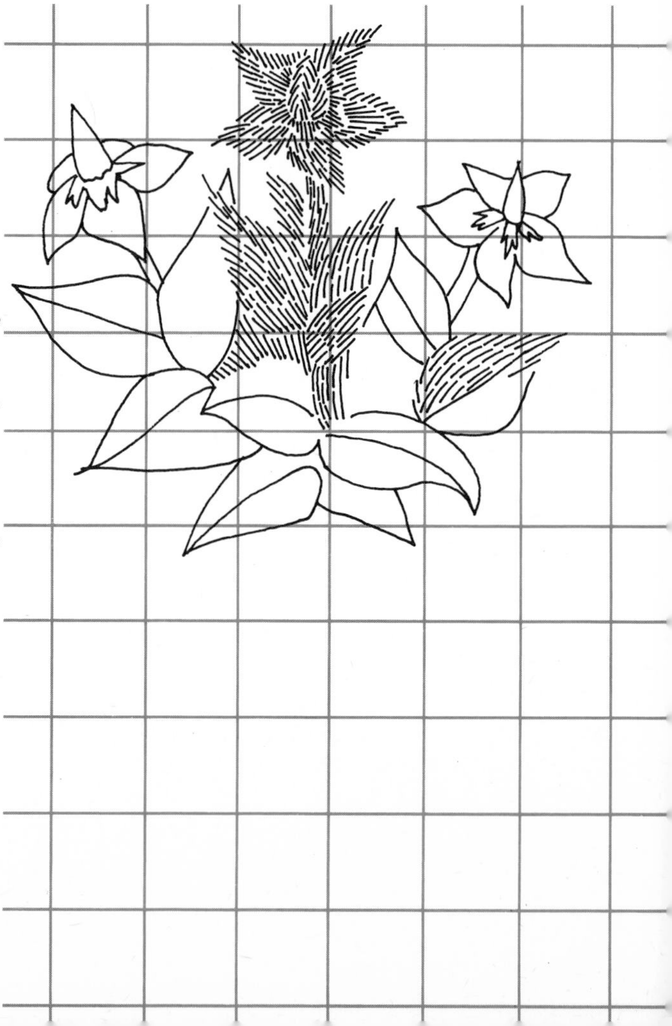

Panel embroidered by May Morris, daughter of William Morris; late 19th century

The panel depicts trees, flowers, fruit, and verse, with a picture of Kelmscott Manor in the centre.

William Morris declared, 'Though the pattern be a veritable flower garden, the embroideress will not forget that she is gardening with silks and gold threads, i.e. the needlewoman must work according to the needle and do what the needle commands best and be content with that.'

The panel is divided vertically by graceful tree and flower motifs with the verse in Gothic lettering. Unrelated motifs of leaves and flowers are embroidered between narrow borders made up of parallel lines enclosing designs of flowers and berries. Main stitches used are satin, outline, stem, chain, and French knots.

Courtesy The William Morris Gallery, Walthamstow

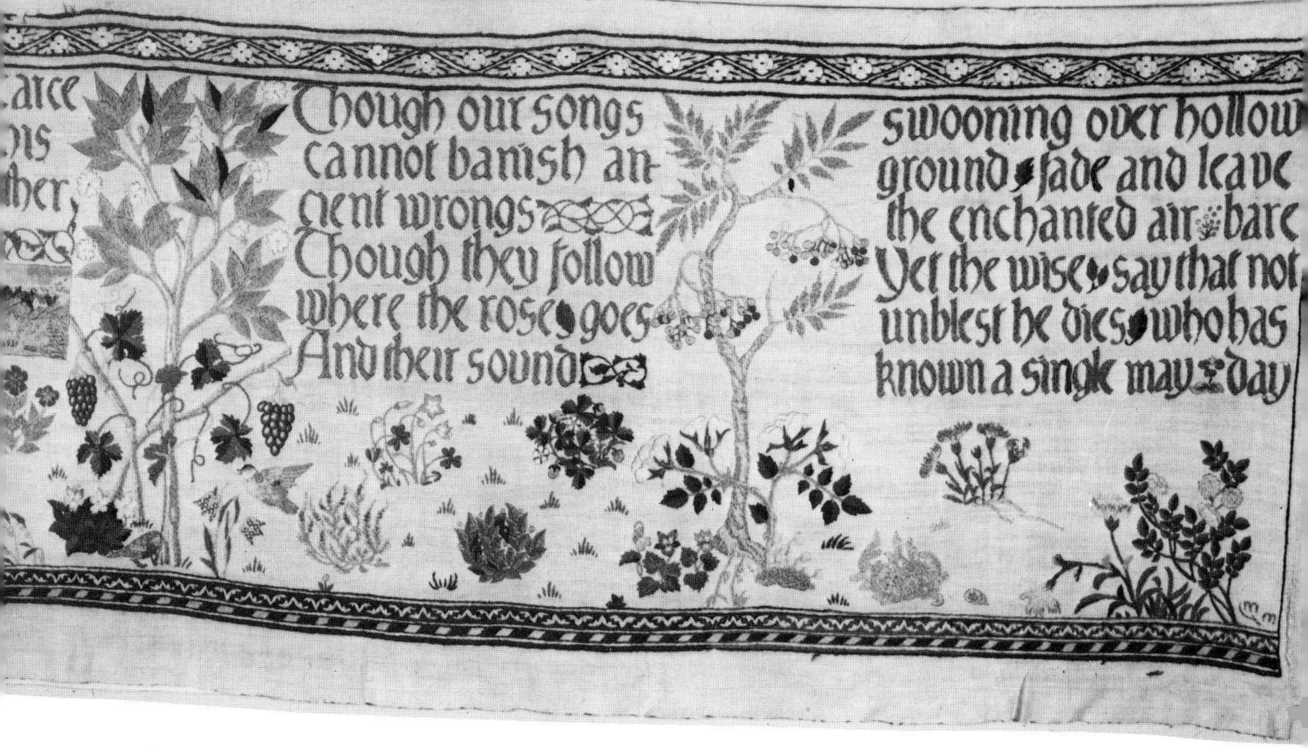
Though our songs
cannot banish an-
cient wrongs
Though they follow
where the rose goes
And their sound
swooning over hollow
ground fade and leave
the enchanted air bare
Yet the wise say that not
unblest he dies who has
known a single may day

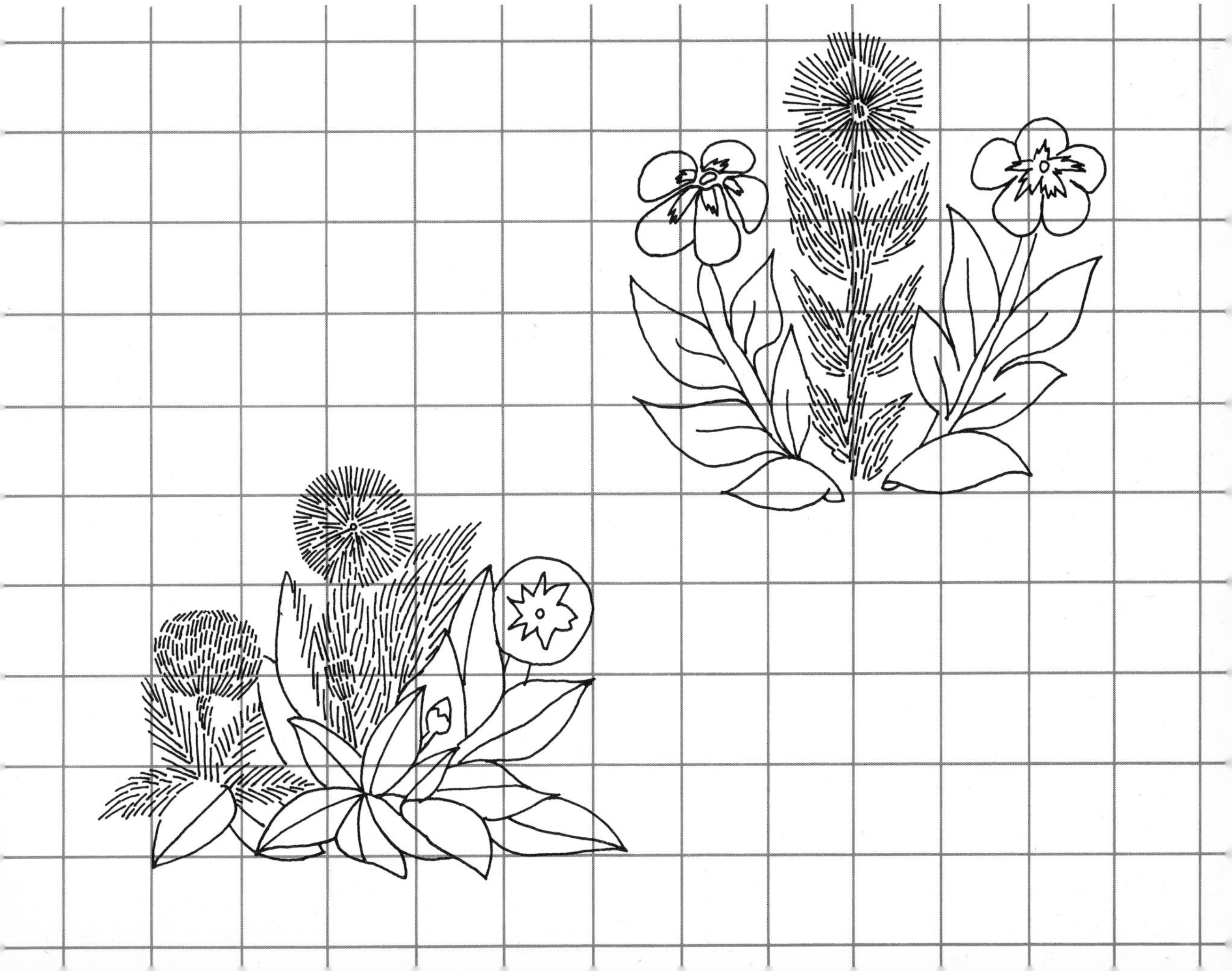

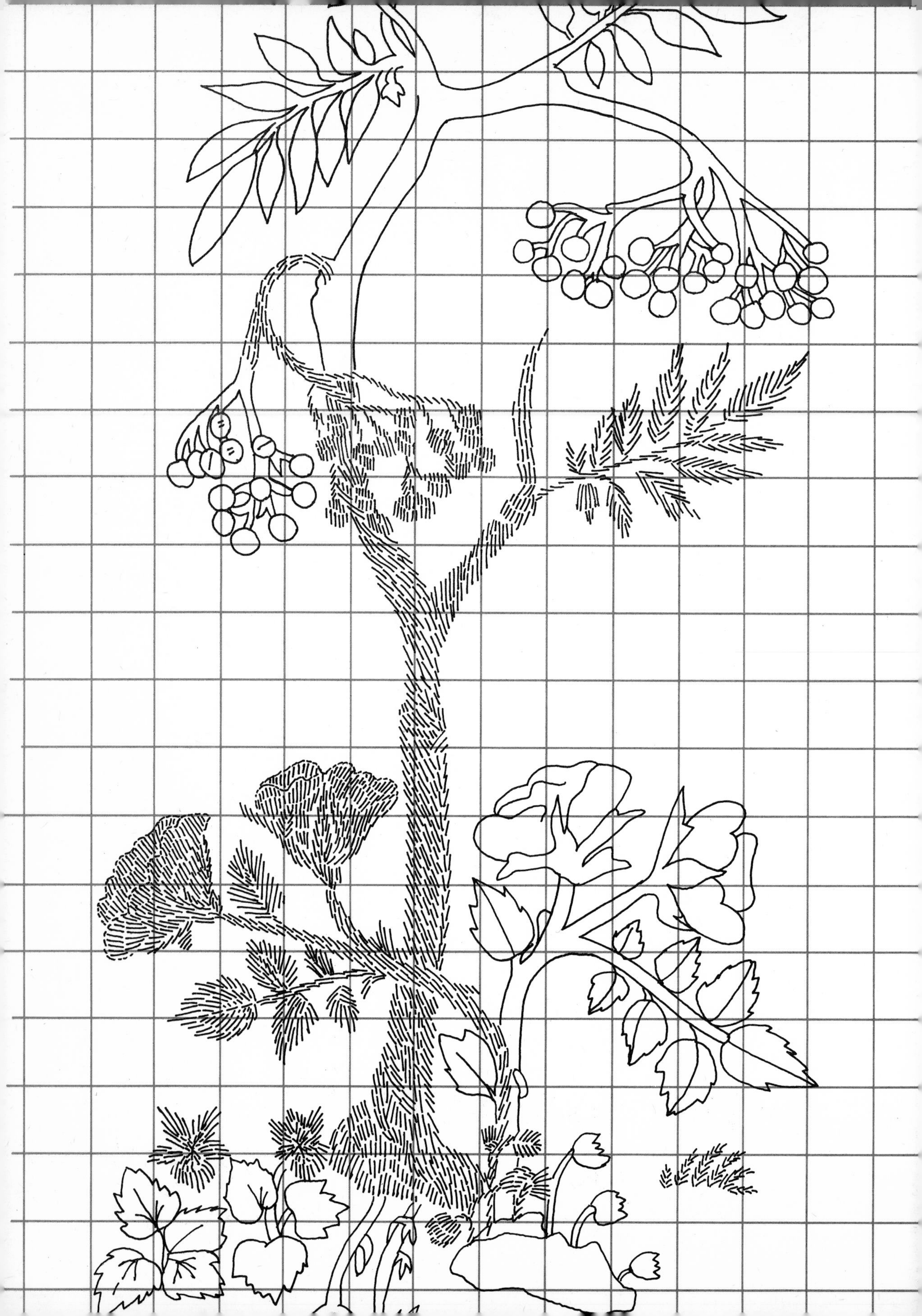

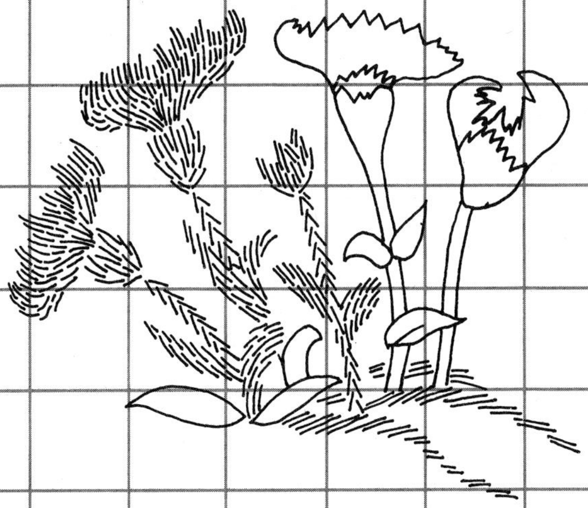

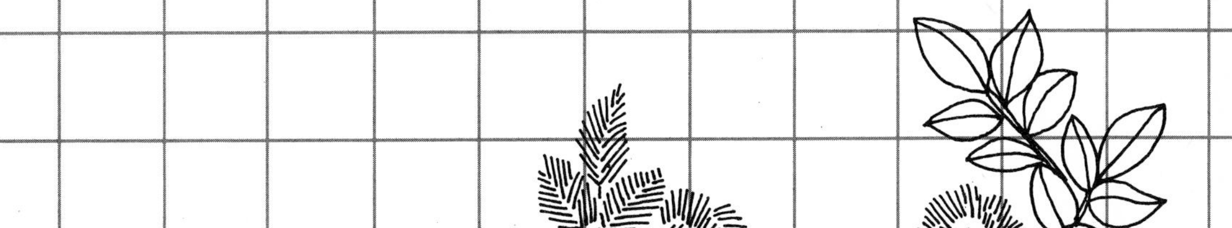

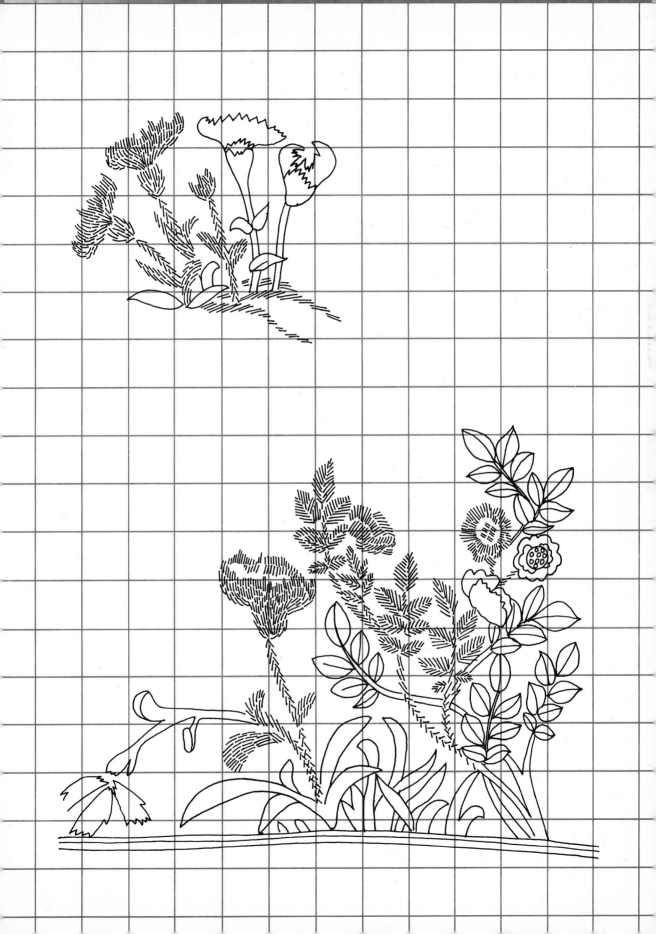

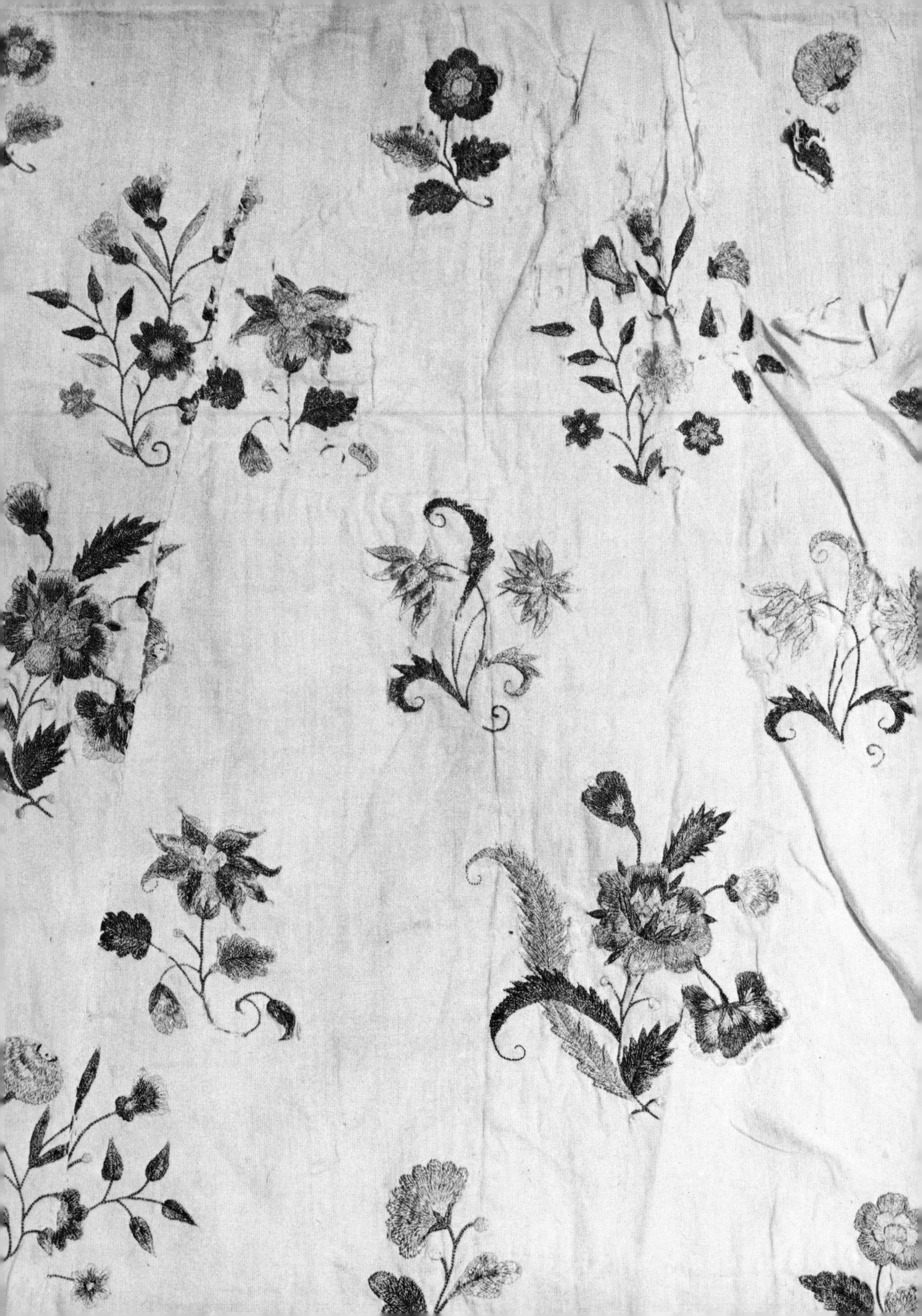

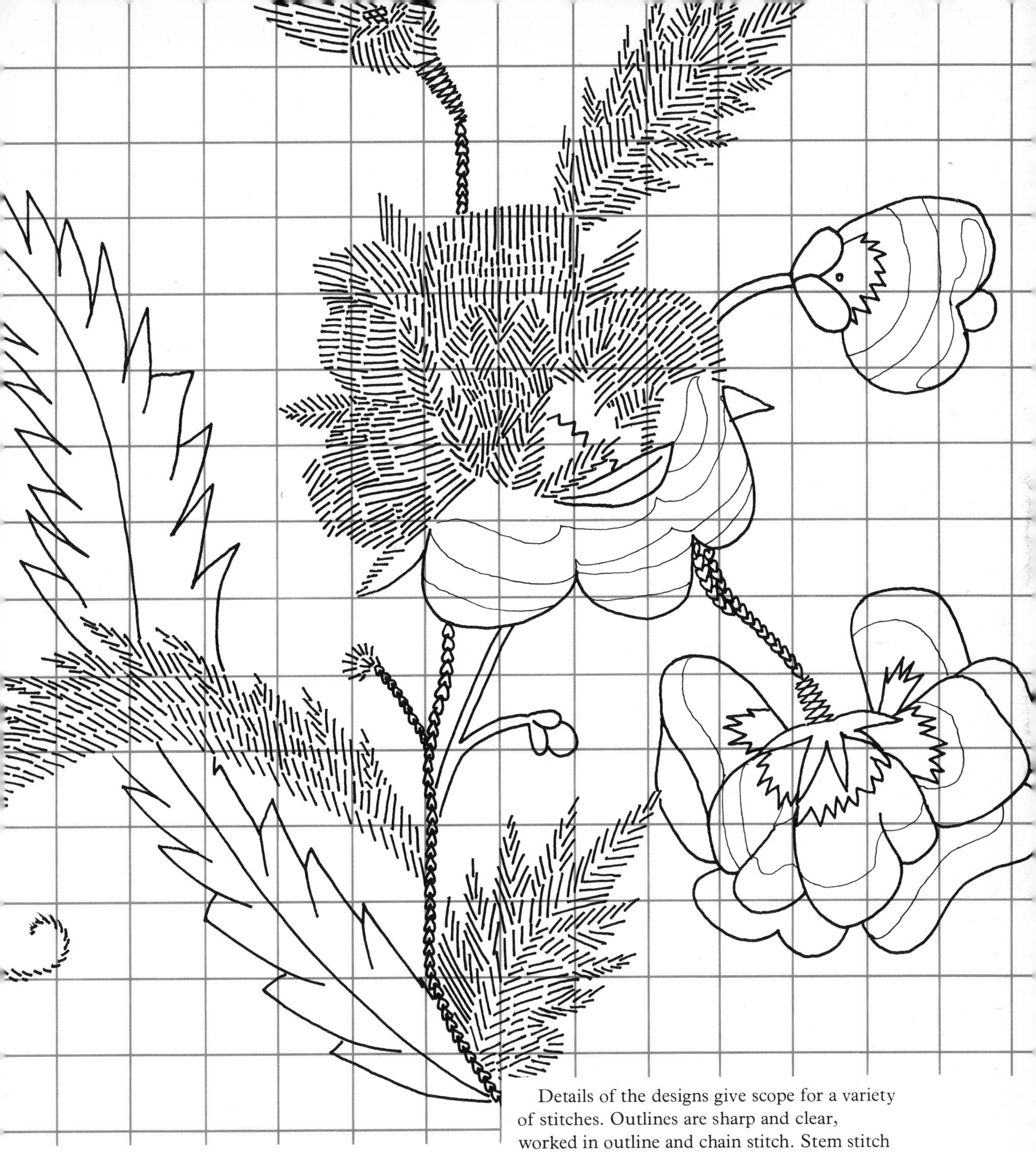

Elizabethan embroidery; 16th century

This pleasing example of an arrangement of separate motifs allows full effect of the background material. Indigenous flowers are embroidered, the designs being inspired by specimens in gardens and illustrations in contemporary herbals. The scrolling stem is apparent in the isolated flower slips.

Details of the designs give scope for a variety of stitches. Outlines are sharp and clear, worked in outline and chain stitch. Stem stitch is used for the finer stems and fine satin stitch for the broader ones. Leaves and petals are in satin and long and short stitch; calyxes in massed effect are in satin stitch. Buttonhole stitch emphasizes details of blossoms.

These motifs have grace and lightness and lend themselves to bright and judicious interpretation in colour.

Courtesy H. E. Kiewe

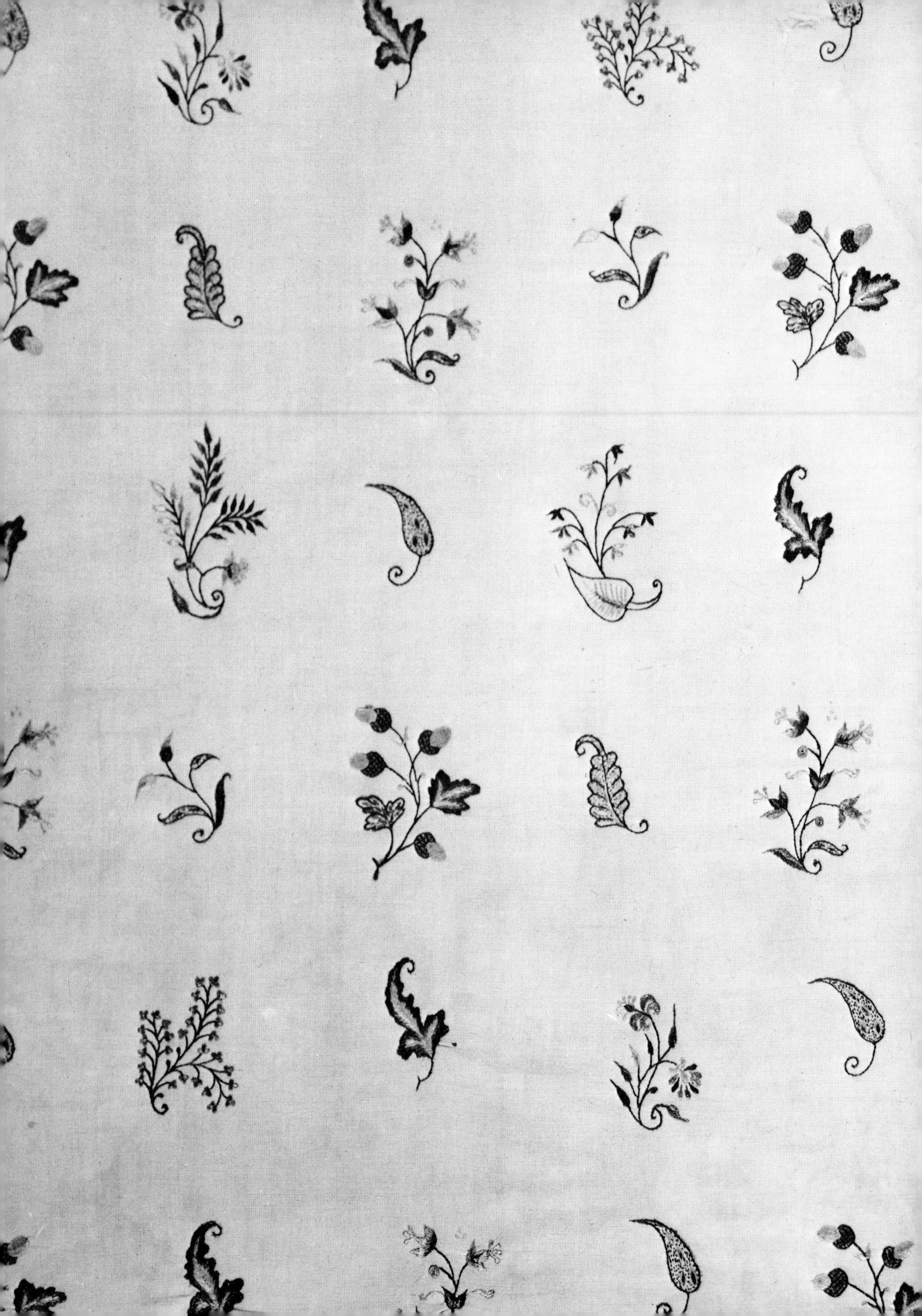

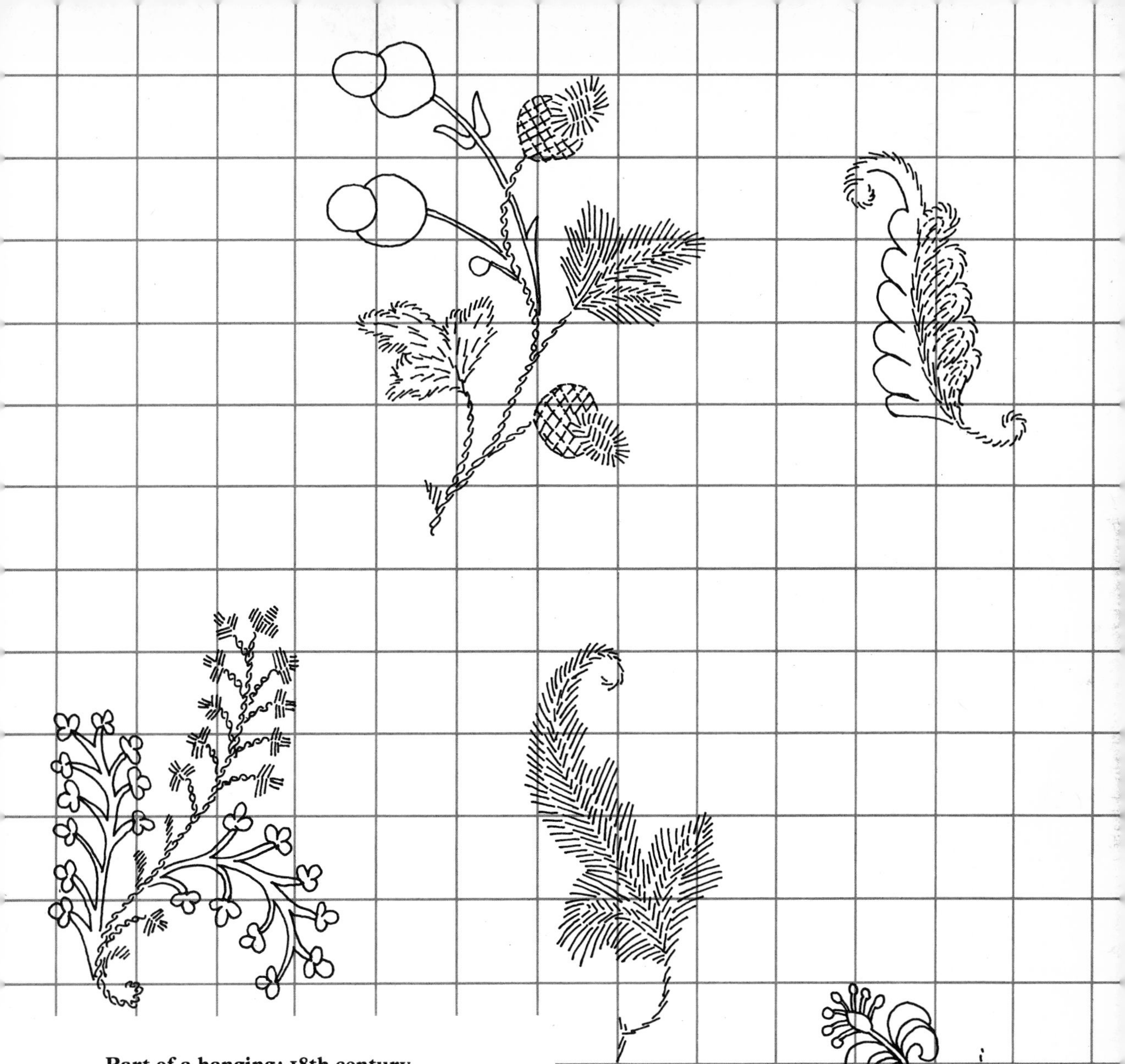

Part of a hanging; 18th century

Naturalistic presentation of separate flower motifs is seen here with a delicate interpretation of flower sprays and of leaves.

The graceful stems are mainly in fine stem stitch. Many leaves are in massed satin stitch worked in darker tones at the edges. Calyxes and petals are likewise in satin stitch; sepals are in bullion stitch. Separate chain stitch and seeding is superimposed on the stitching of leaves to indicate veining and other details. The specimen shows that the oak leaf and acorn, which were greatly loved by Stuart embroiderers, were already established. The delicate colourings of the flowers are enhanced by the use of several shades of green in leaves and stems.

Courtesy The Needlework Development Scheme, Glasgow

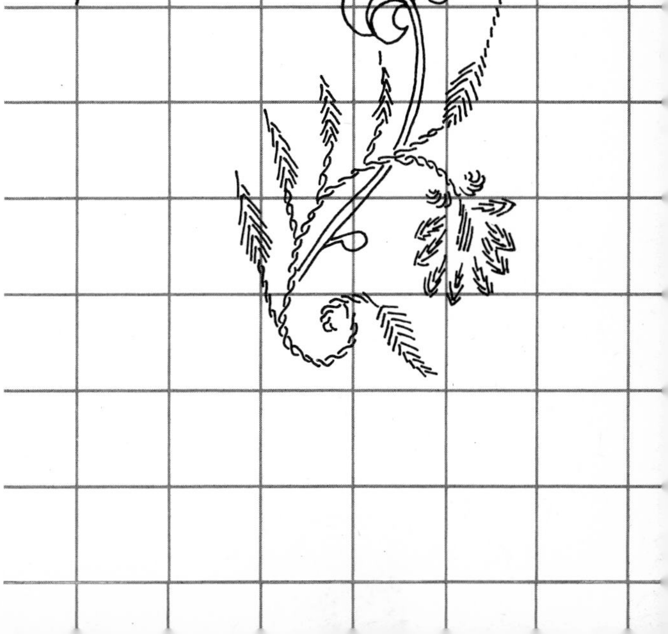

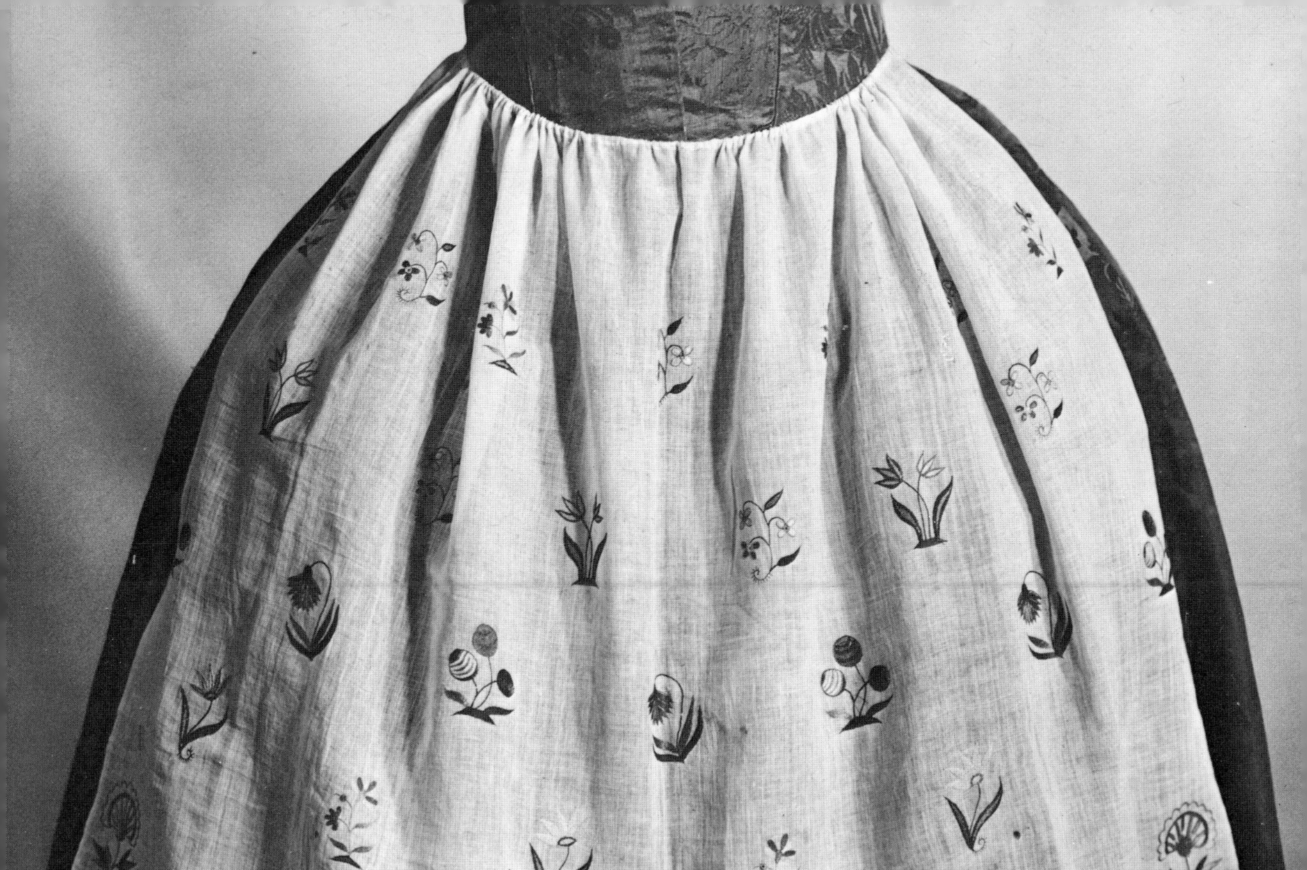

Muslin apron embroidered in crewel wools; 18th century

This decorative apron gathered into a waistband features indigenous flowers embroidered separately, the arrangement possibly being inspired by patterns on delicate porcelain. A light effect is produced by the judicious use of background with the coiling stem effect evident in the small blooms.

The range of stitches is wide, separate motifs being frequently inspired by sampler work. They include stem, outline, coral and double coral, bullion, and seeding, with some use of satin and feather stitch.

Courtesy The City Art Gallery, Manchester

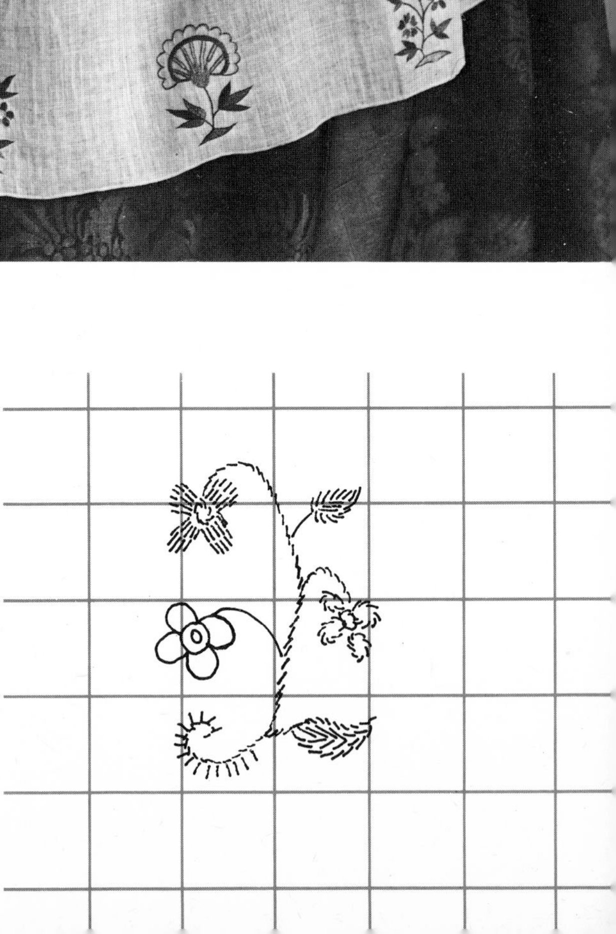

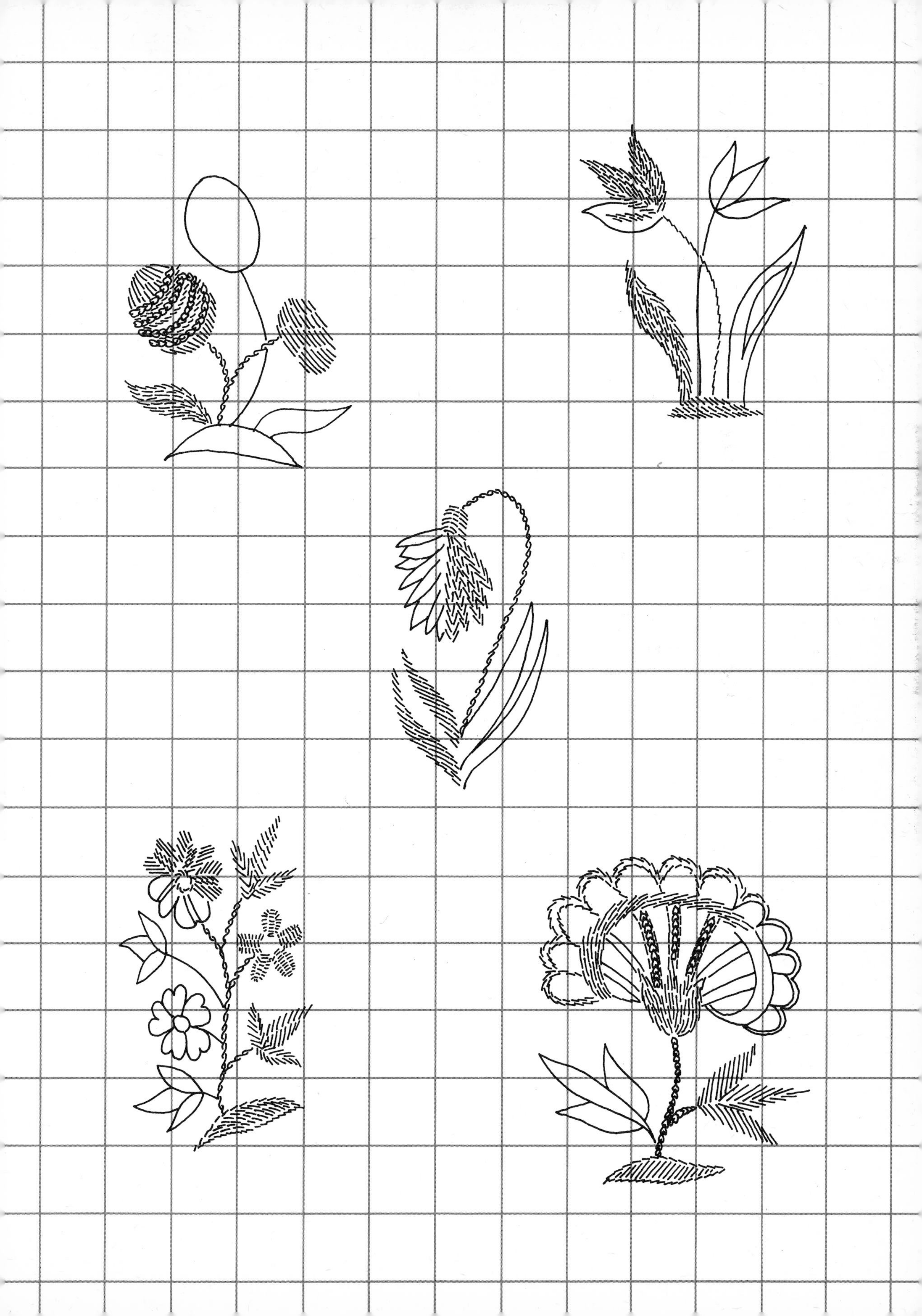

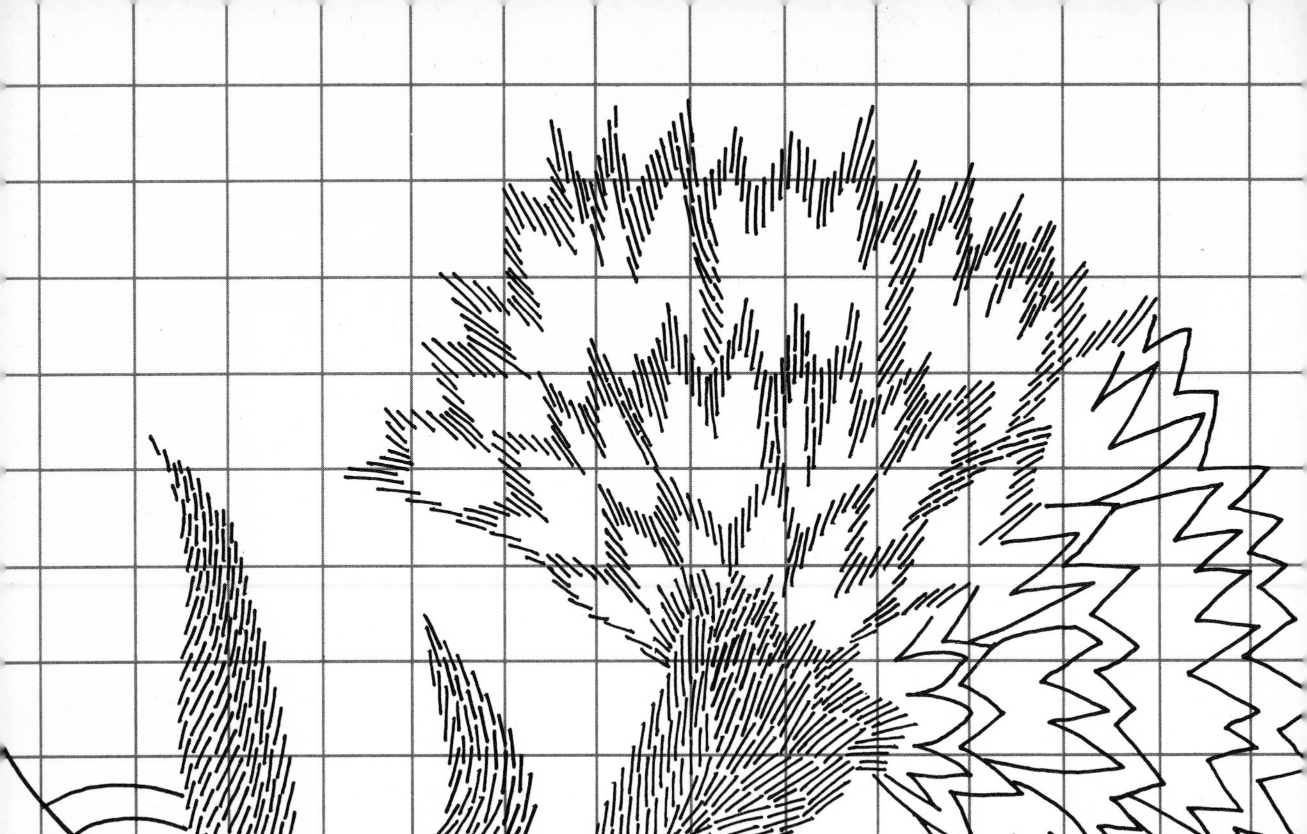

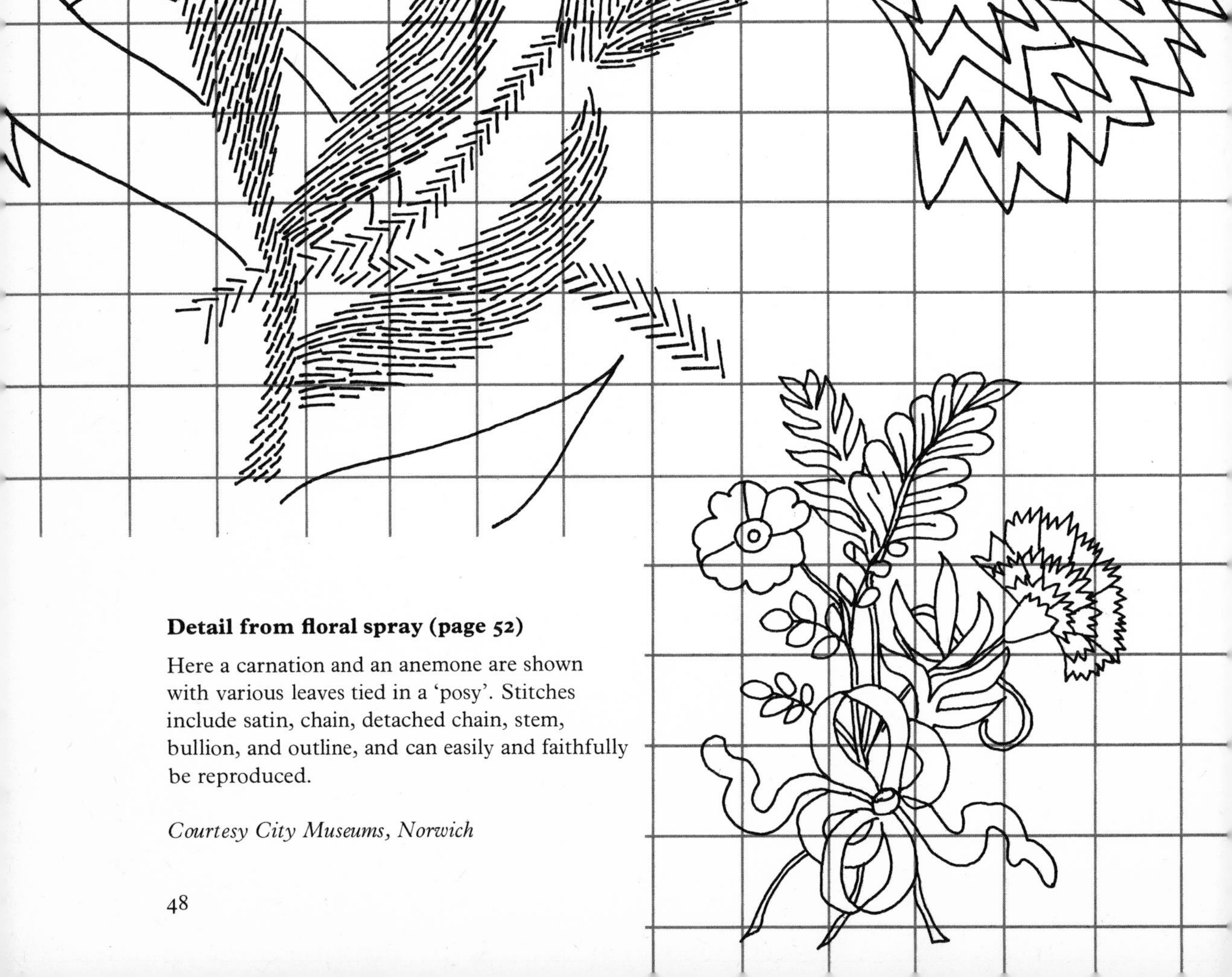

Detail from floral spray (page 52)

Here a carnation and an anemone are shown with various leaves tied in a 'posy'. Stitches include satin, chain, detached chain, stem, bullion, and outline, and can easily and faithfully be reproduced.

Courtesy City Museums, Norwich

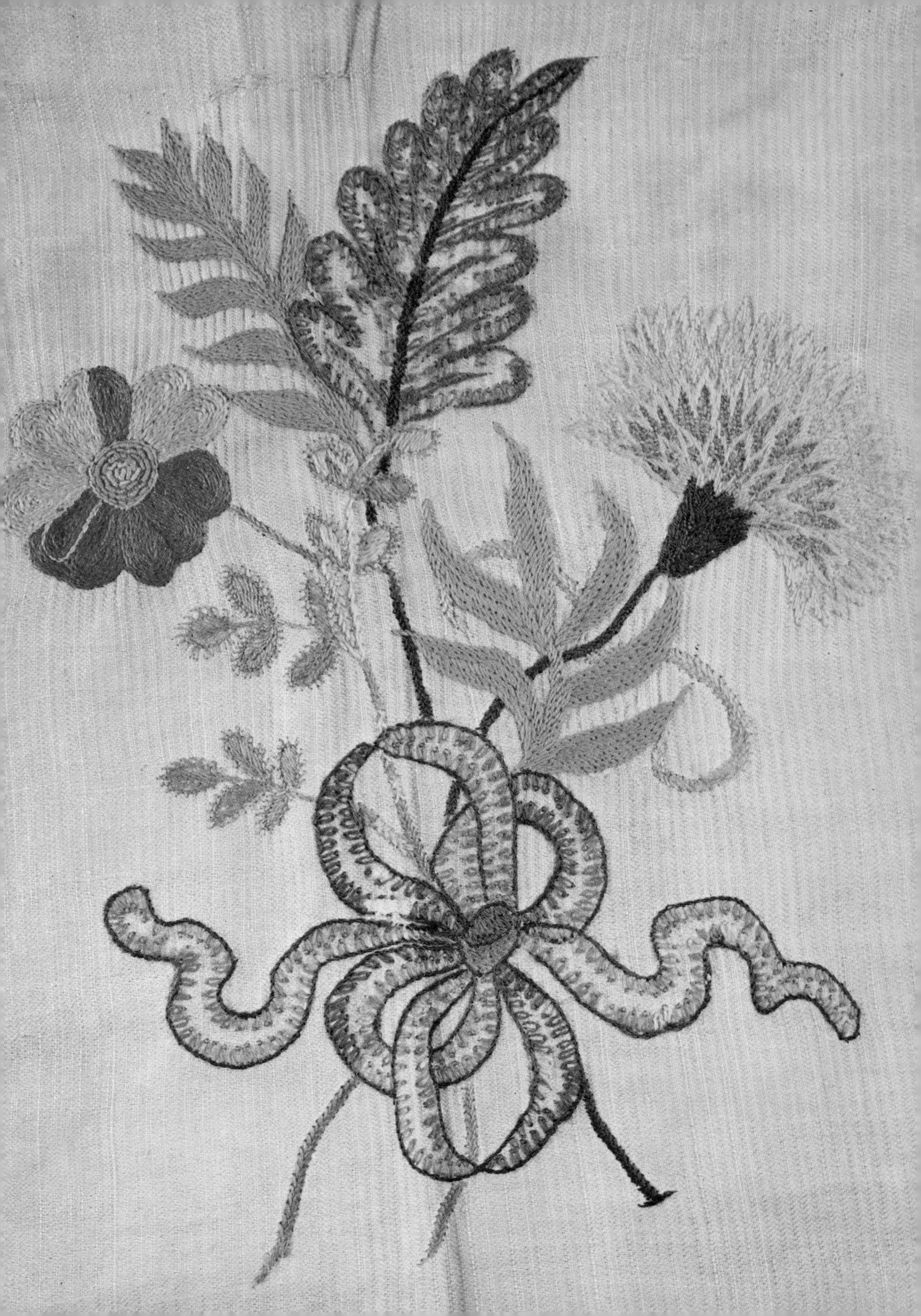

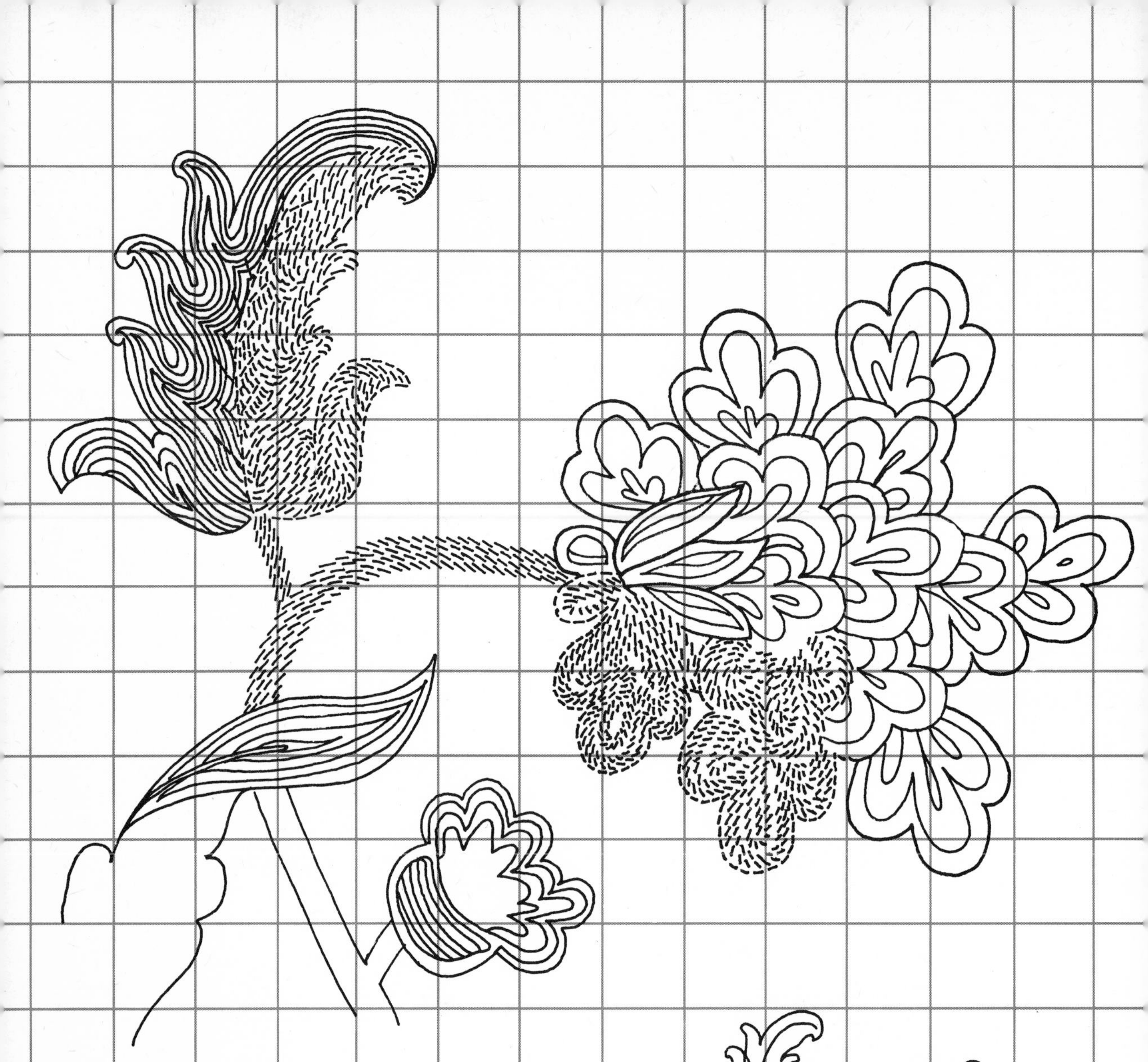

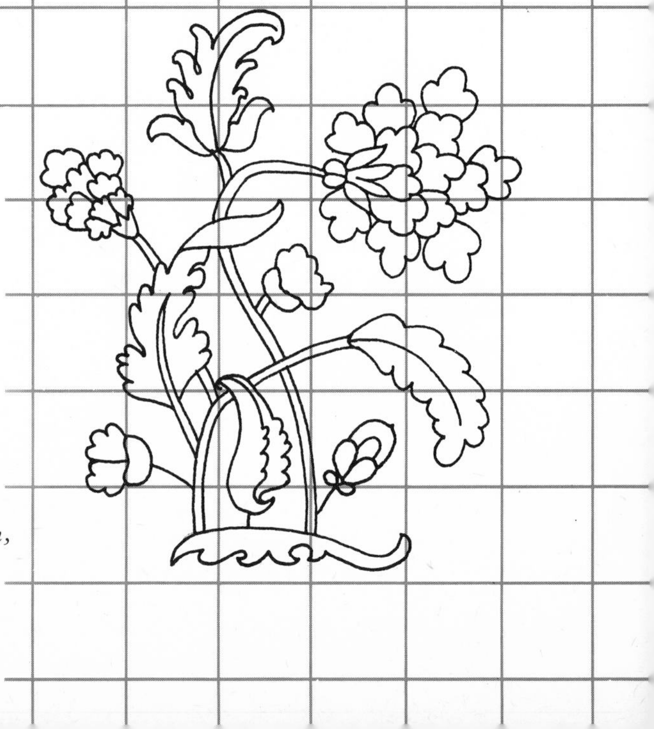

Detail of stylized floral motif from bed furnishings; 1908–18

This attractive motif from the hanging shown on page 32 is worked in satin, stem, chain and outline stitches.

The small drawing on the right is for enlarging the whole design, whereas the large drawing above gives details of the stitches that can be used.

Courtesy The Rachel Kay-Shuttleworth Collection, Gawthorpe Hall, Lancashire

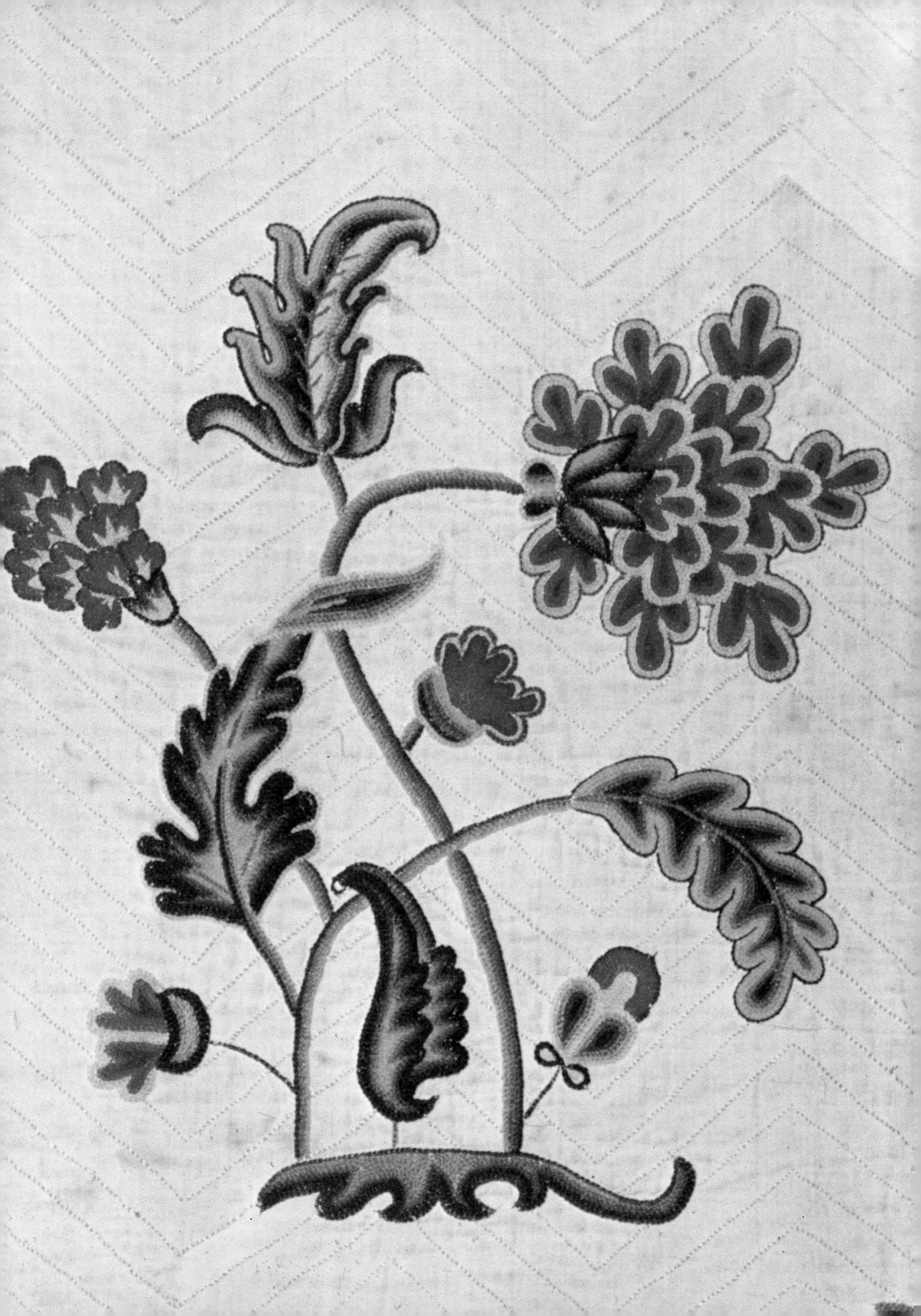

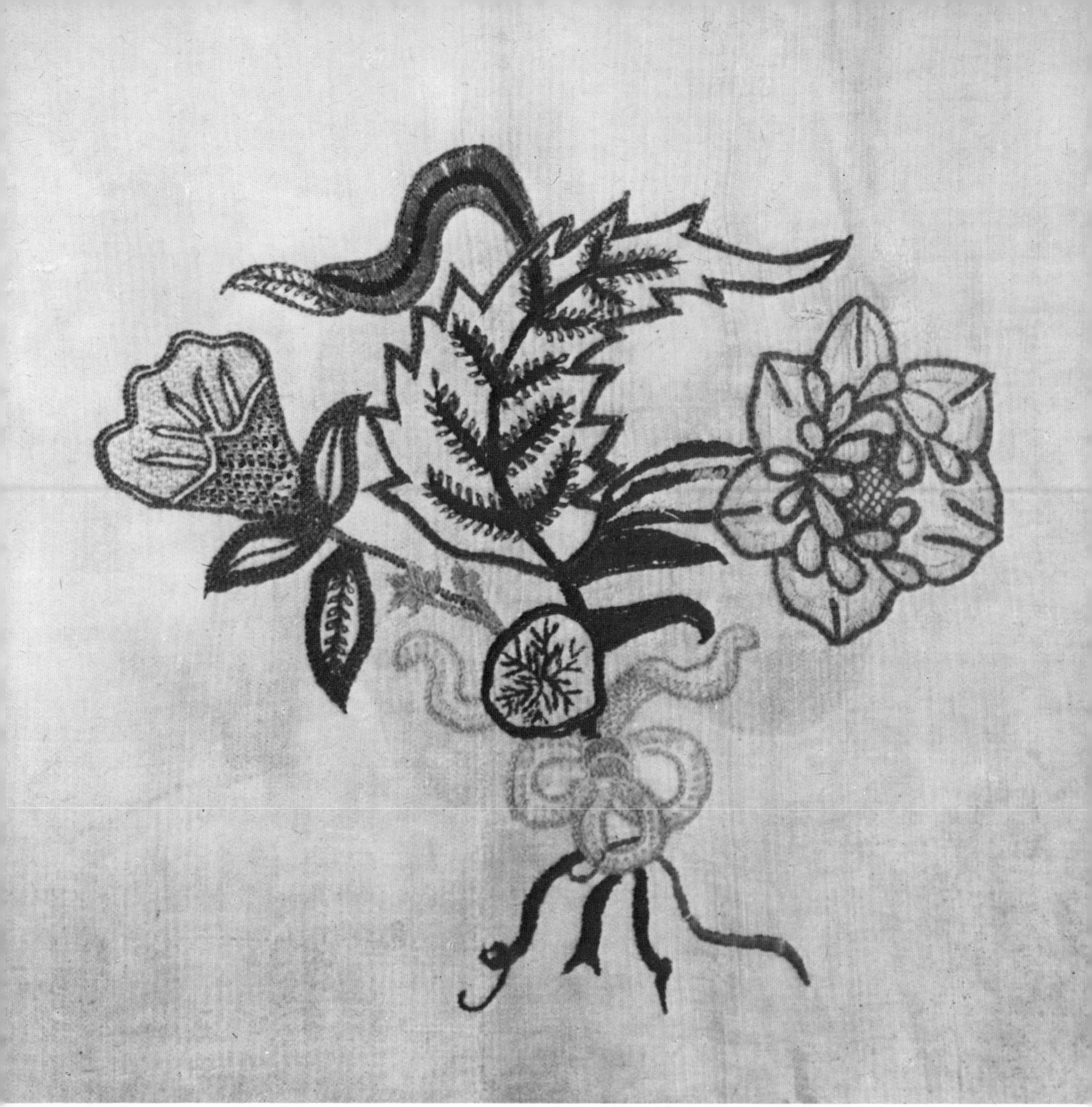

Floral spray from a bed curtain; late 17th to mid 18th century

From the curtain border on page 54, the stitches include chain, satin, split, Cretan, and French knots.

Courtesy City Museums, Norwich

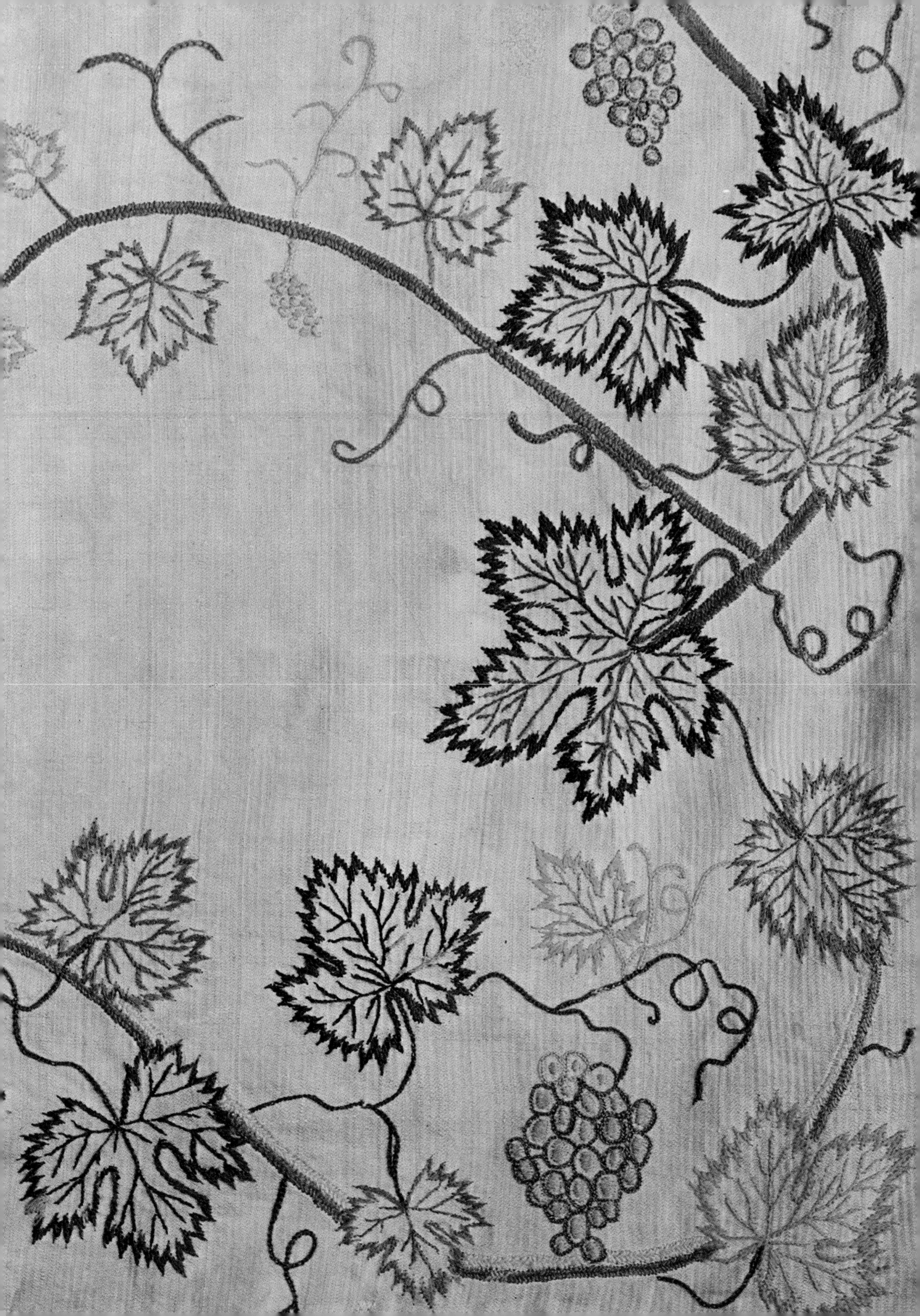

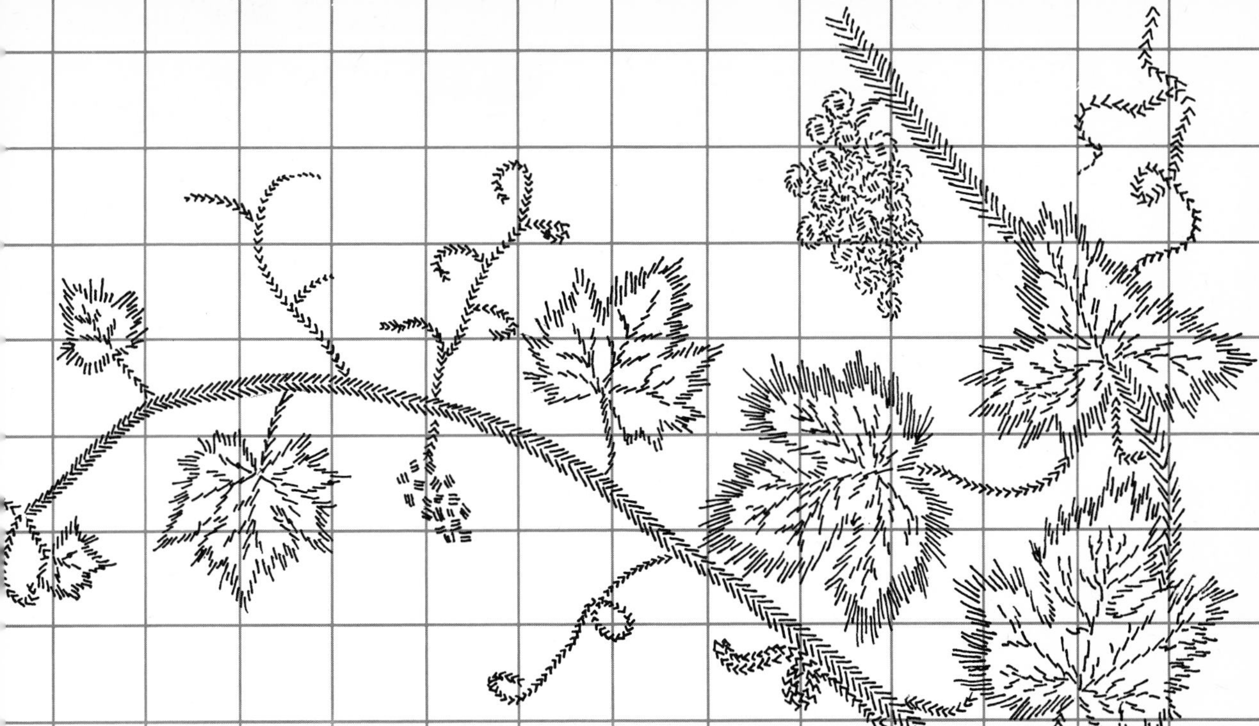

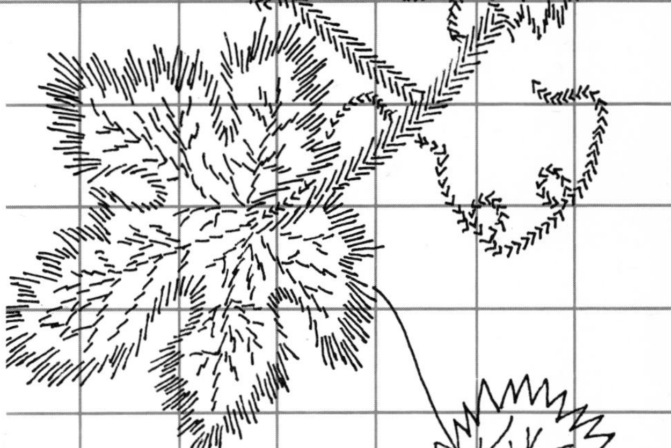

Detail from a bed curtain; late 17th to mid-18th century

The distinct grapevine pattern forms a border on the curtain, the ground being covered with various floral sprays. Stitches used in this detail include chain, outline, stem, feather, Cretan, satin, and long and short. Further details are shown on pages 49 and 52.

Courtesy City Museums, Norwich

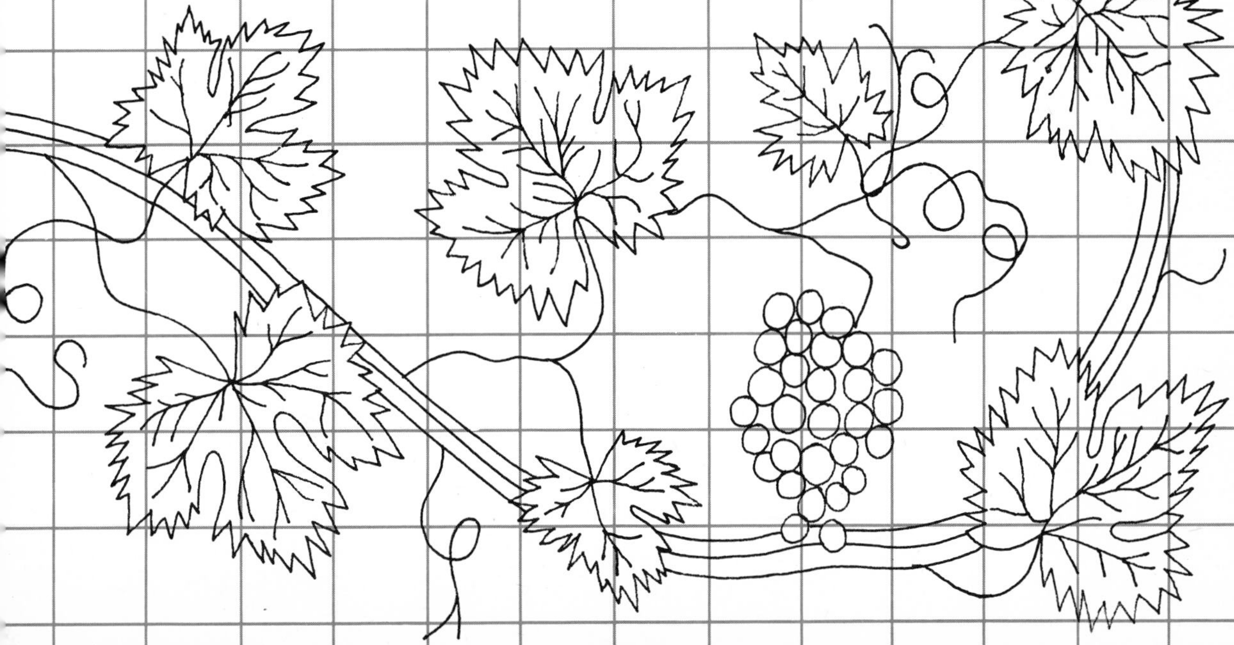

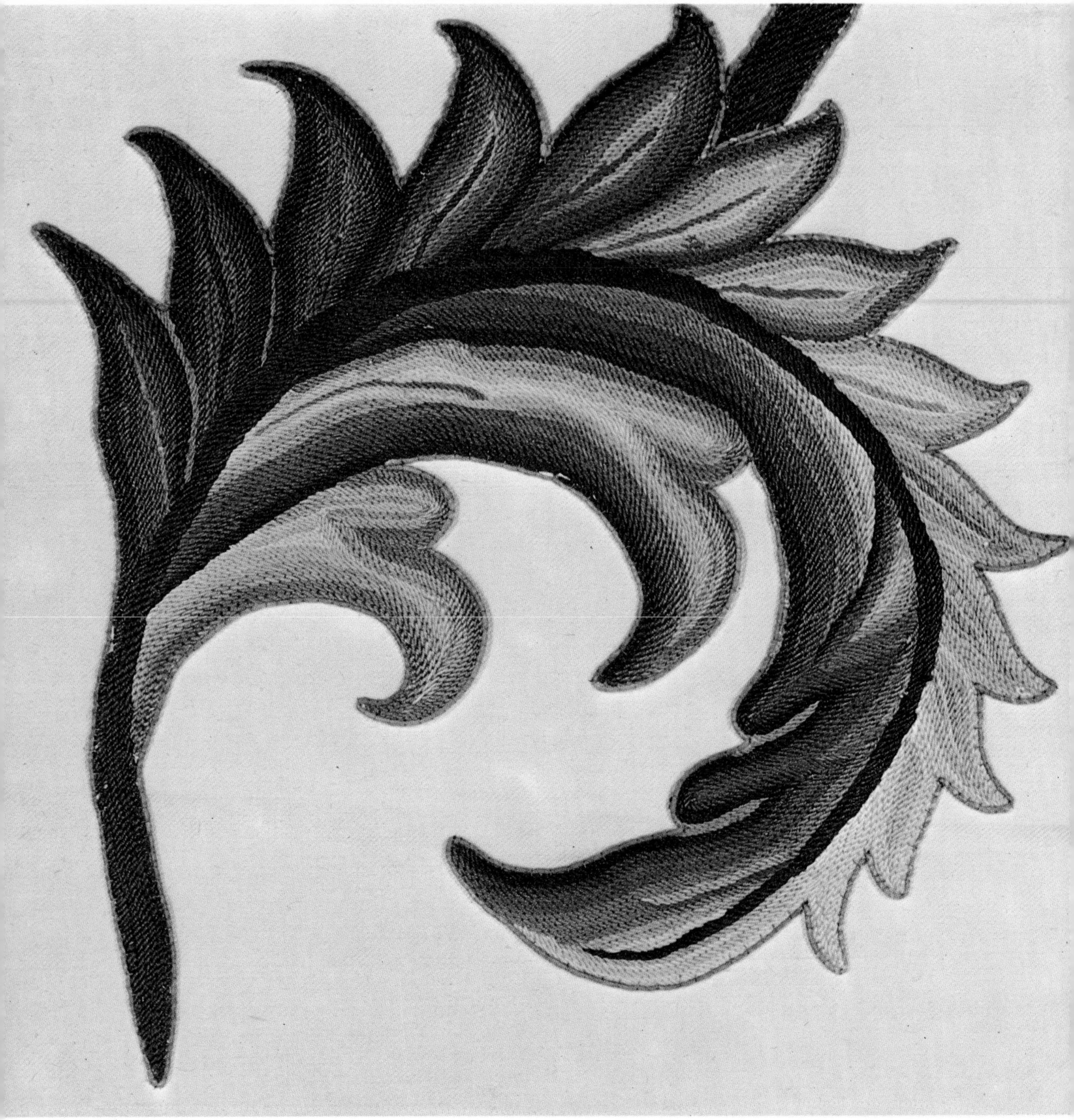

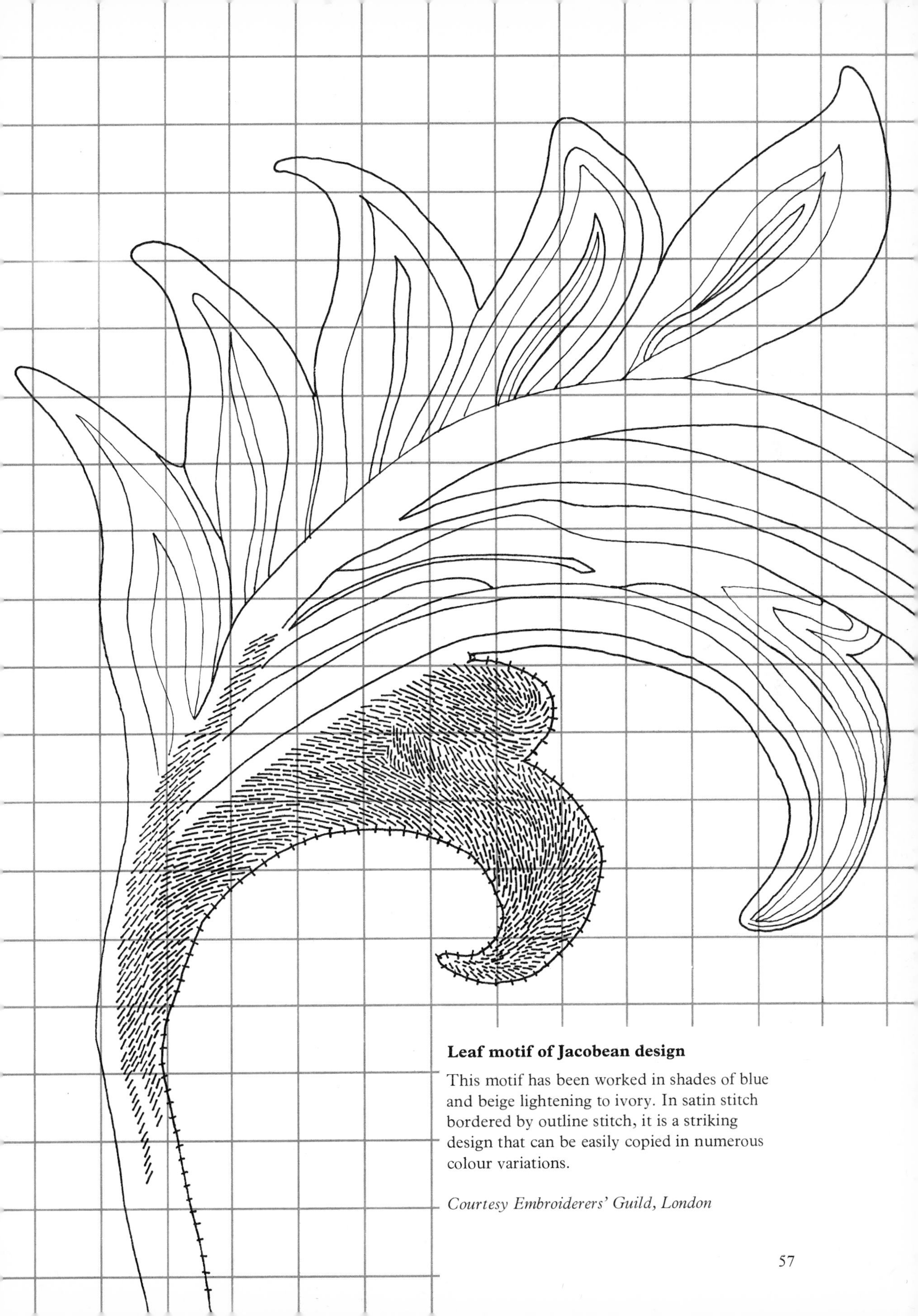

Leaf motif of Jacobean design

This motif has been worked in shades of blue and beige lightening to ivory. In satin stitch bordered by outline stitch, it is a striking design that can be easily copied in numerous colour variations.

Courtesy Embroiderers' Guild, London

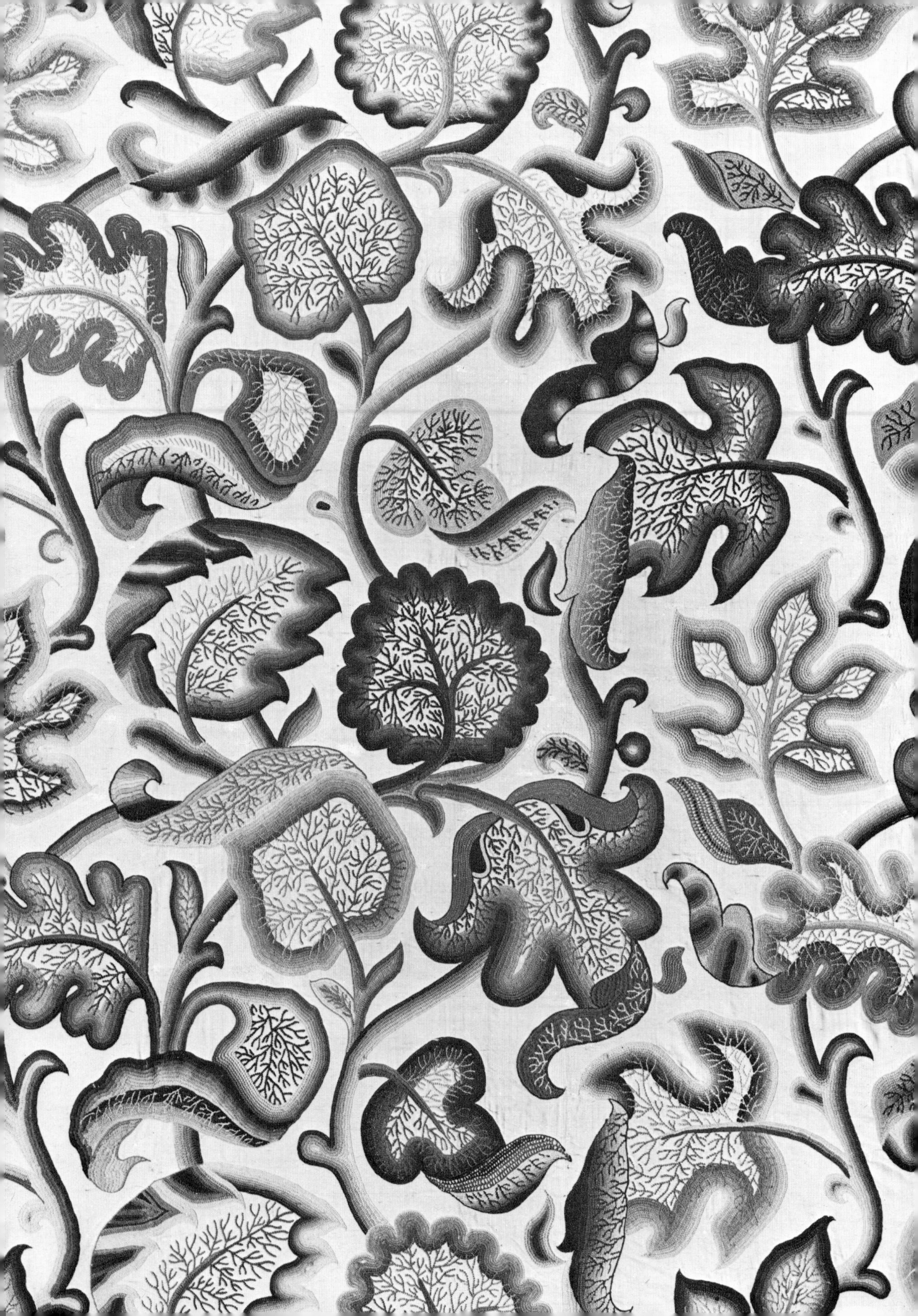

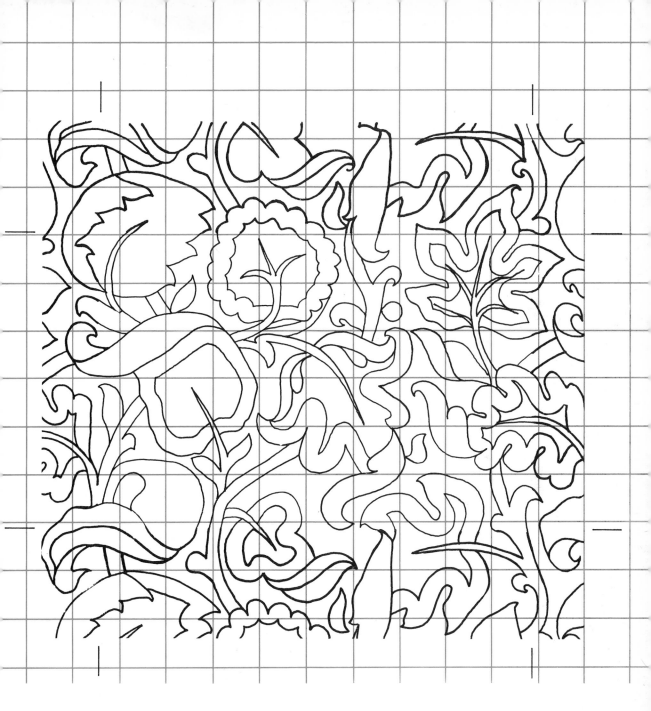

Hanging; mid 17th century

An individual treatment of a leaf motif with a
variation of leaves, tendrils, and patterns
superimposed on the main structure. The whole
is emphasized by strong and flowing outlines
worked in thick threads using closely worked
Cretan stitch, satin stitch, stem, and chain
stitches. By clever use of colour shades, relief
is suggested. The unfilled background, the

flowing lines of the design, and spaced seeding
give a suggestion of lightness.

The drawing is one unit of the whole design,
which can be repeated as many times as
necessary. The bold lines and registration
marks indicate the start of adjacent units.
Each motif may be varied in colour and stitch.

*Crown copyright, Victoria and Albert Museum,
London*

59

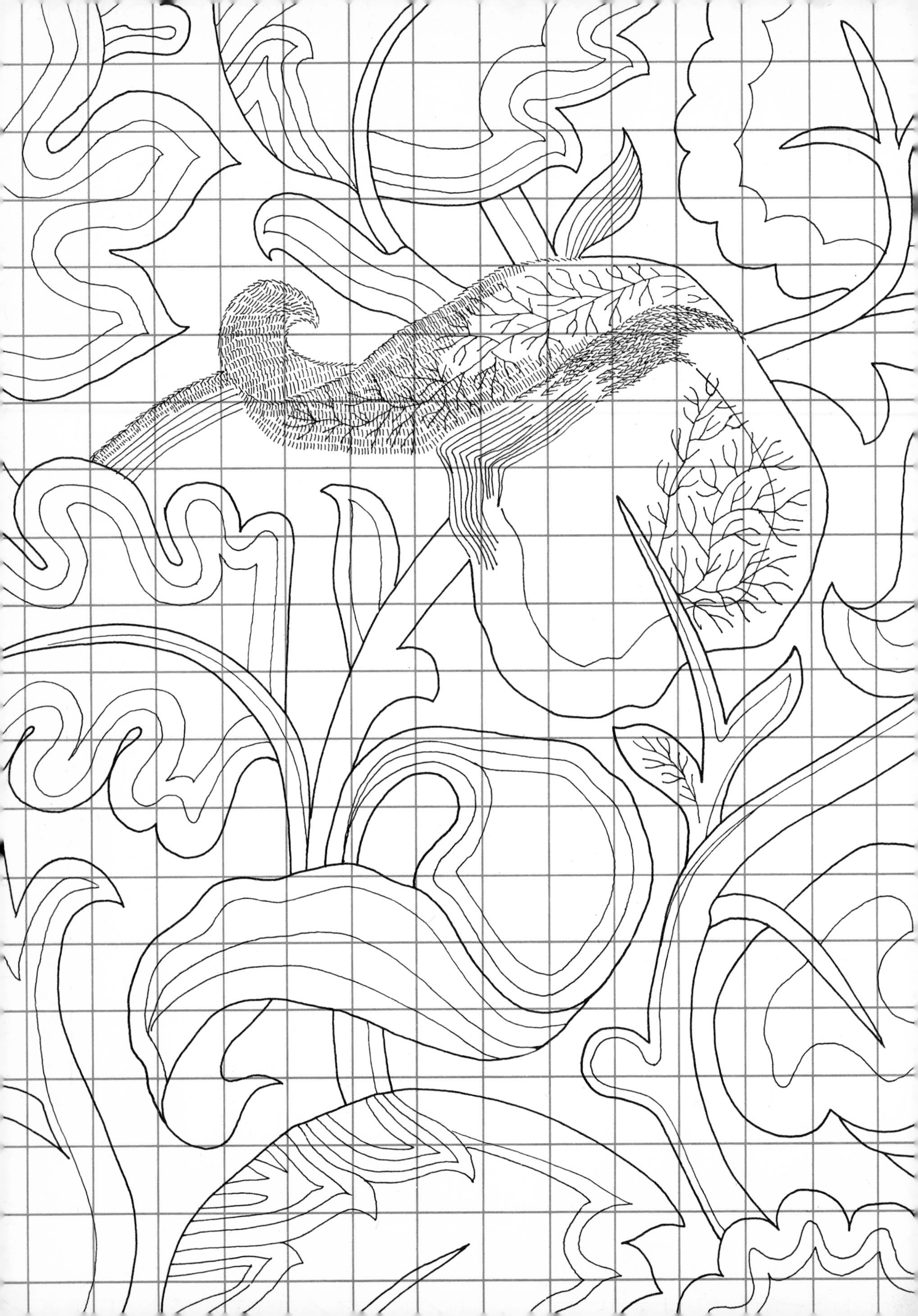

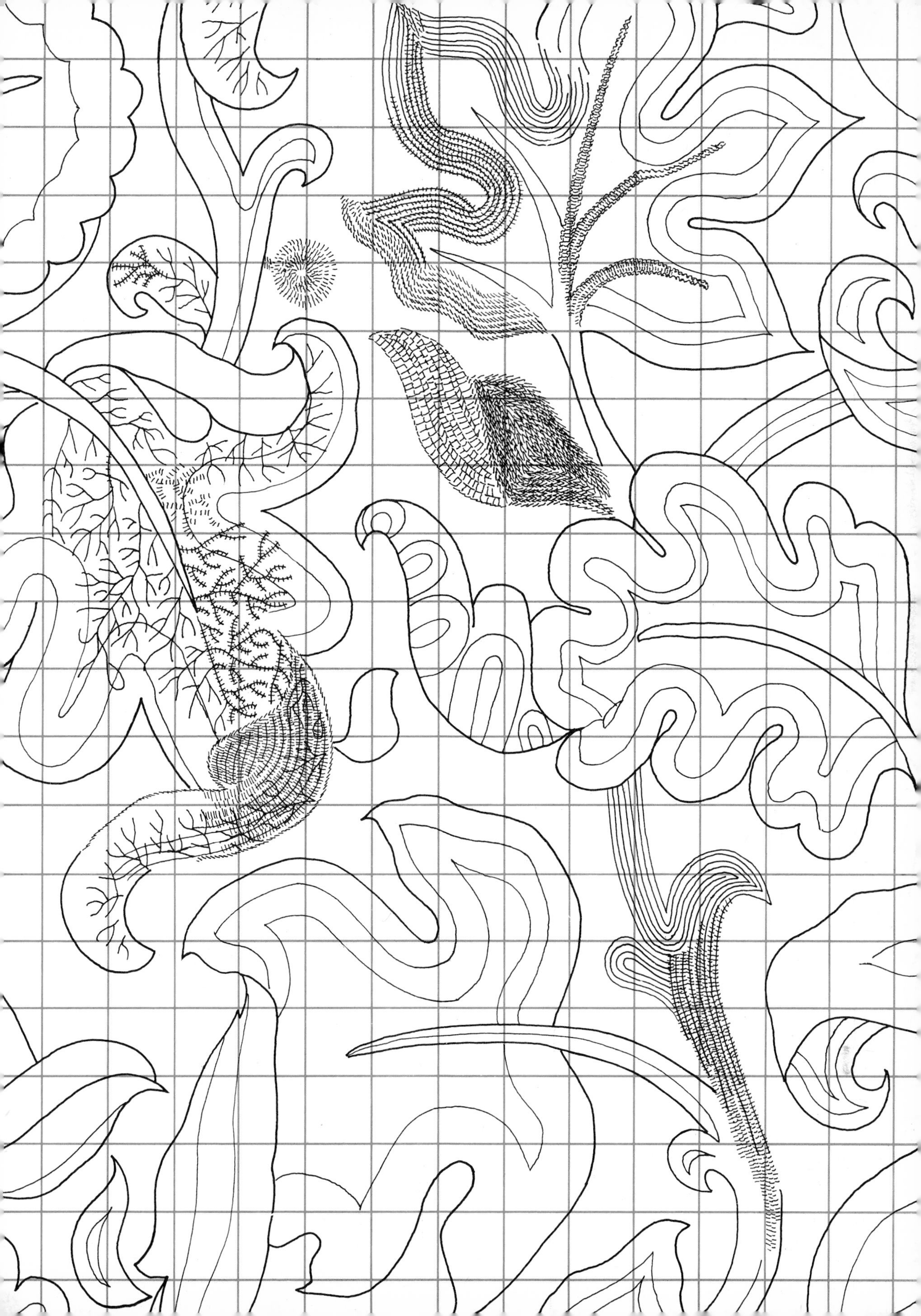

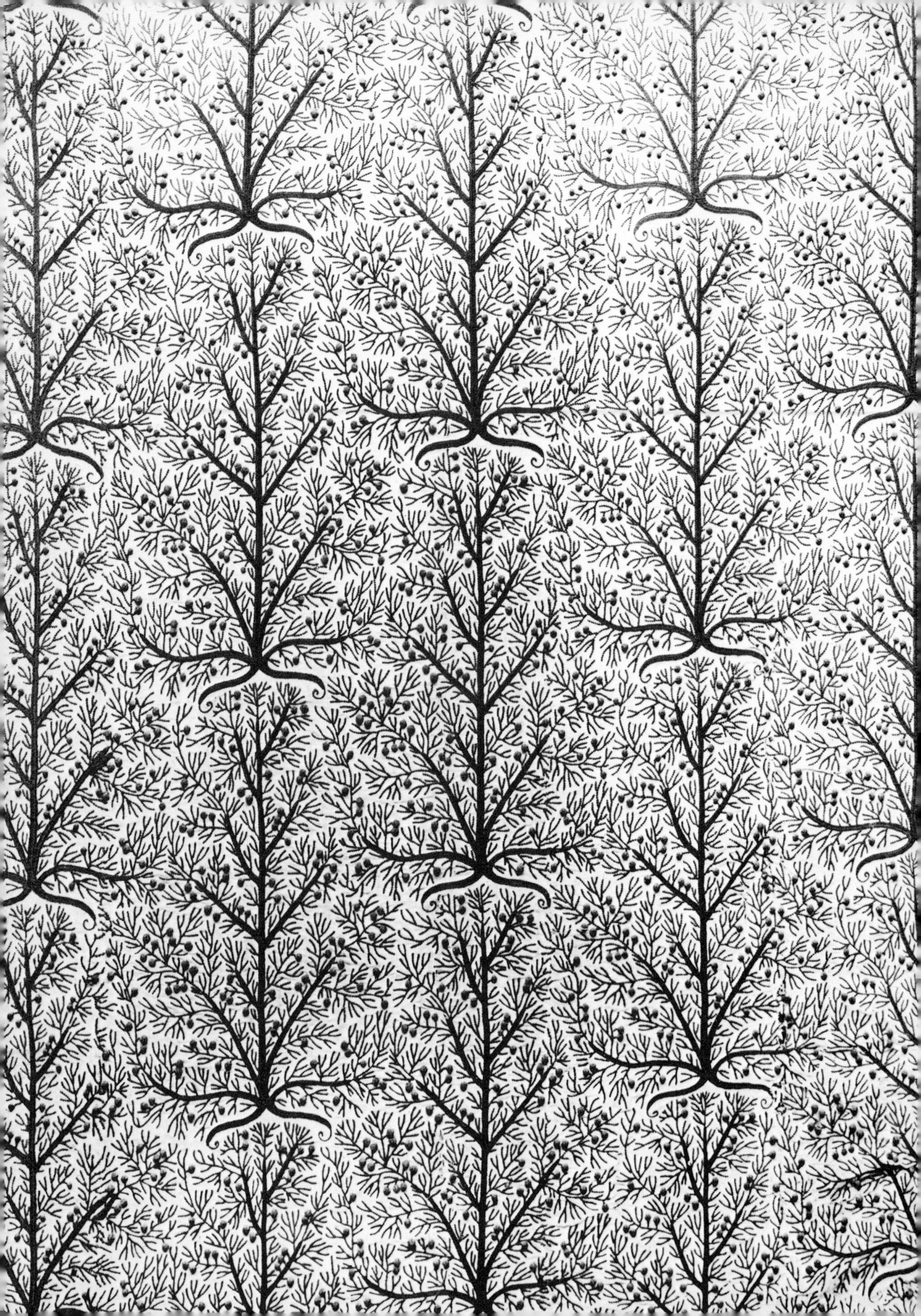

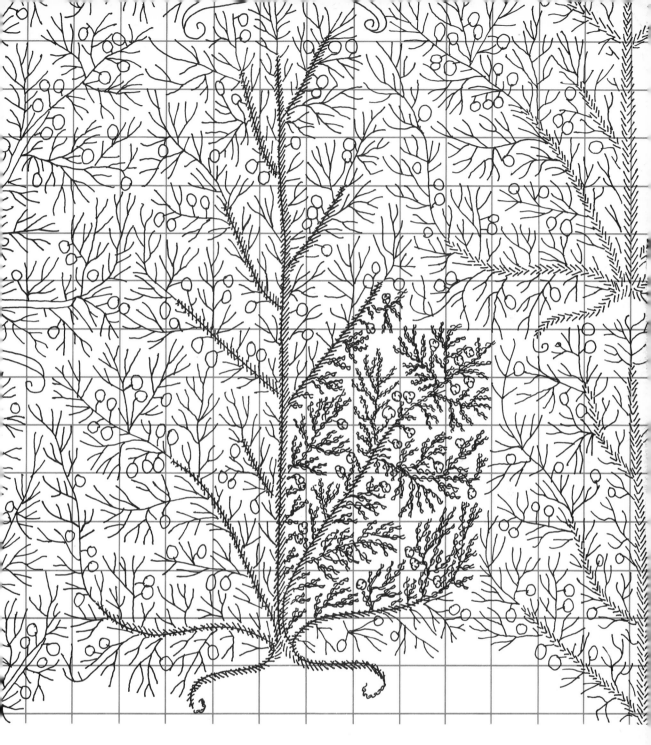

Curtain embroidered in crewel wools on cotton and linen twill; late 17th century

The all-over design of delicate detail shows slender tree trunks, branches, leaves, and berries. The work owes its charm to fine needlework and to a measure of uniformity and restraint in the number of stitches used.

The horizontal lines within the pattern are well adapted to a curtain, with the close design and finely worked embroidery giving an air of lightness and delicacy. Stitches include coral, stem, herringbone, and plaited knots.

Crown copyright, Victoria and Albert Museum, London

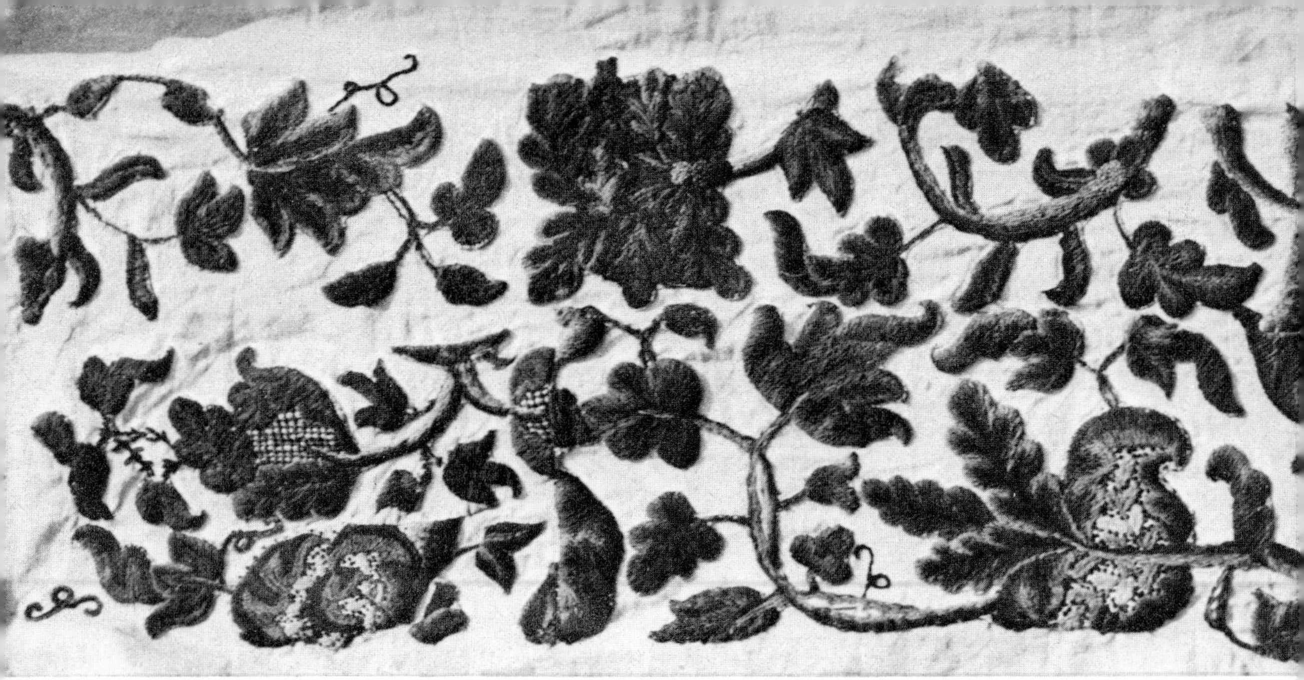

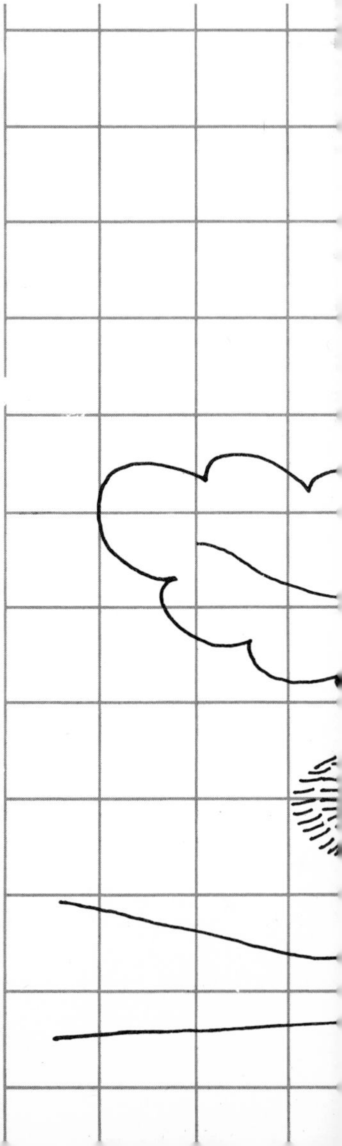

Foliate border of massed pattern, closely arranged and conventionally treated; mid 17th century

The different frets and lattices, interlacings and traceries are clear-cut, facilitating embroidering and allowing for variation in stitch and the introduction of subtle shading.

The larger areas of the design are in stem and satin stitches. Smaller leaves are in satin stitch, with some use of long and short. Subtle tones of green enhance the work.

Courtesy H. E. Kiewe

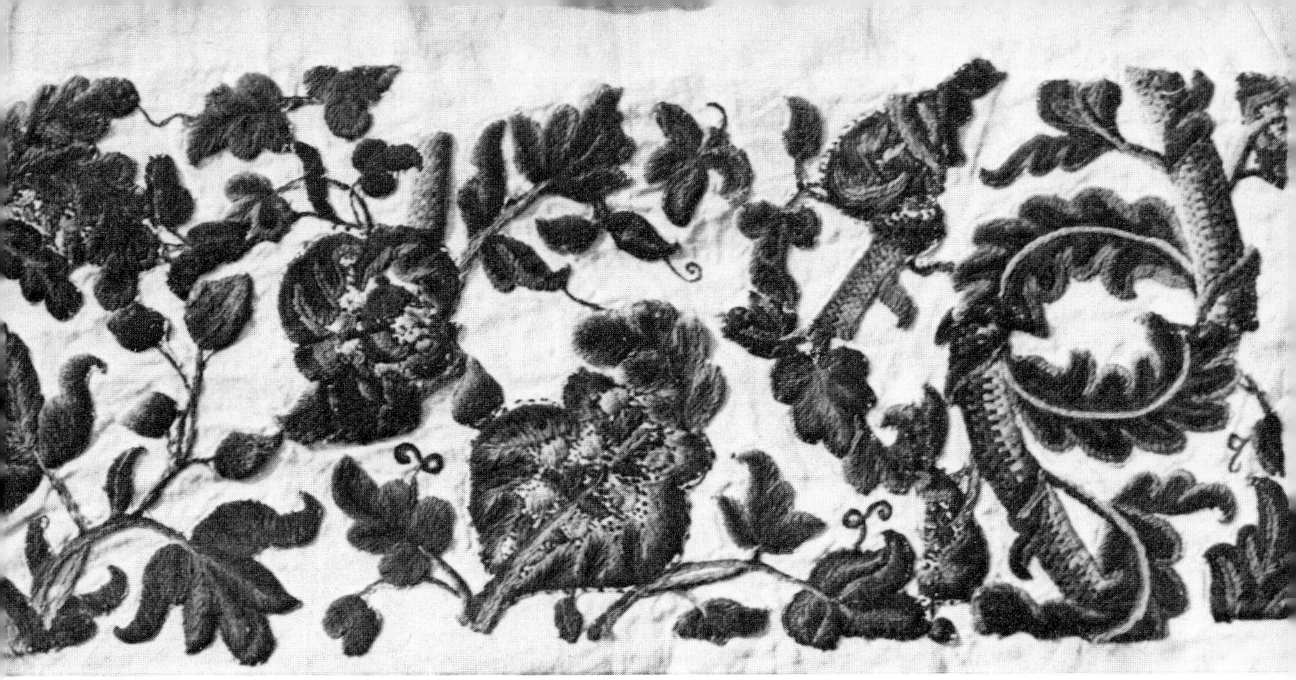

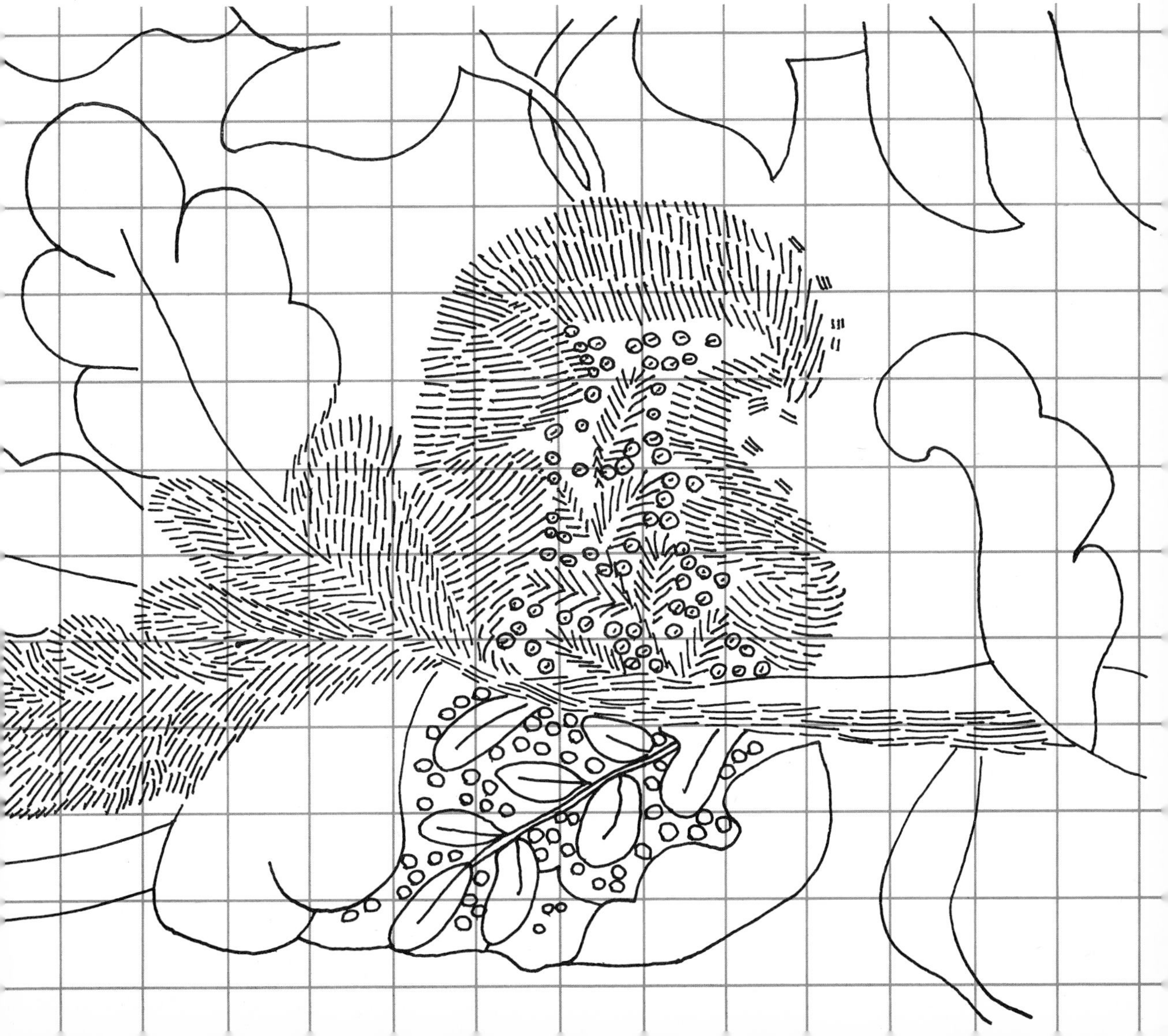

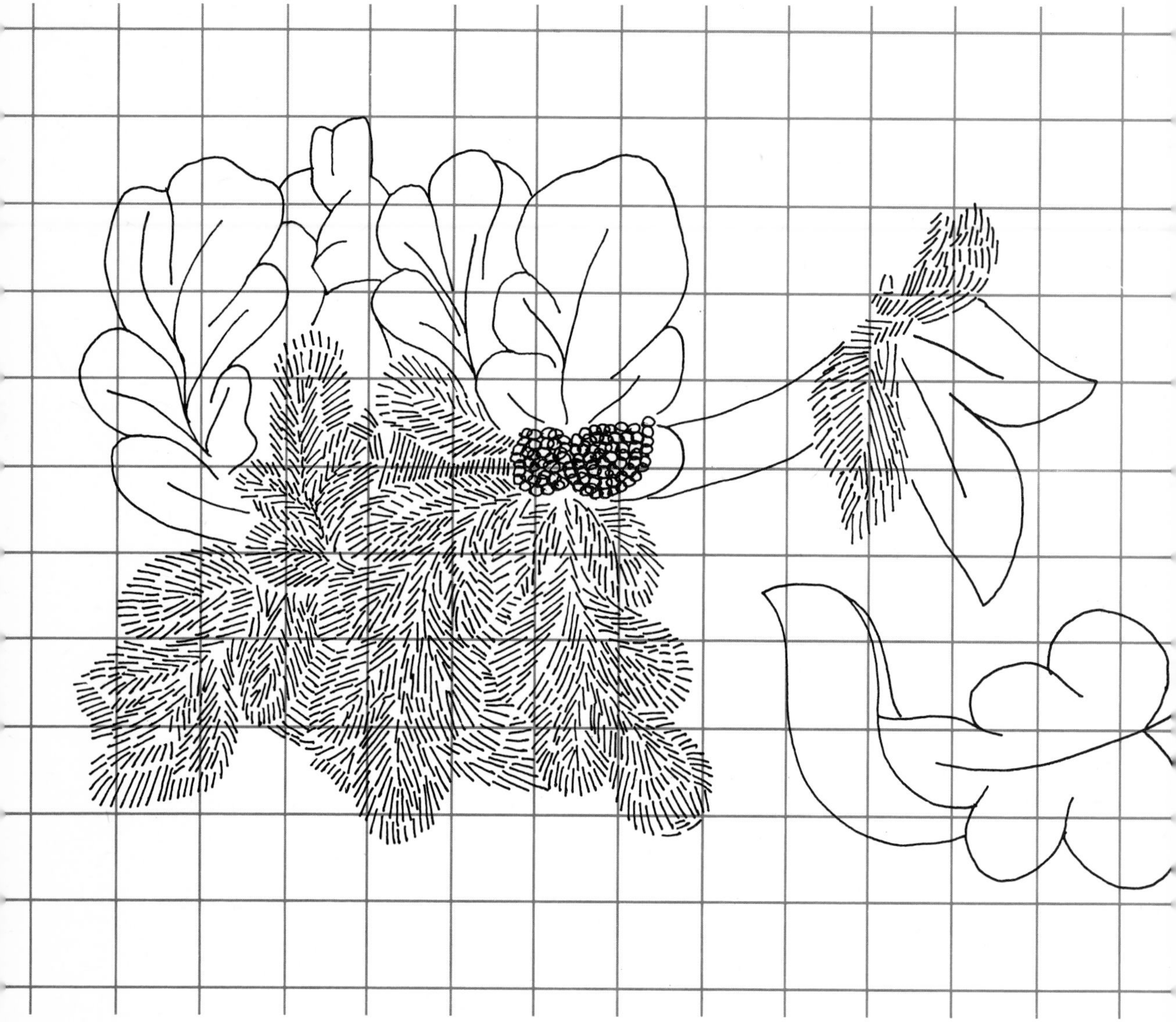

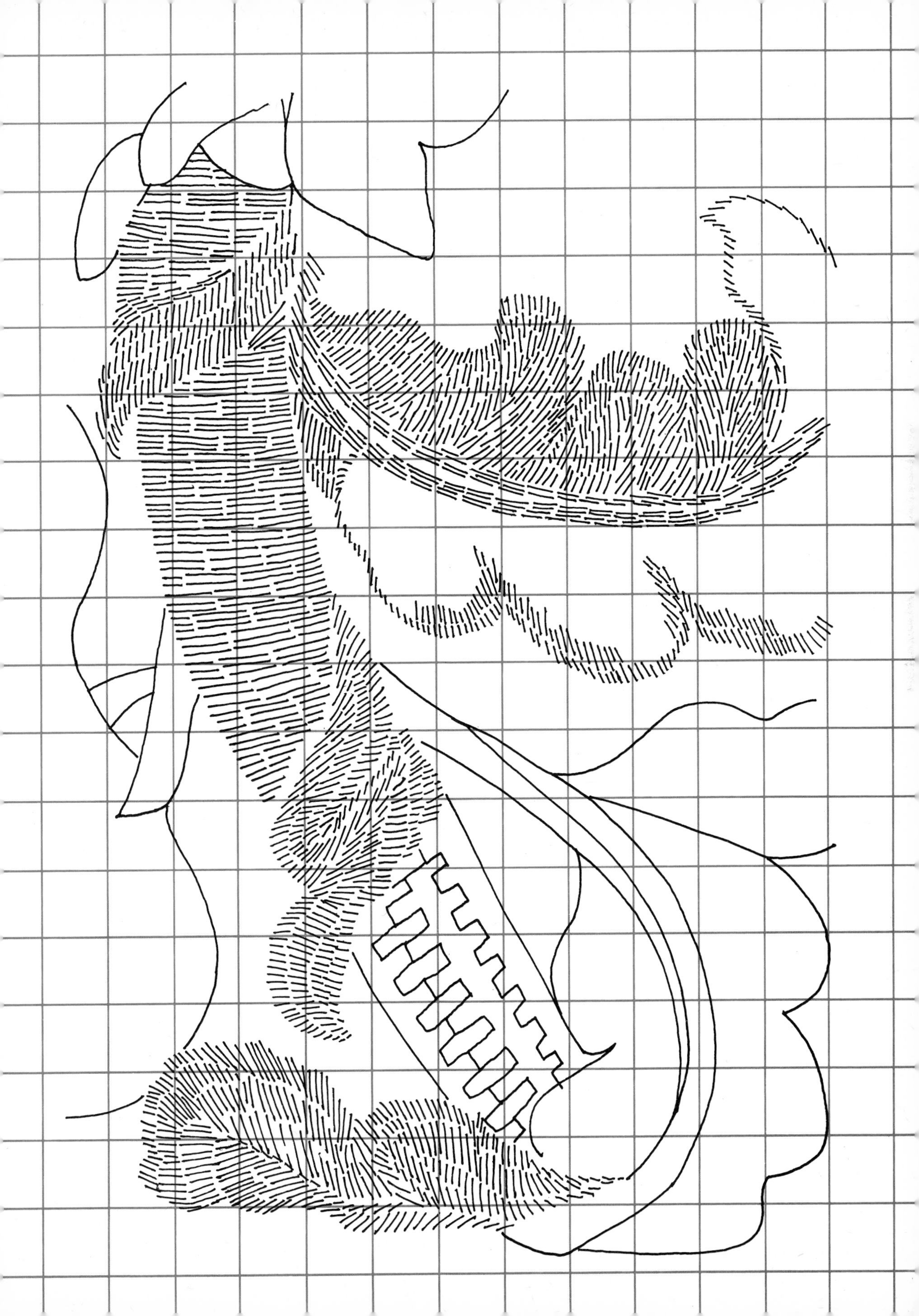

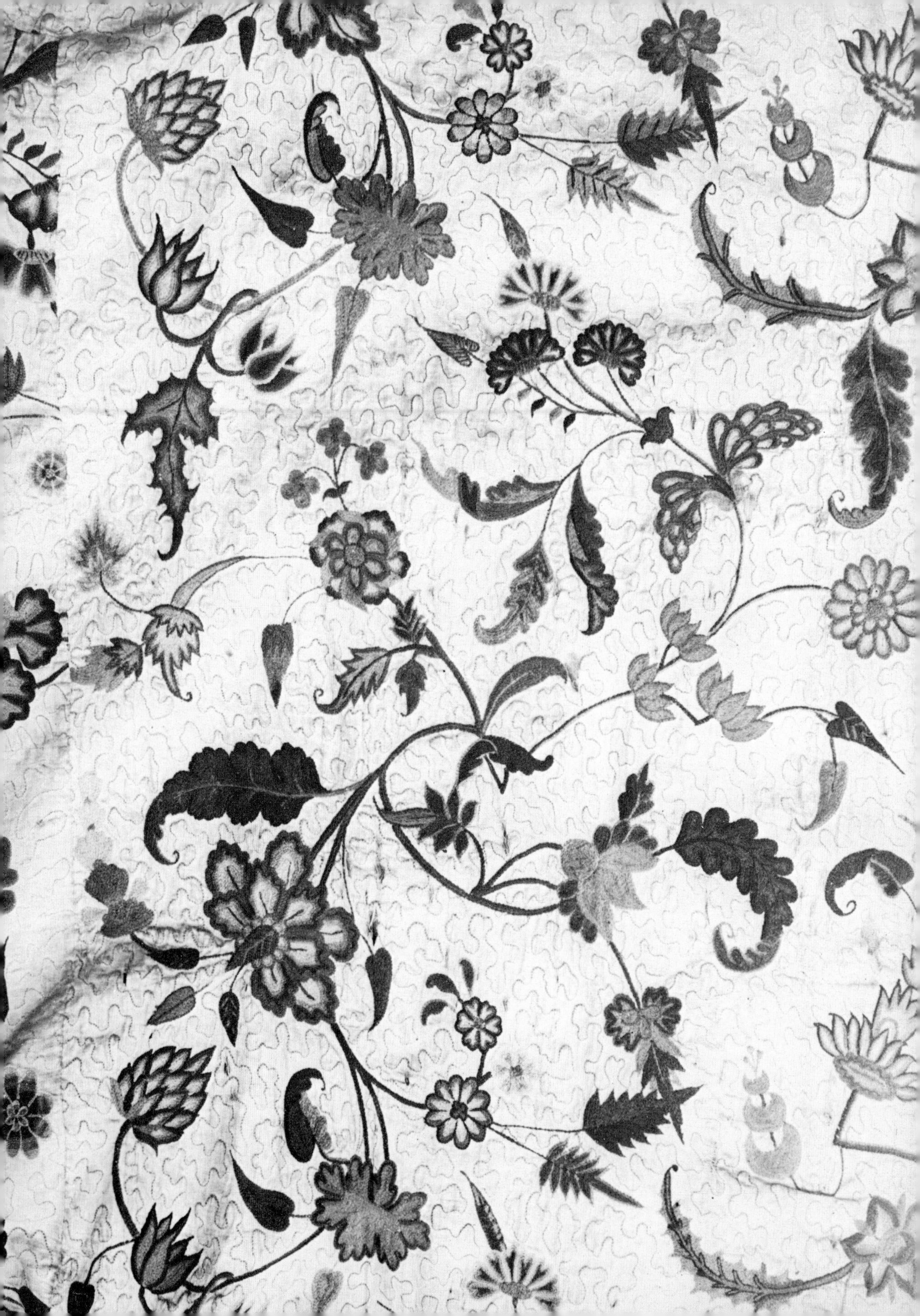

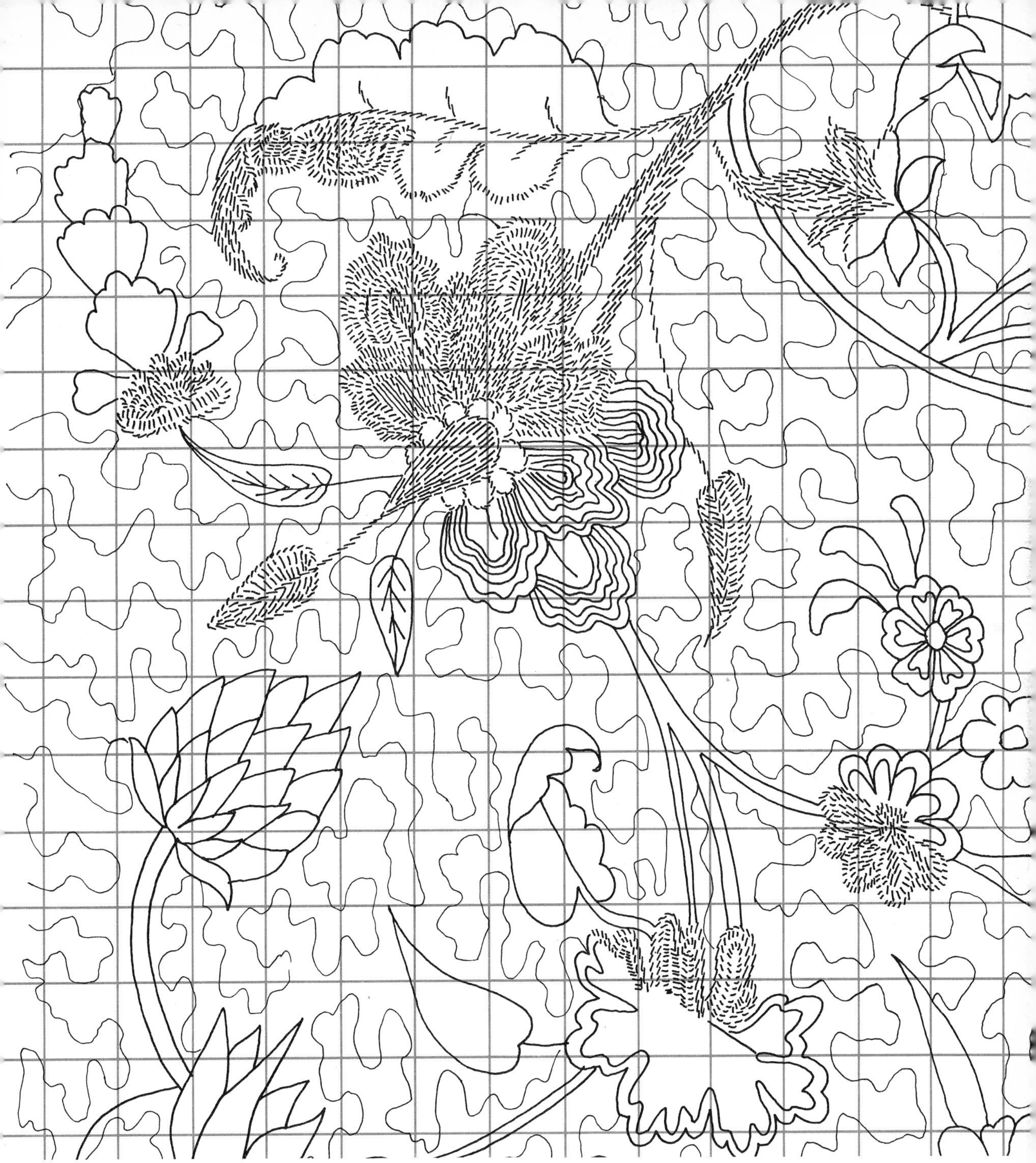

Detail of skirt of woman's dress embroidered in crewel wools; late 17th century

An attractive floral pattern with cursive stems and foliage, it is worked in satin, long and short, stem, outline, and chain stitches.

Courtesy The Whitworth Art Gallery, Manchester

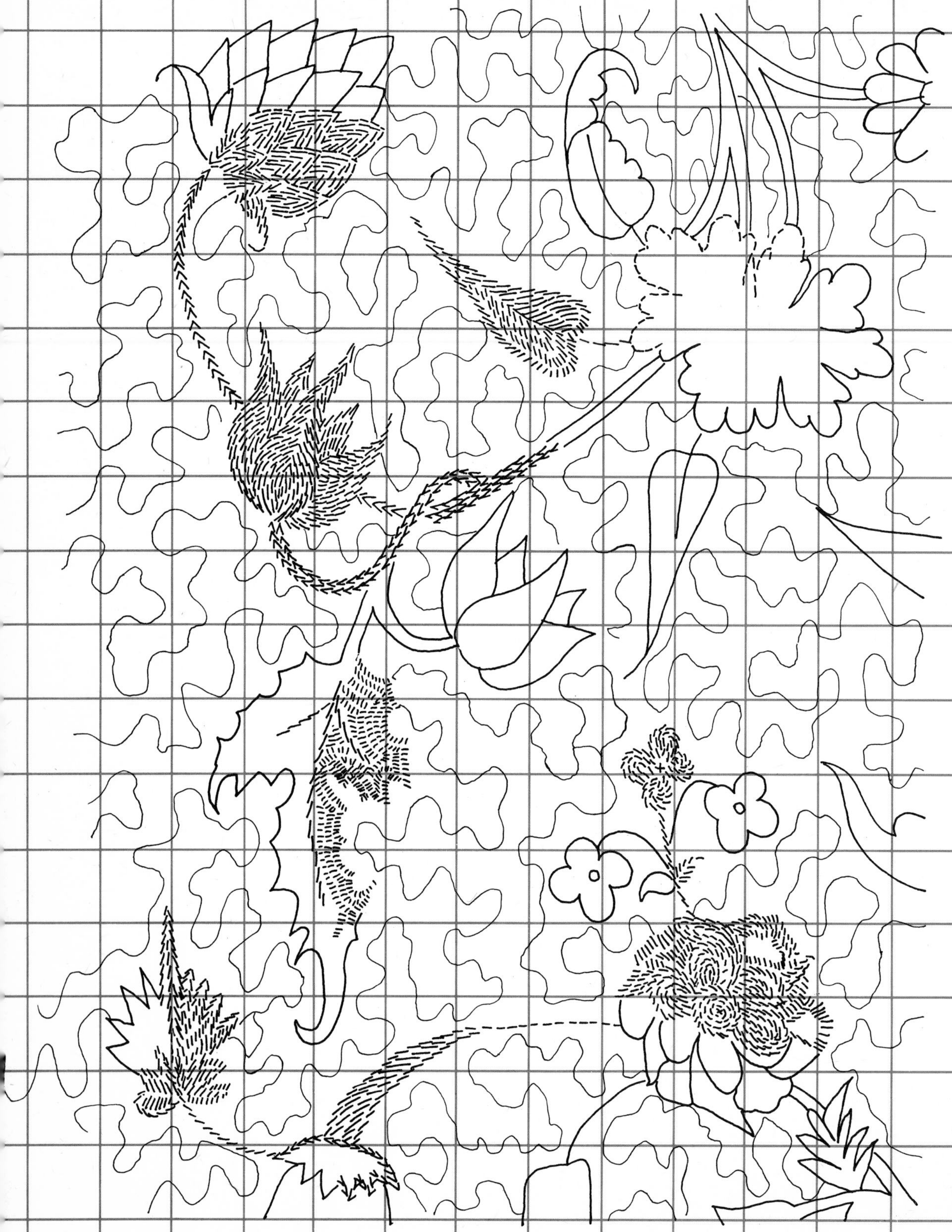

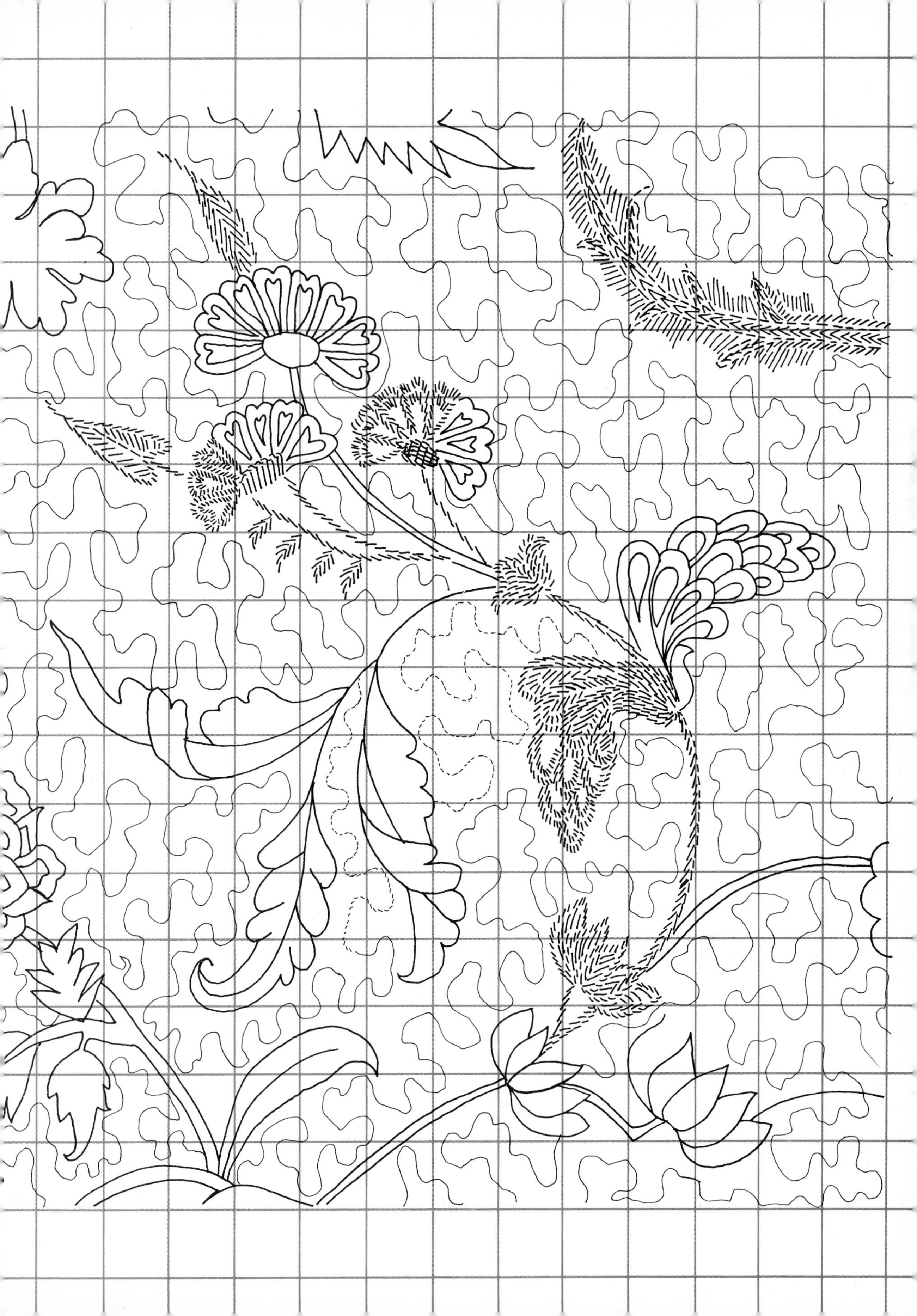

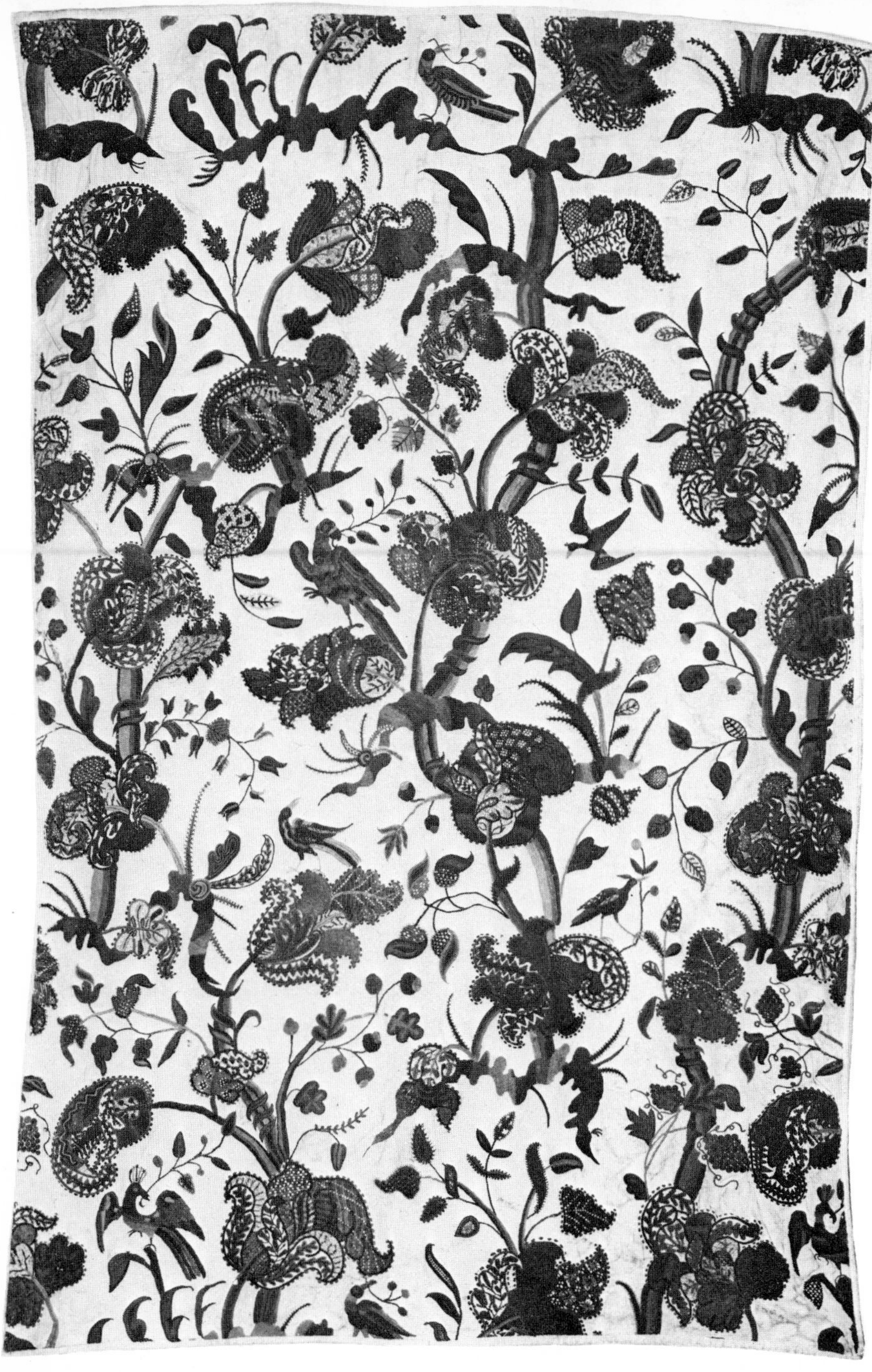

Curtain in crewel wools; about 1696

Crewel wools on linen and cotton twill are worked in a wide variety of stitches including stem, long and short, satin, chain, detached chain, coral, buttonhole, Roumanian, French knots, and seeding.

The design is of the type inspired by Indian cottons, here an elaborate palampore. A graceful presentation of sprays with flowers represented in several different positions calls for uniformity of colour and of stitchery. Birds of bright plumage are interspersed among the branches and the total effect is of vivid colour and clarity.

The drawing is one unit of the whole design, which can be repeated as many times as necessary. The bold lines and registration marks indicate the start of adjacent units. Each motif may be varied in colour and stitch.

Crown copyright, Victoria and Albert Museum, London

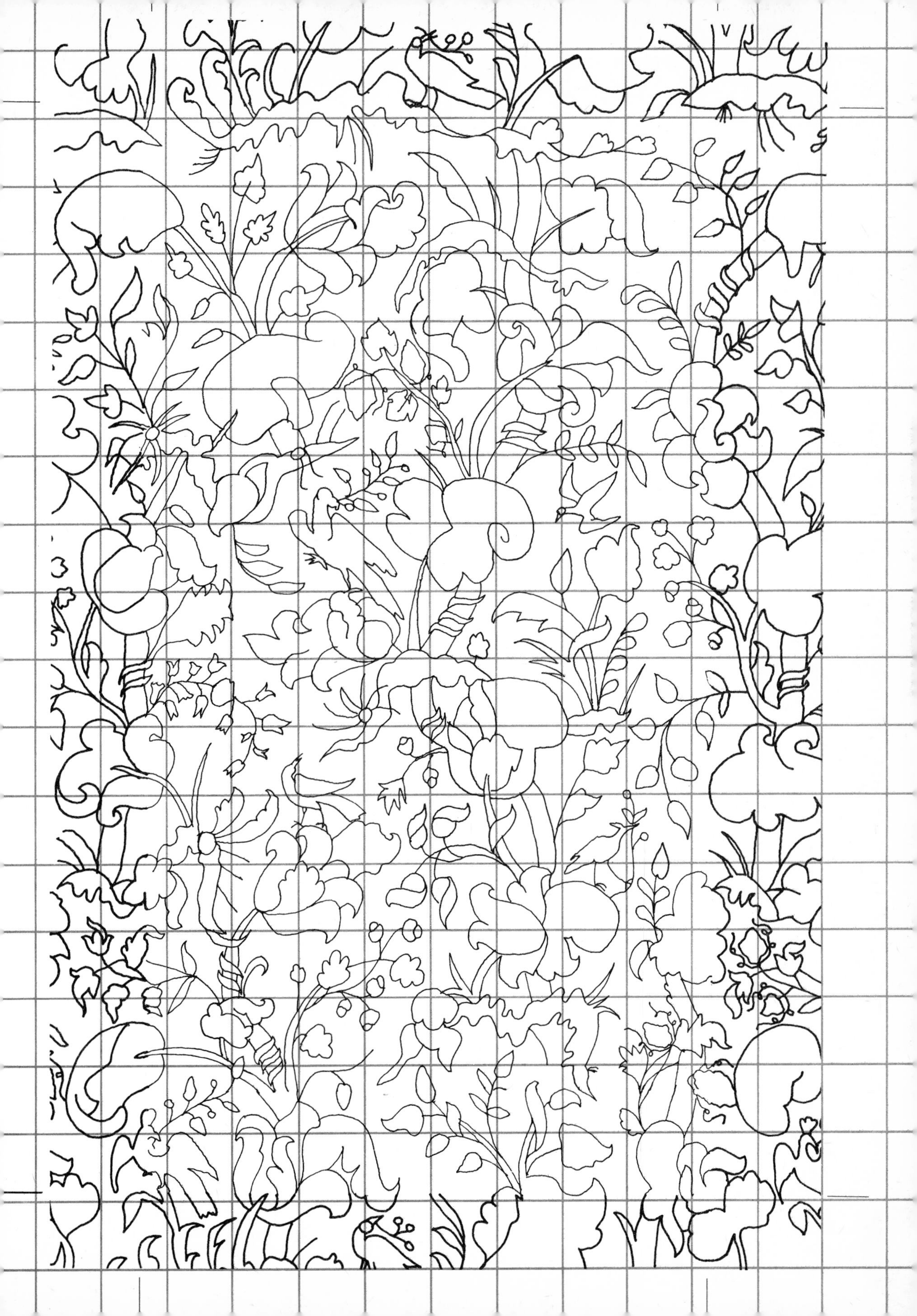

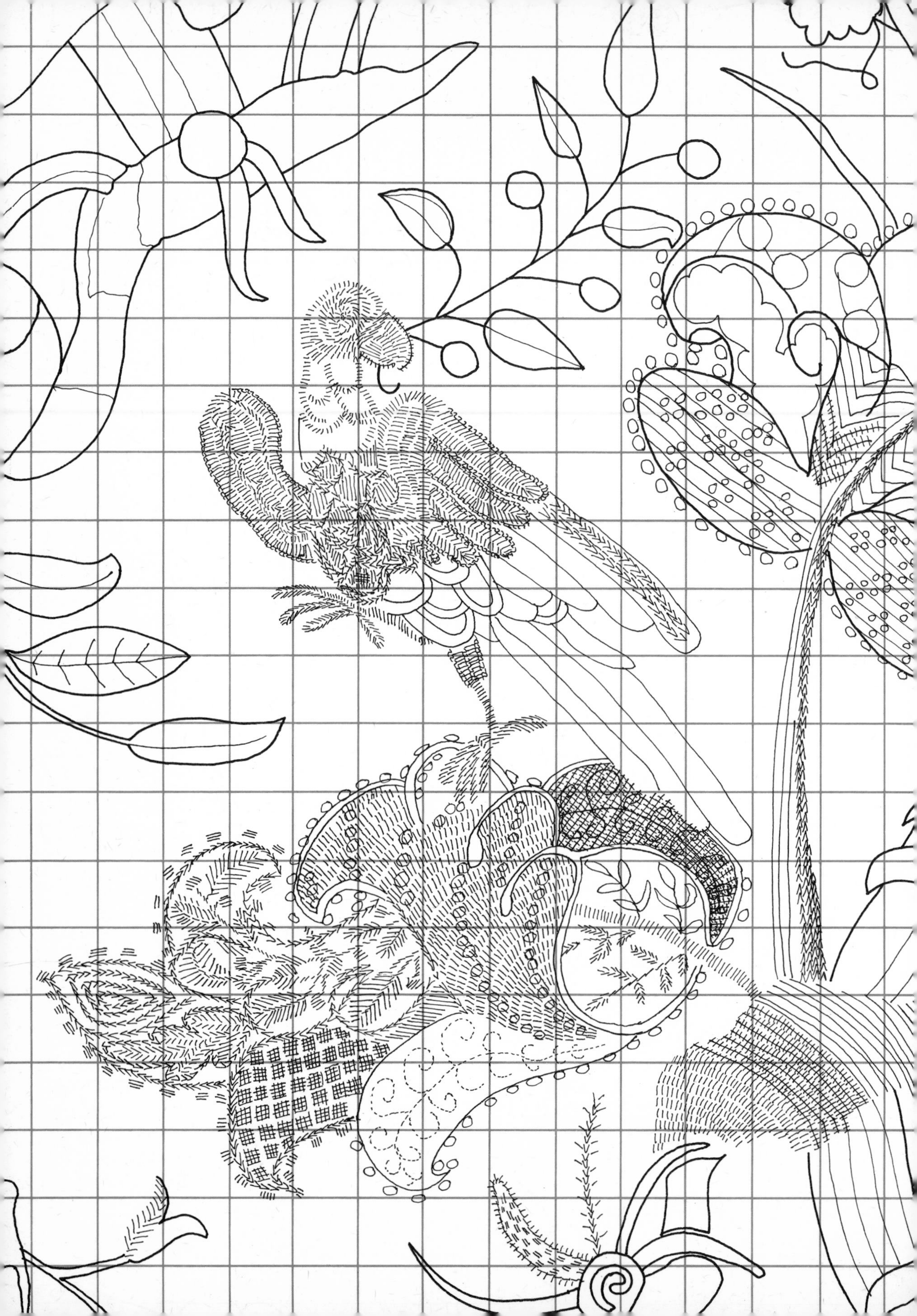

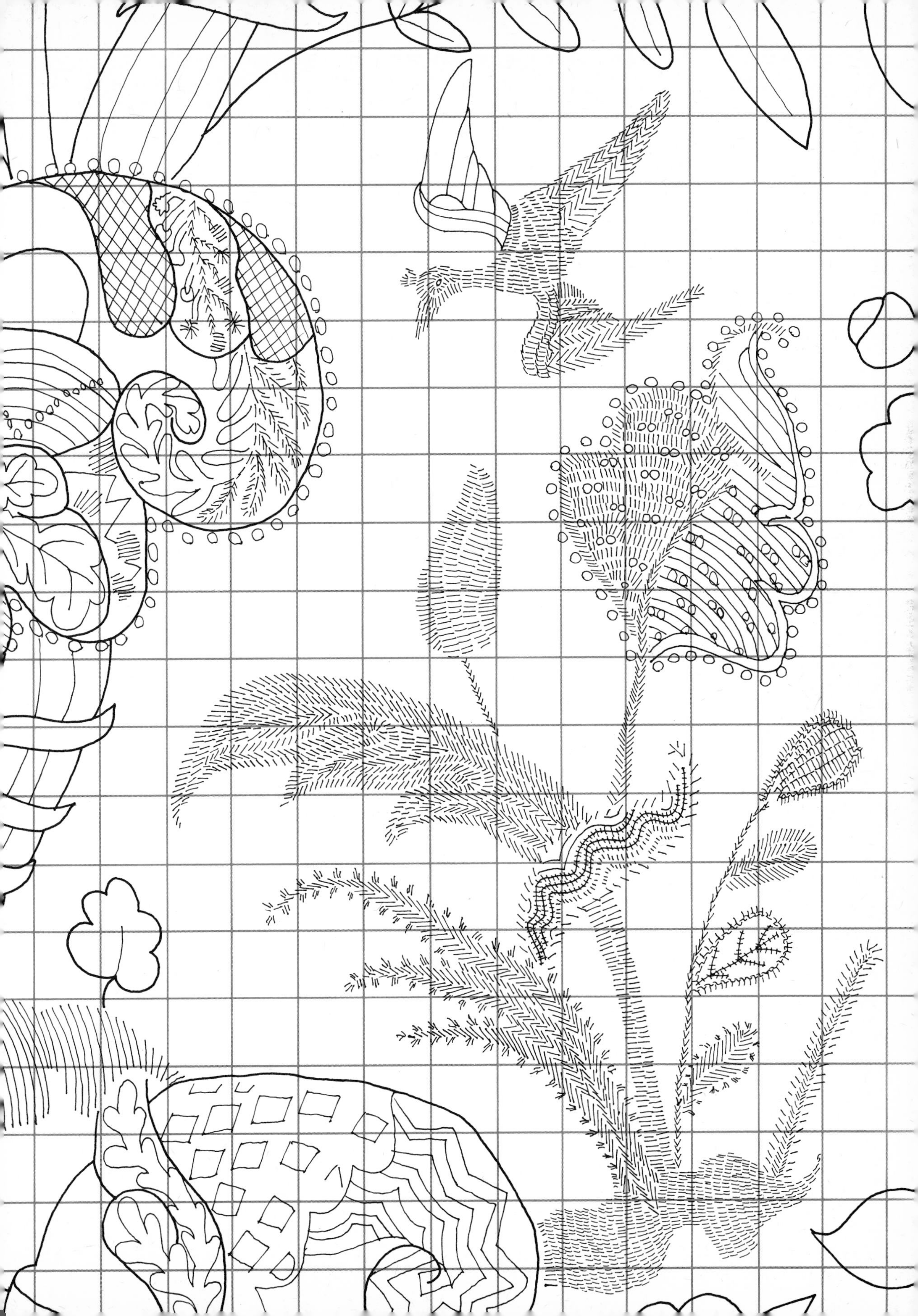

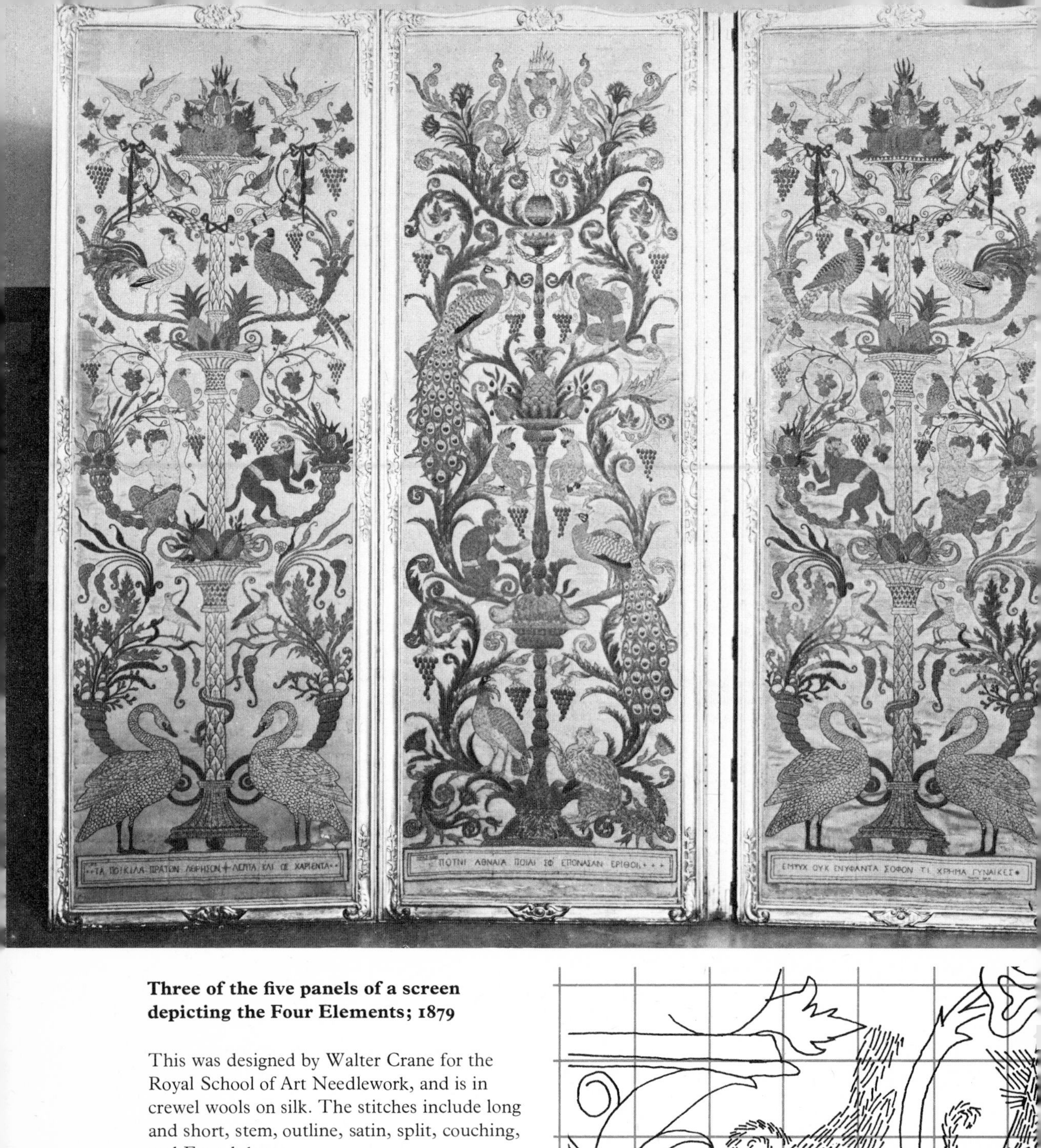

Three of the five panels of a screen depicting the Four Elements; 1879

This was designed by Walter Crane for the Royal School of Art Needlework, and is in crewel wools on silk. The stitches include long and short, stem, outline, satin, split, couching, and French knots.

Crown copyright, Victoria and Albert Museum, London

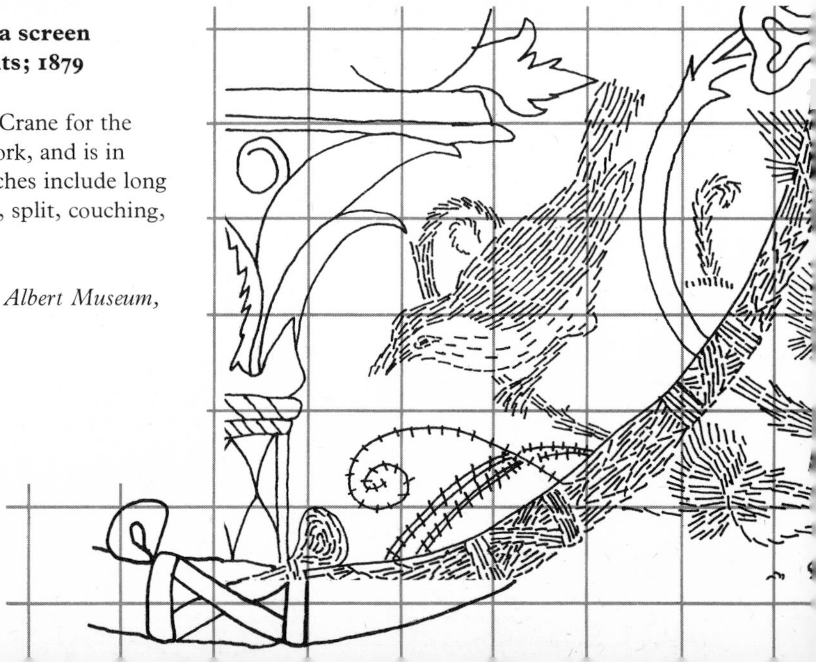

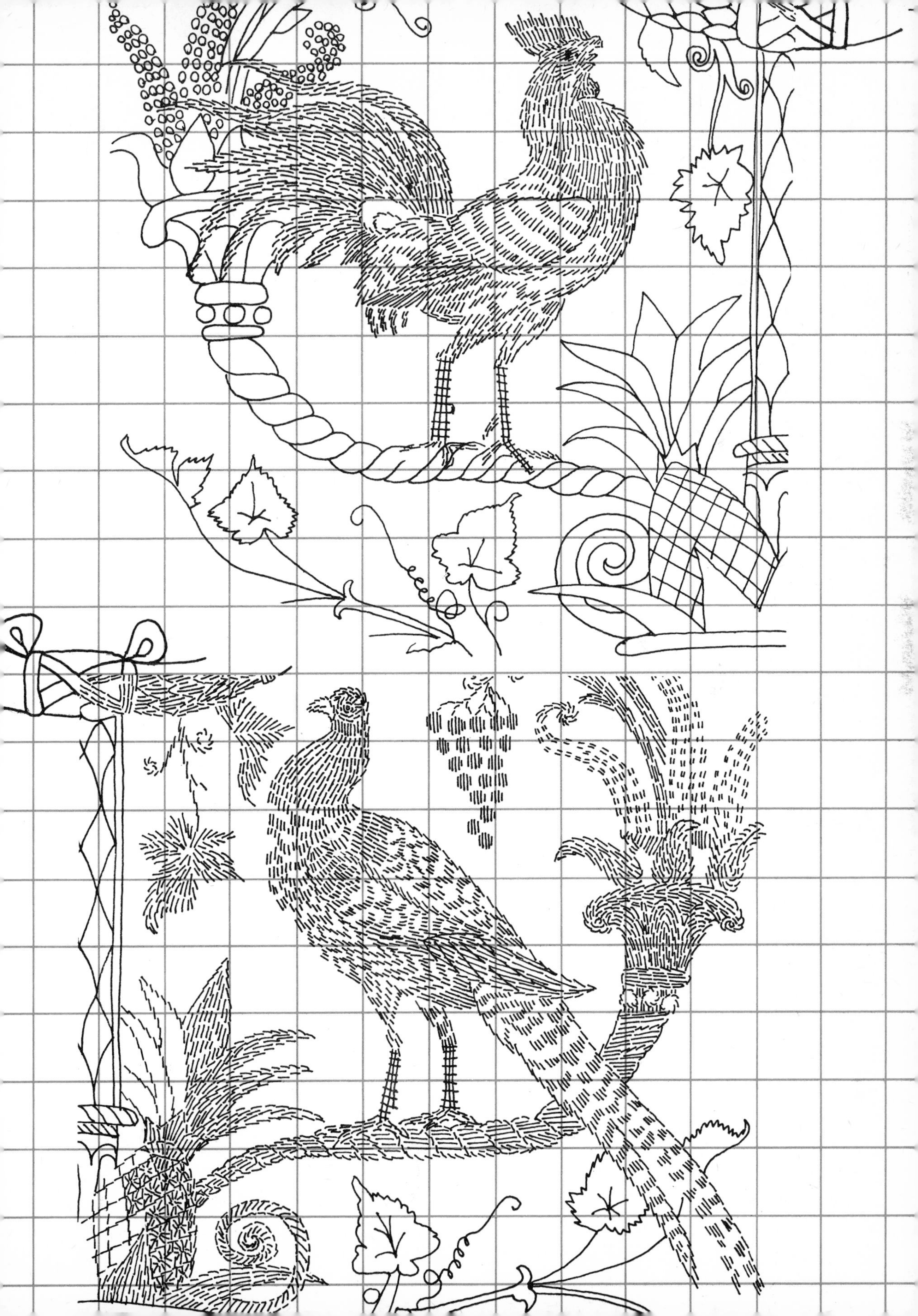

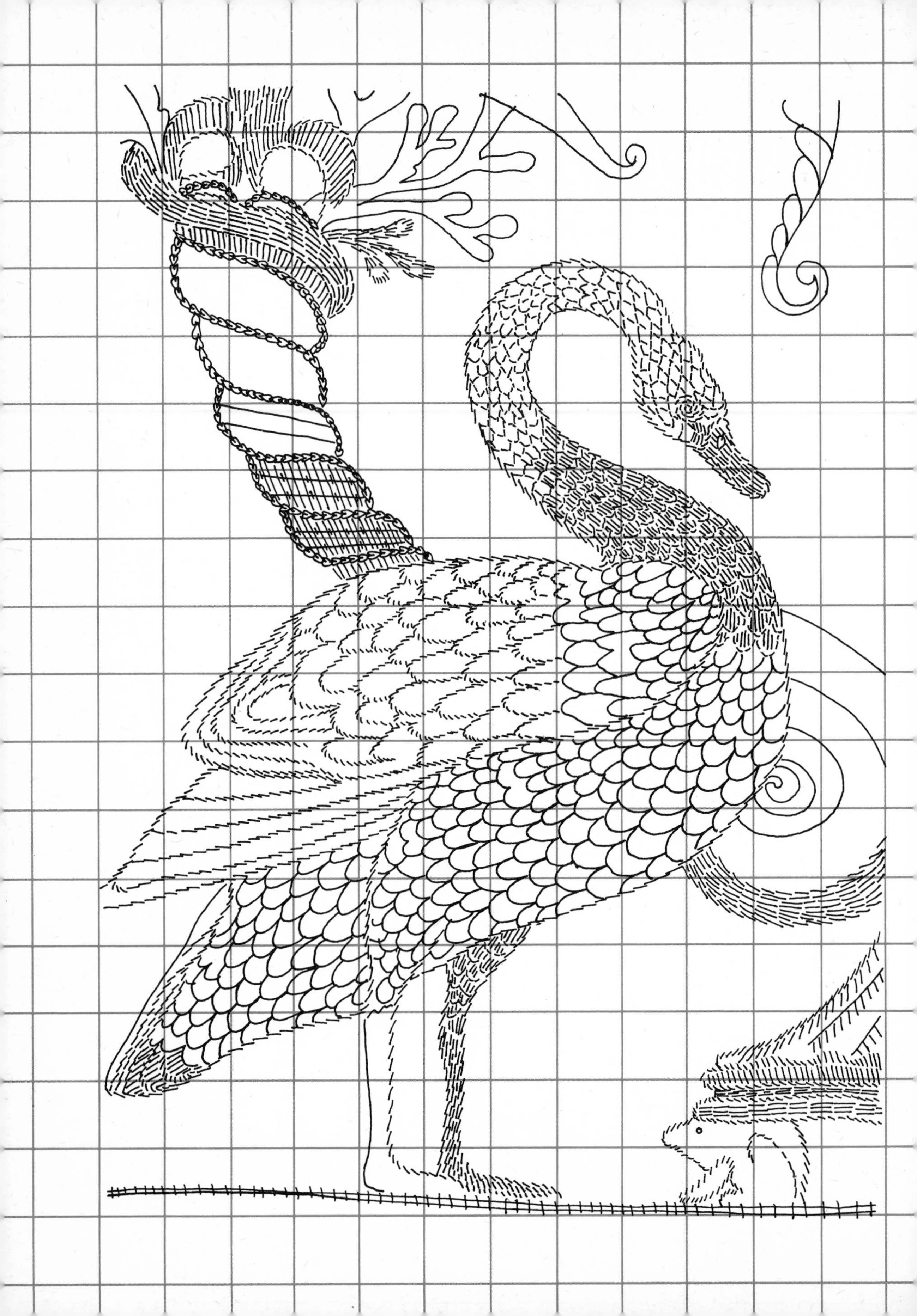

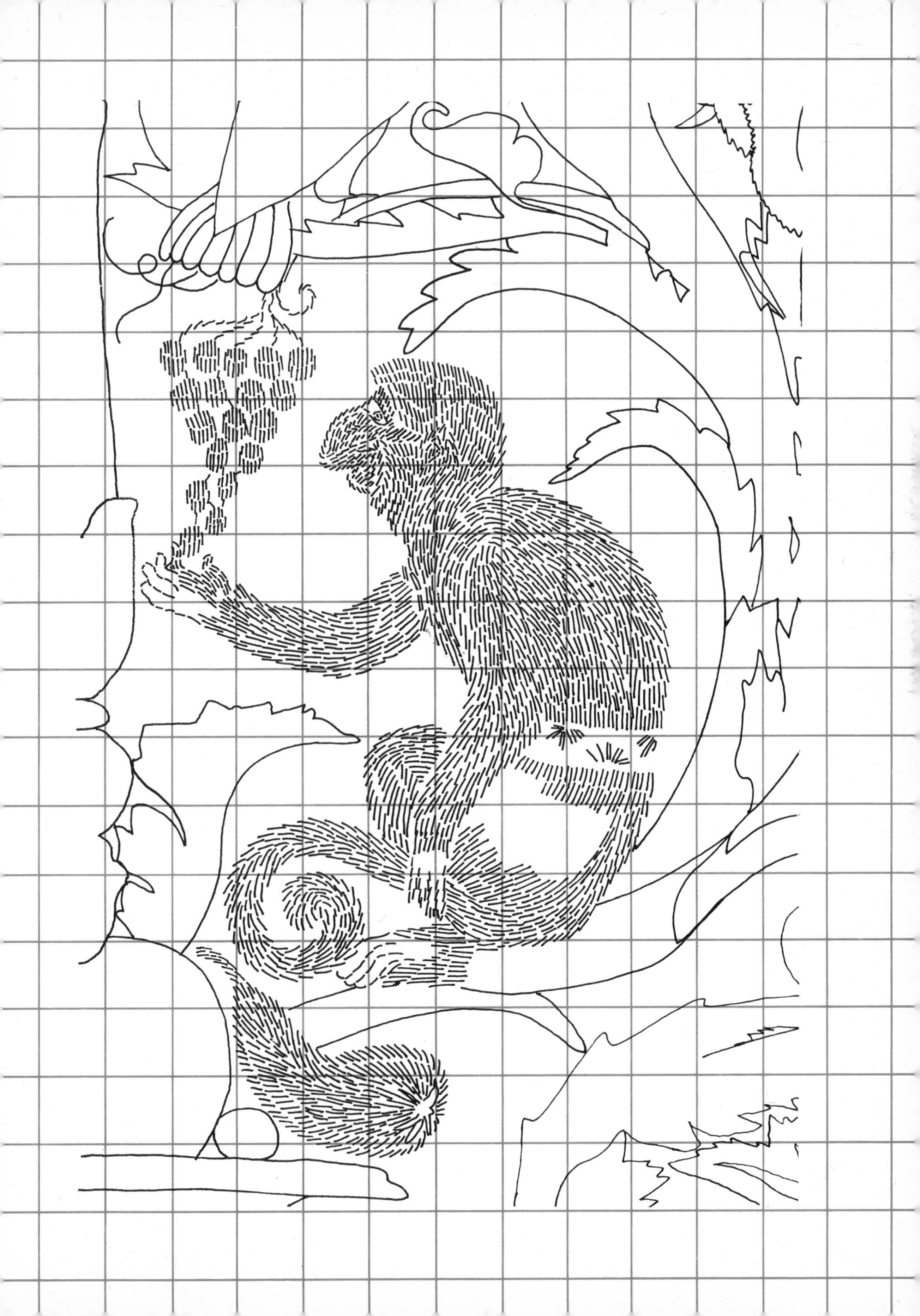

Stump-work panel; 17th century

The two central figures appear in relief in
stump-work against a crowded background
made up of a medley of motifs. Like this
example, stump-work was traditionally done on
silk or other fine fabrics with the flat background
motifs worked in silk thread. However, these
motifs were frequently copied by needlewomen
in crewel wools and are easily adapted to this
medium.

The significance of the background motifs
is as follows. *Castle*: buildings were a focal
point of interest in stump-work pictures. They
lack perspective and are seldom topographical.
Lion: it was ubiquitous in embroidery. Where it
had heraldic and symbolic significance it stood
for the king. A lifeless lion is usual; the
humorous rendering here is in direct contrast.

Stag: this persisted as a favourite motif down
to Victorian times. It was a heraldic device
belonging to Edward III. *Butterfly*: it was a
special badge of Charles I.

When working these motifs in crewels, it is
still advisable to use the same stitches that were
done in silk on the original. These are satin,
long and short, outline, coral, and brick stitch.

*Crown copyright, Victoria and Albert Museum,
London*

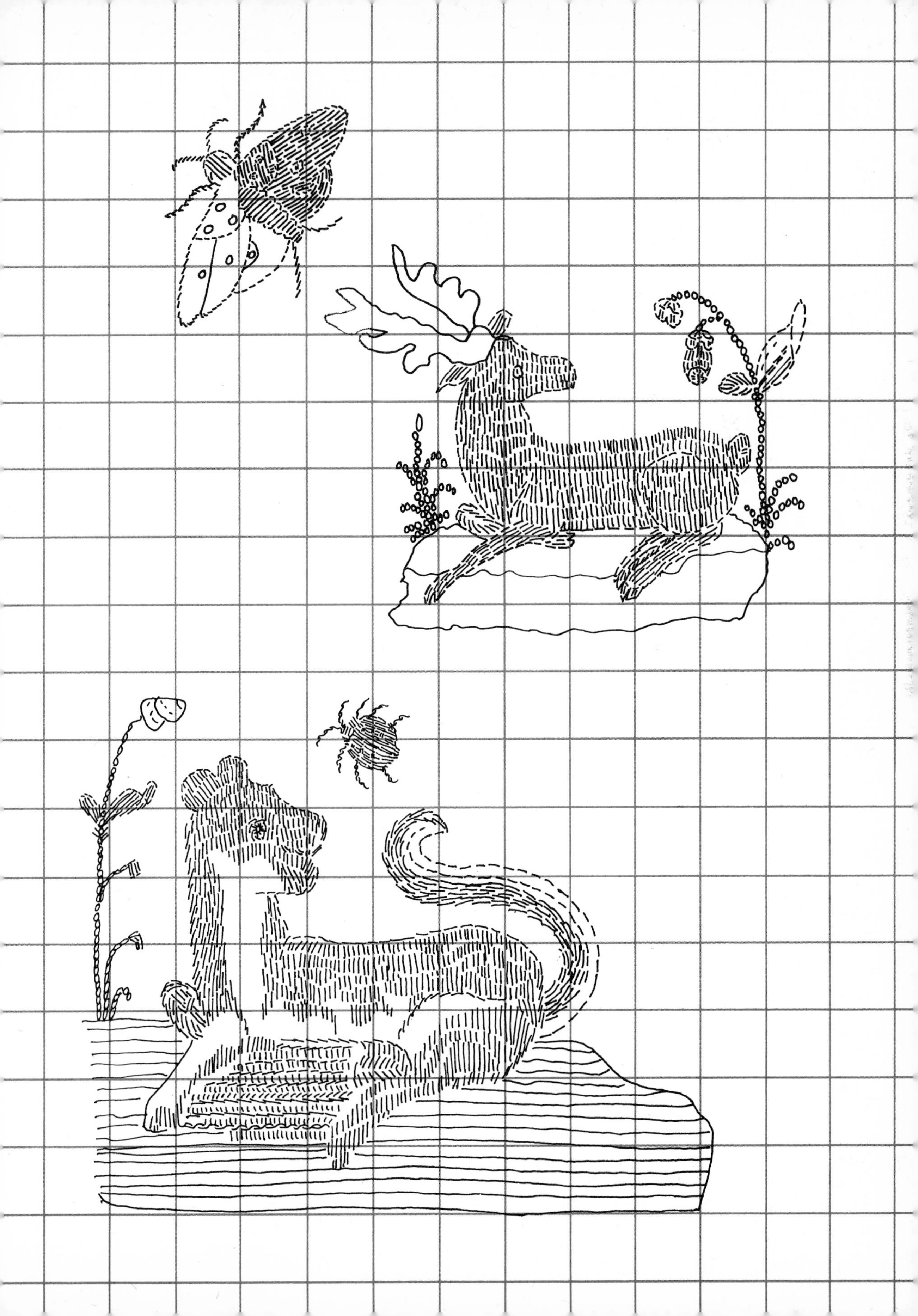

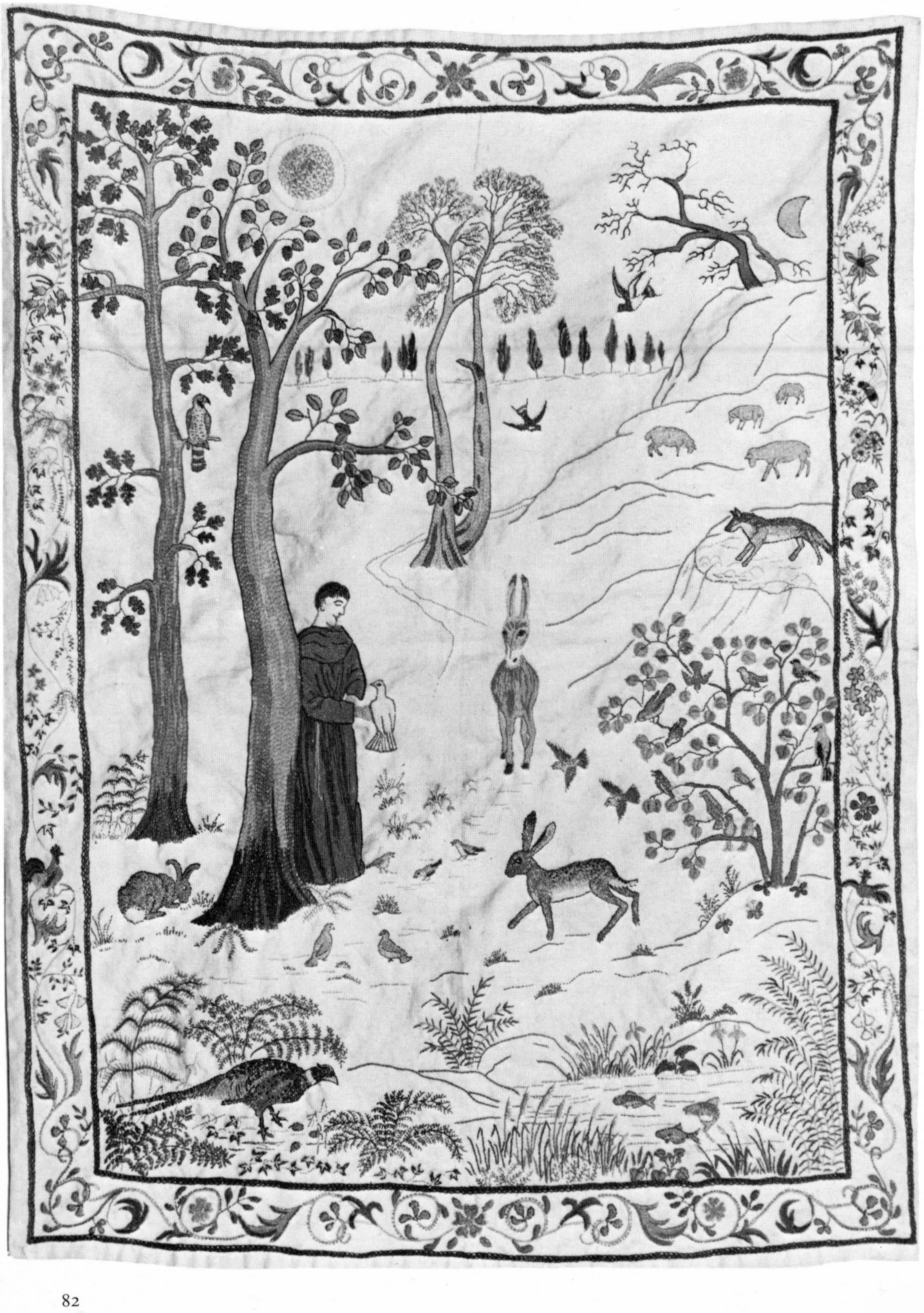

**Panel depicting St Francis of Assisi;
20th century**

The panel is worked in crewel wools on linen
twill. Split, long and short, stem, satin, chain,
couching, and running stitches are used.

Courtesy Mrs Joyce Knowles

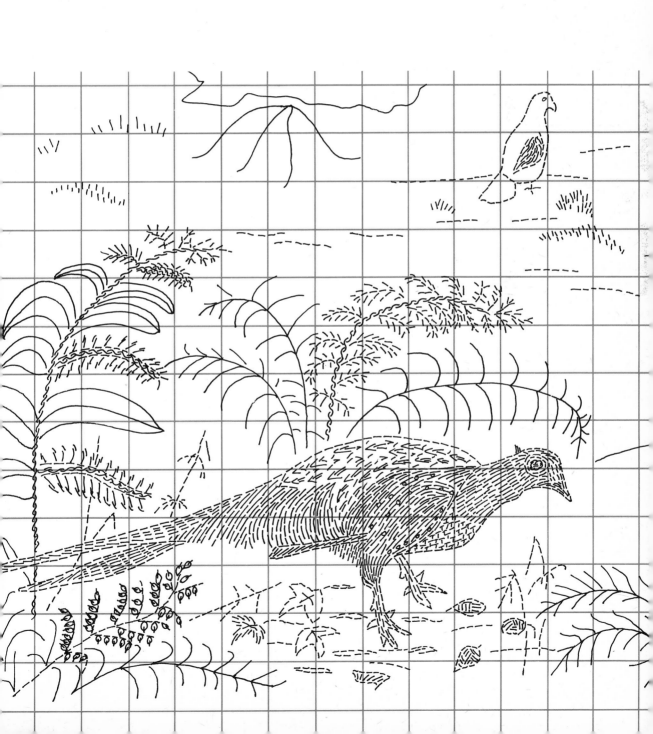

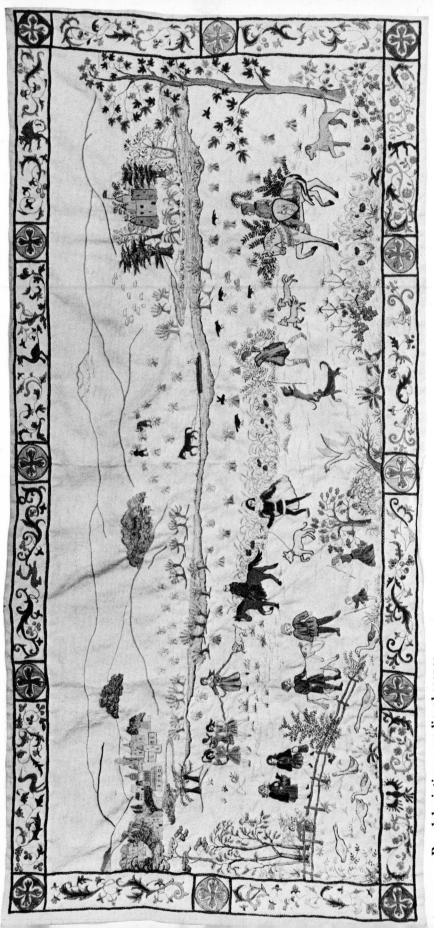

**Panel depicting a medieval scene;
20th century**

The stitches used are split, chain, stem, satin,
long and short, running, and couching. The
panel is worked in crewel wools on linen twill.

Courtesy Mrs Joyce Knowles

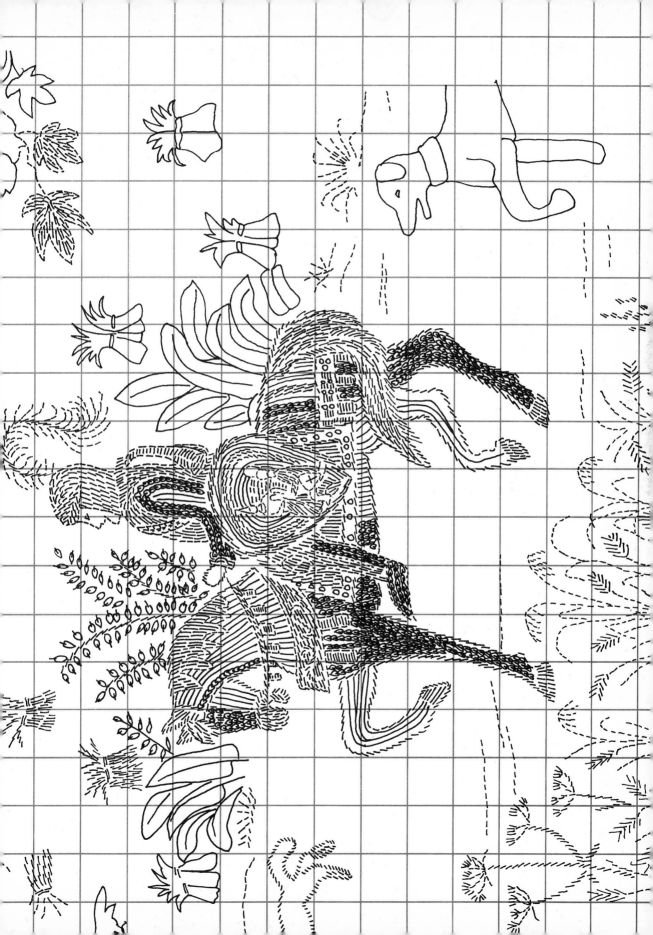

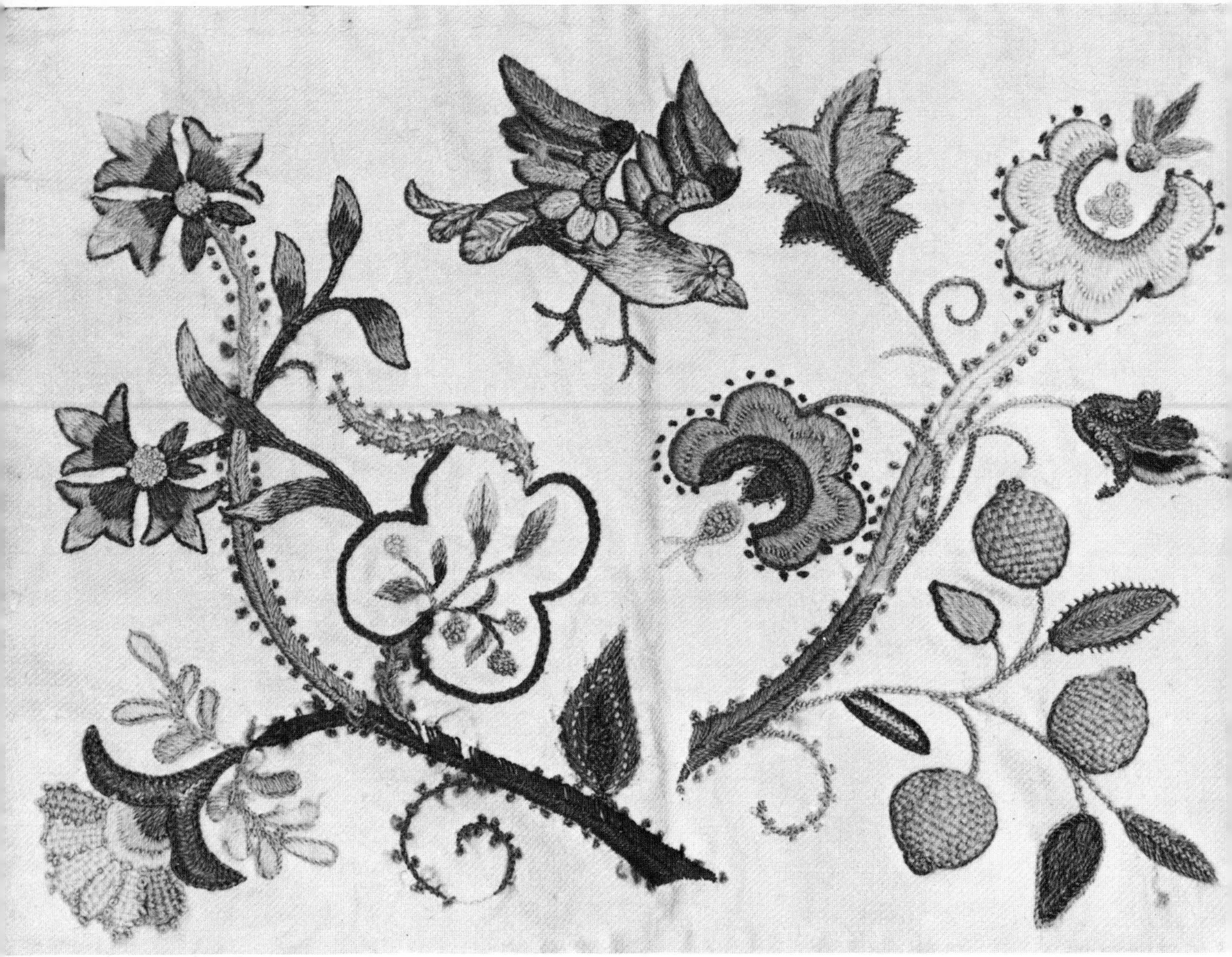

Floral spray and bird in crewel wools on wool fabric; neo-crewel period, 1910

There is a suggestion of wide and coiling stems. Flowers are in full blossom and the leaves large. The bird on the wing gives an opportunity for artistic stitchery in portraying feathers. This is done largely in satin and split stitches with strong outline stitch enclosing the whole. A broken outline stitch suggests serrated edges to leaves and this is supported by outlines in French knots. There is wide variation in leaf forms but a measure of unity is achieved by mass fillings mainly in close satin stitch with seeding and some detached chain stitch superimposed. Brick stitch has also been used as a filling.

Courtesy H. E. Kiewe

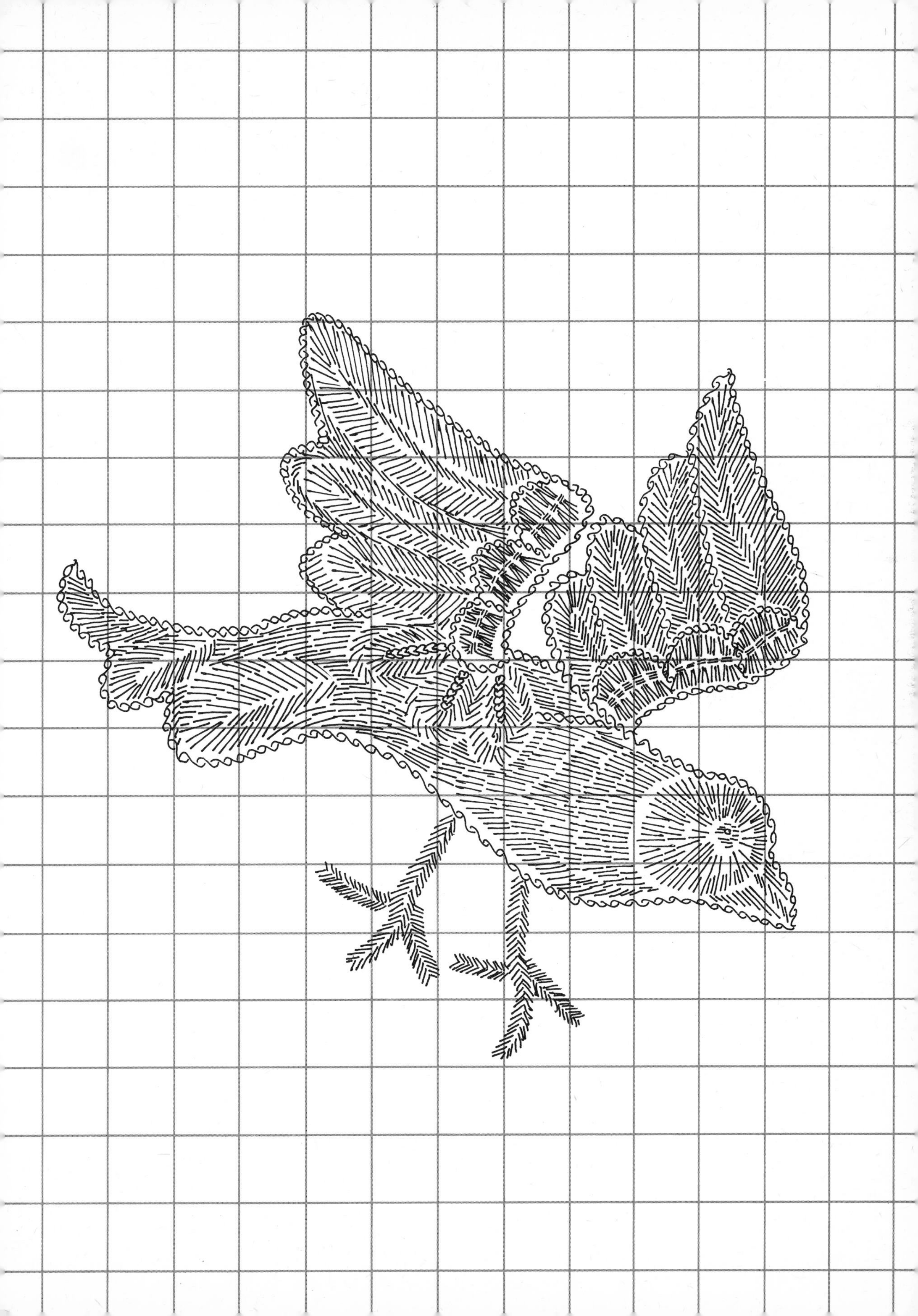

Brown owl design; modern

This piece was originally a semi-collage, but the interesting design readily lends itself to crewel embroidery. The stitches that are suggested here include stem, laced running, back, satin, split, long and short, herringbone, fly, chain, cable chain, French knots, and couching.

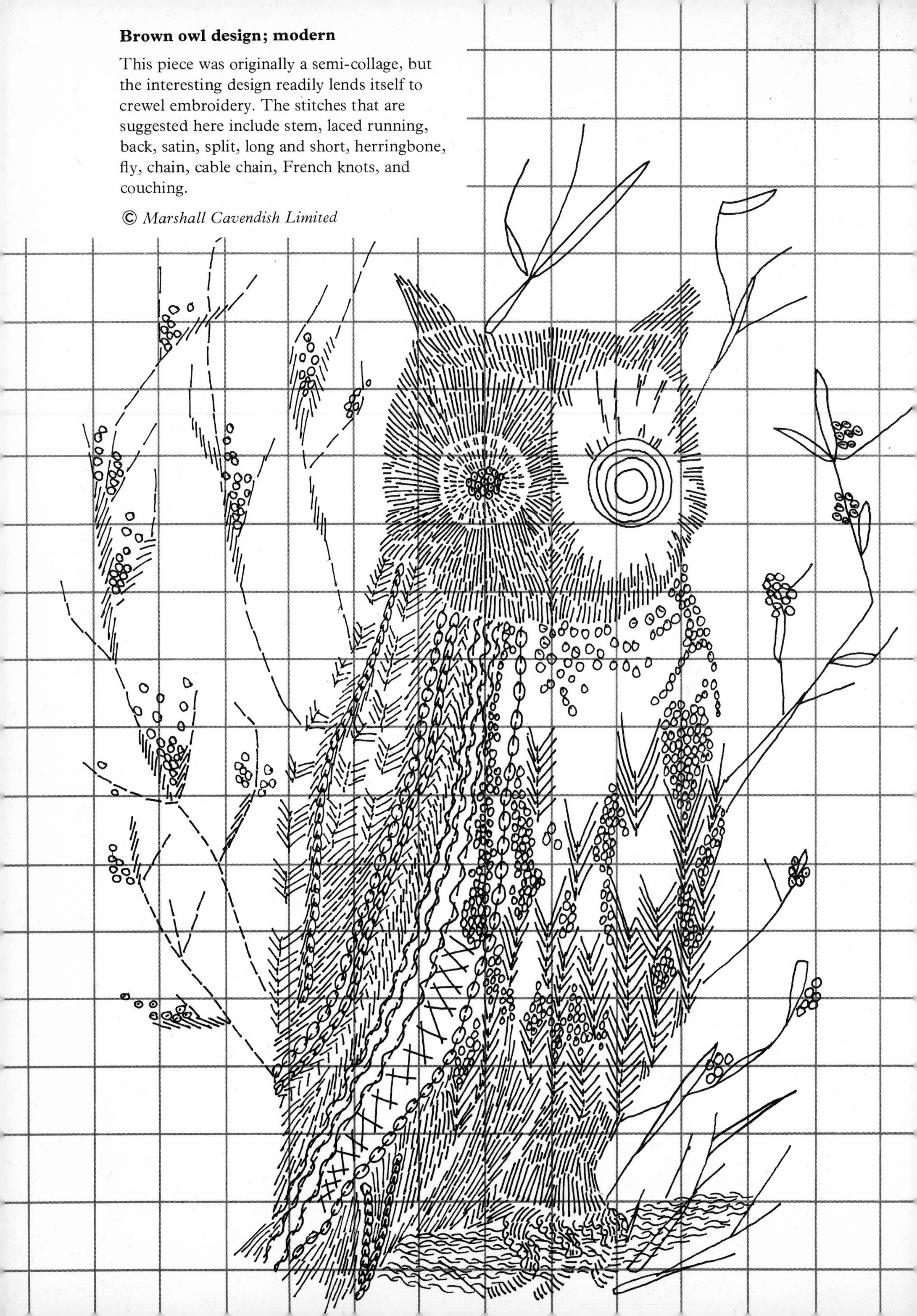

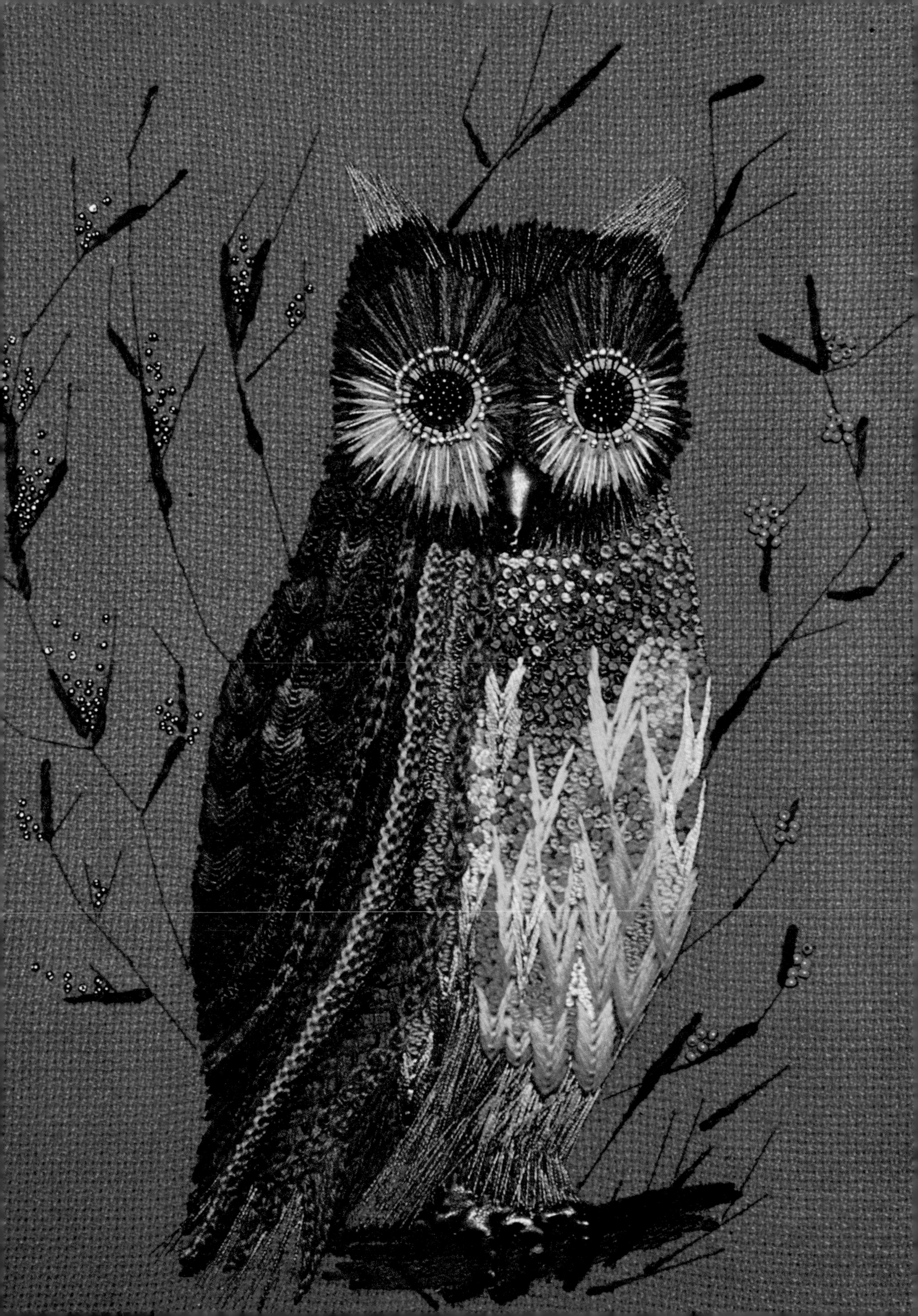

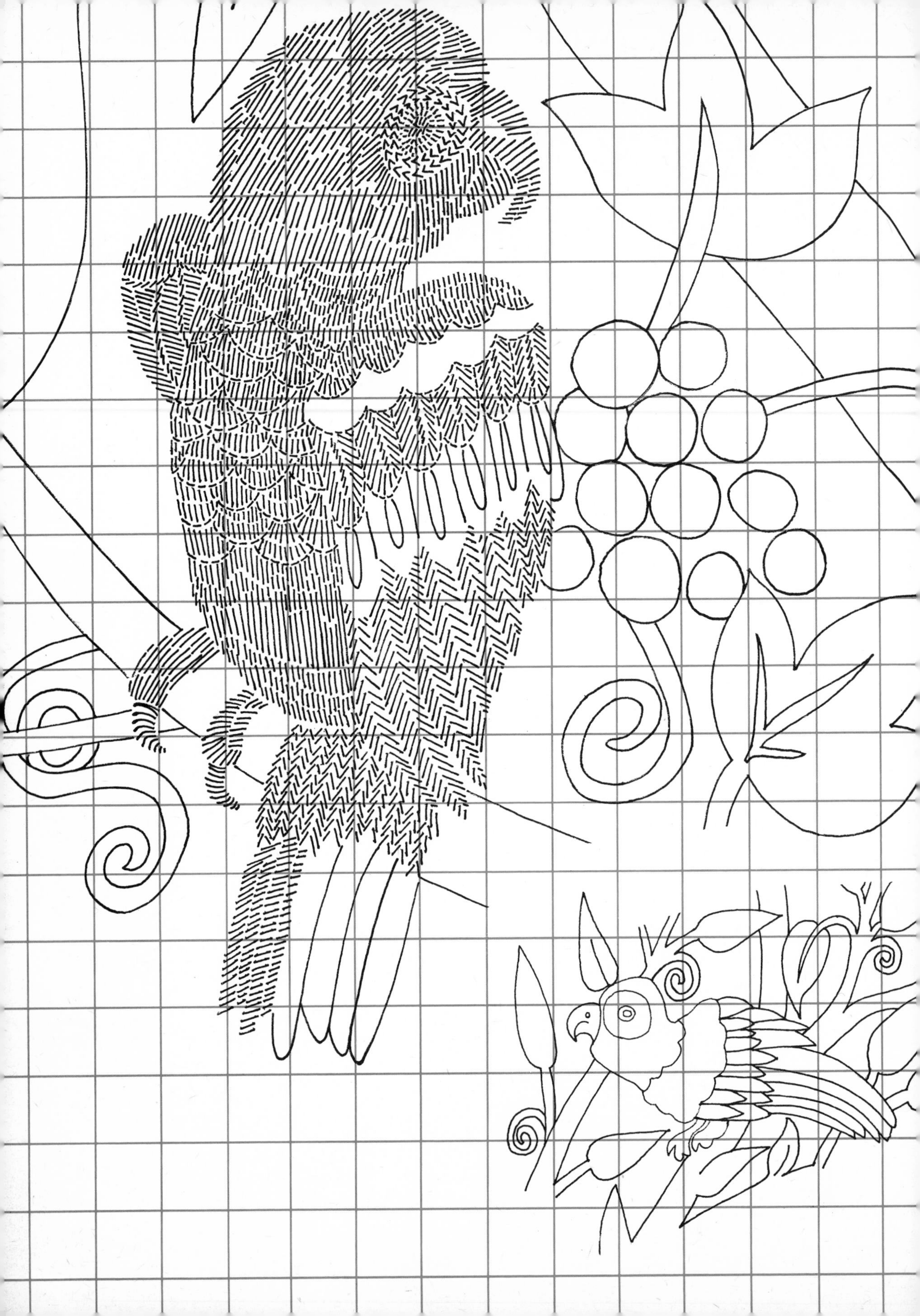

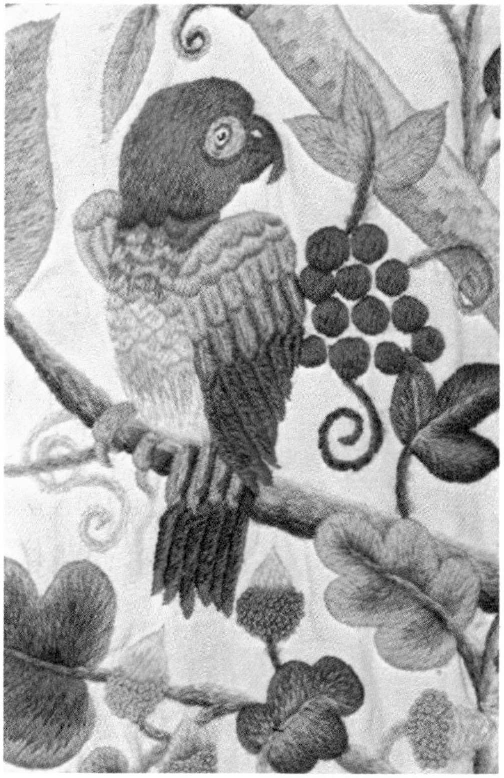

Details from bed furnishings; 1908–18

These two parrots are from the curtain of the bed furnishings shown on page 32. The stitches used are long and short, satin, stem, split and French knots.

The small drawing on the right is for enlarging the whole bird, whereas the large drawing above gives details of the stitches that can be used.

Courtesy The Rachel Kay-Shuttleworth Collection, Gawthorpe Hall, Lancashire

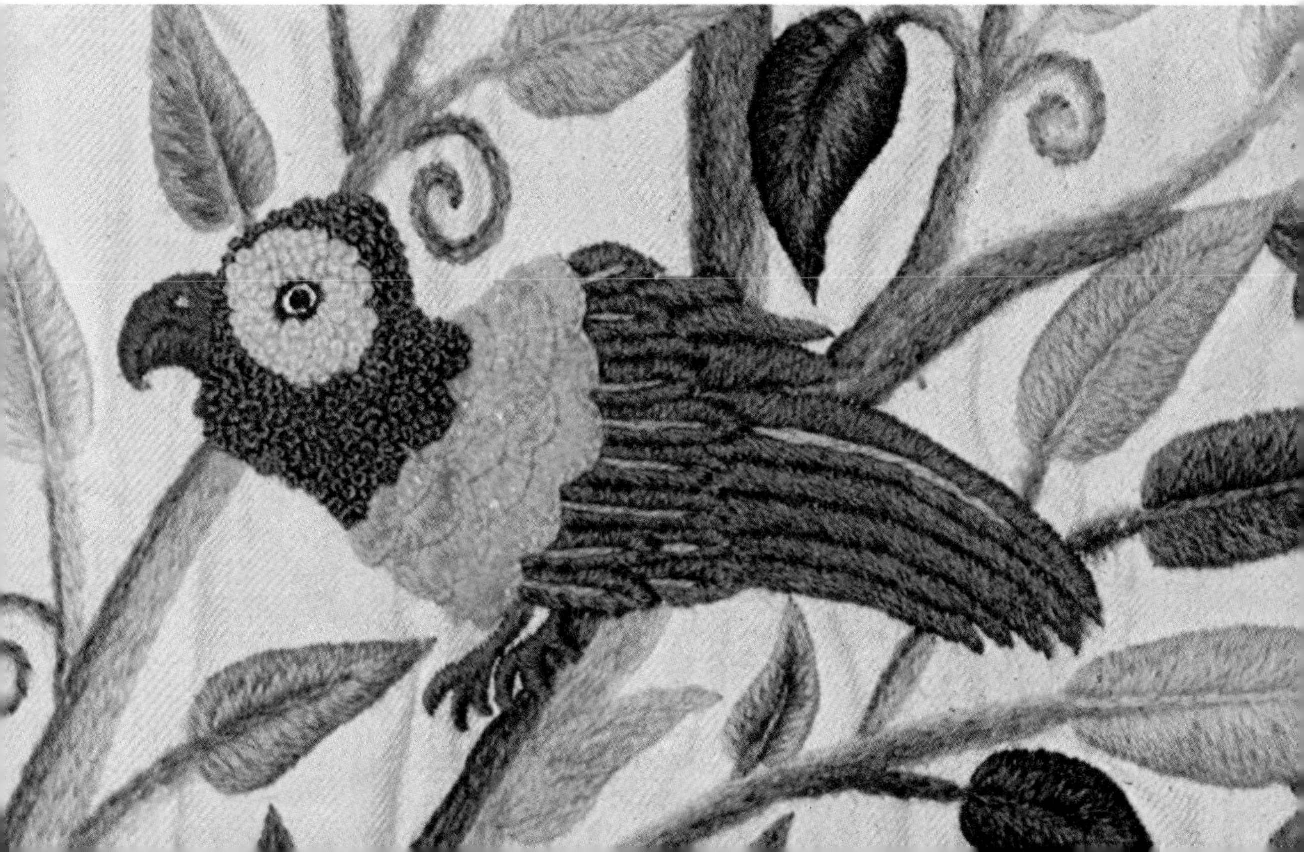

Part of an apron; Queen Anne period

In the early 18th century an apron was an orthodox accessory of formal dress. This example is in the floral tradition and the flowers are arranged in a neat border. Although a little formal, the flower motifs amid trailing leaves are shown naturally, the latter introducing flexibility and movement into the design. Common flowers of field and garden are used here in contrast to the more exotic blooms. A dainty effect is achieved by fine stitchery in satin, outline, and chain, with fillings in seeding, French knots, and herringbone.

Courtesy Embroiderers' Guild, London

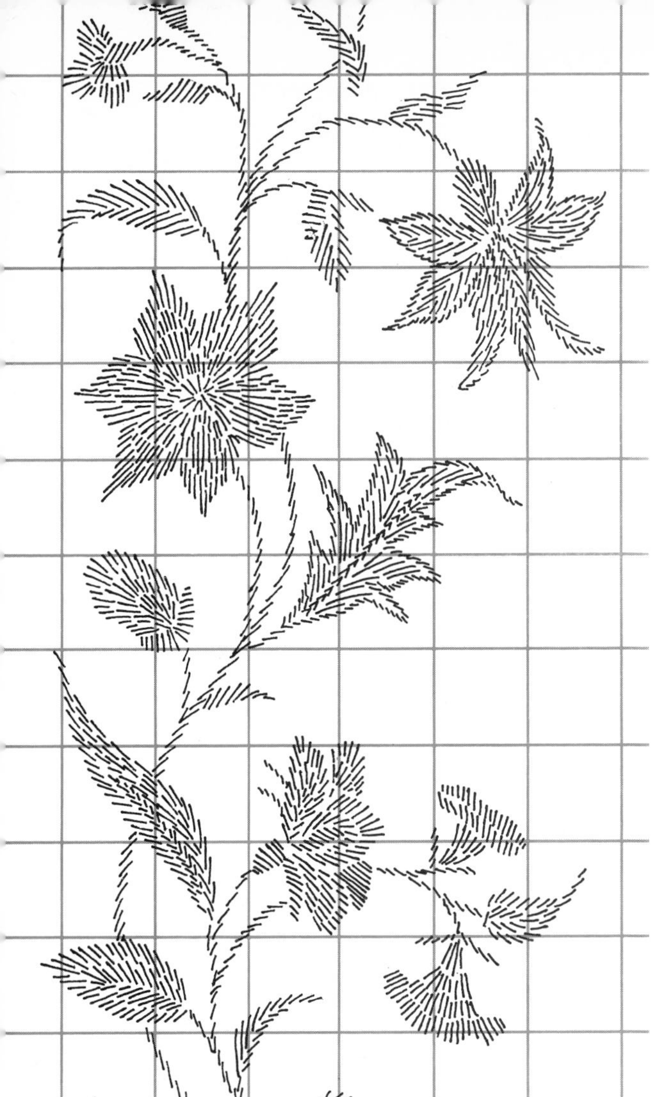

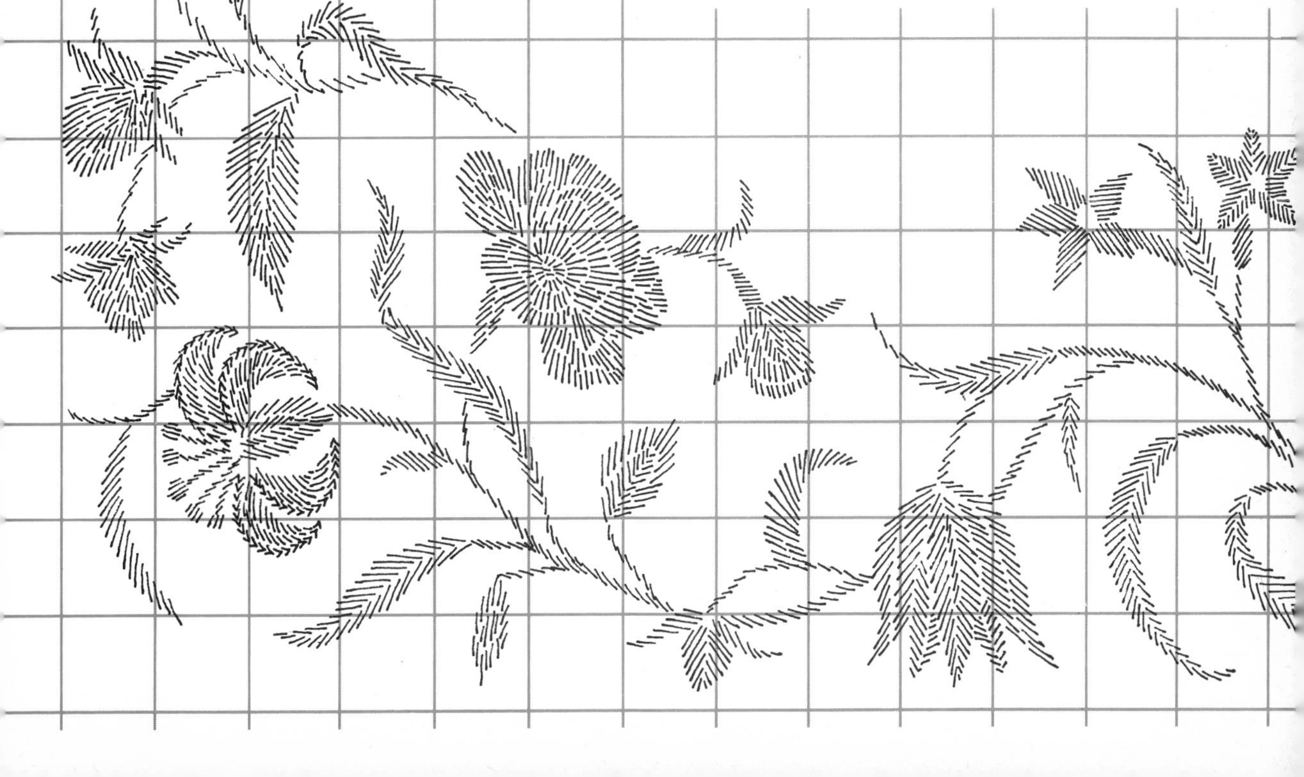

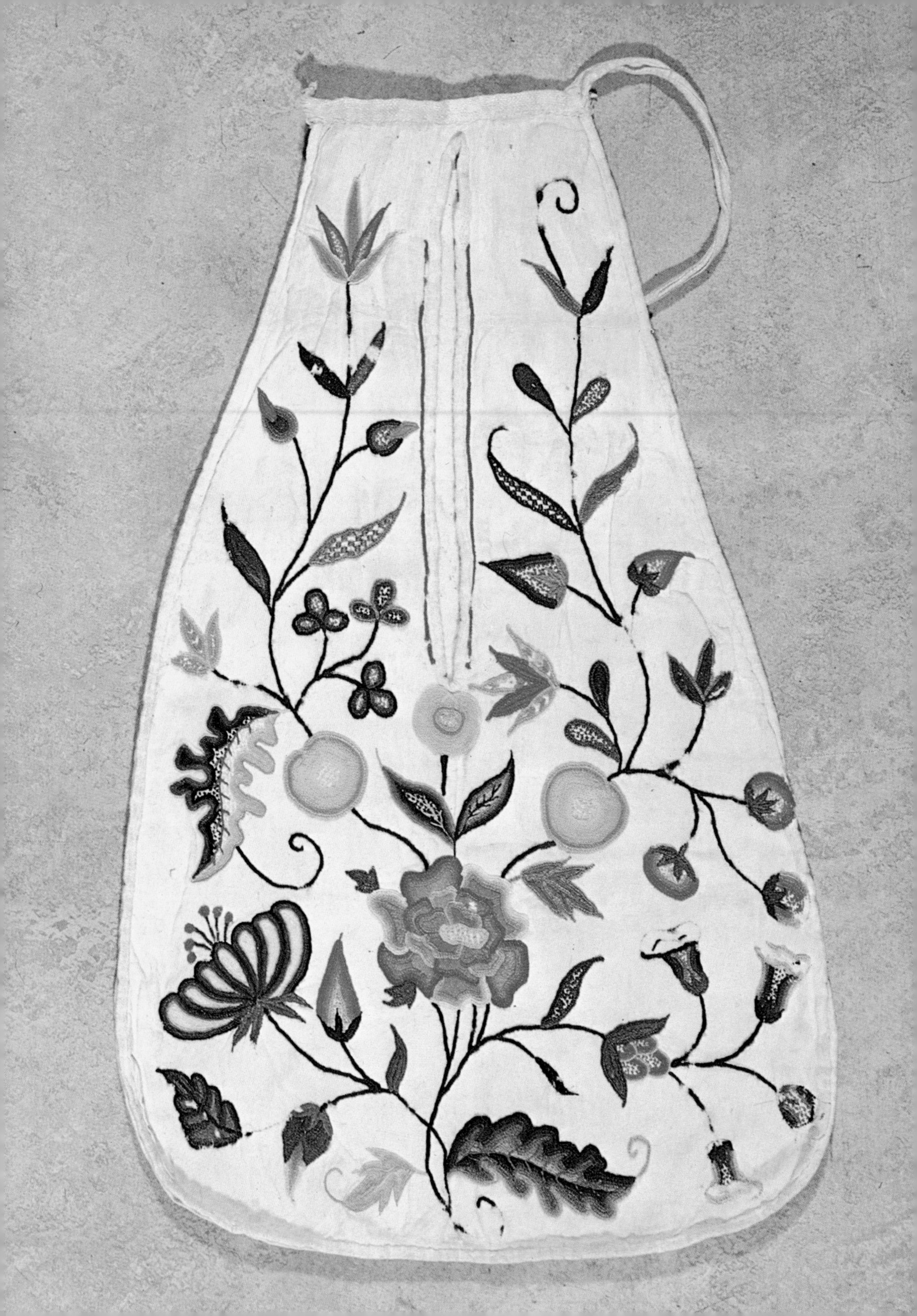

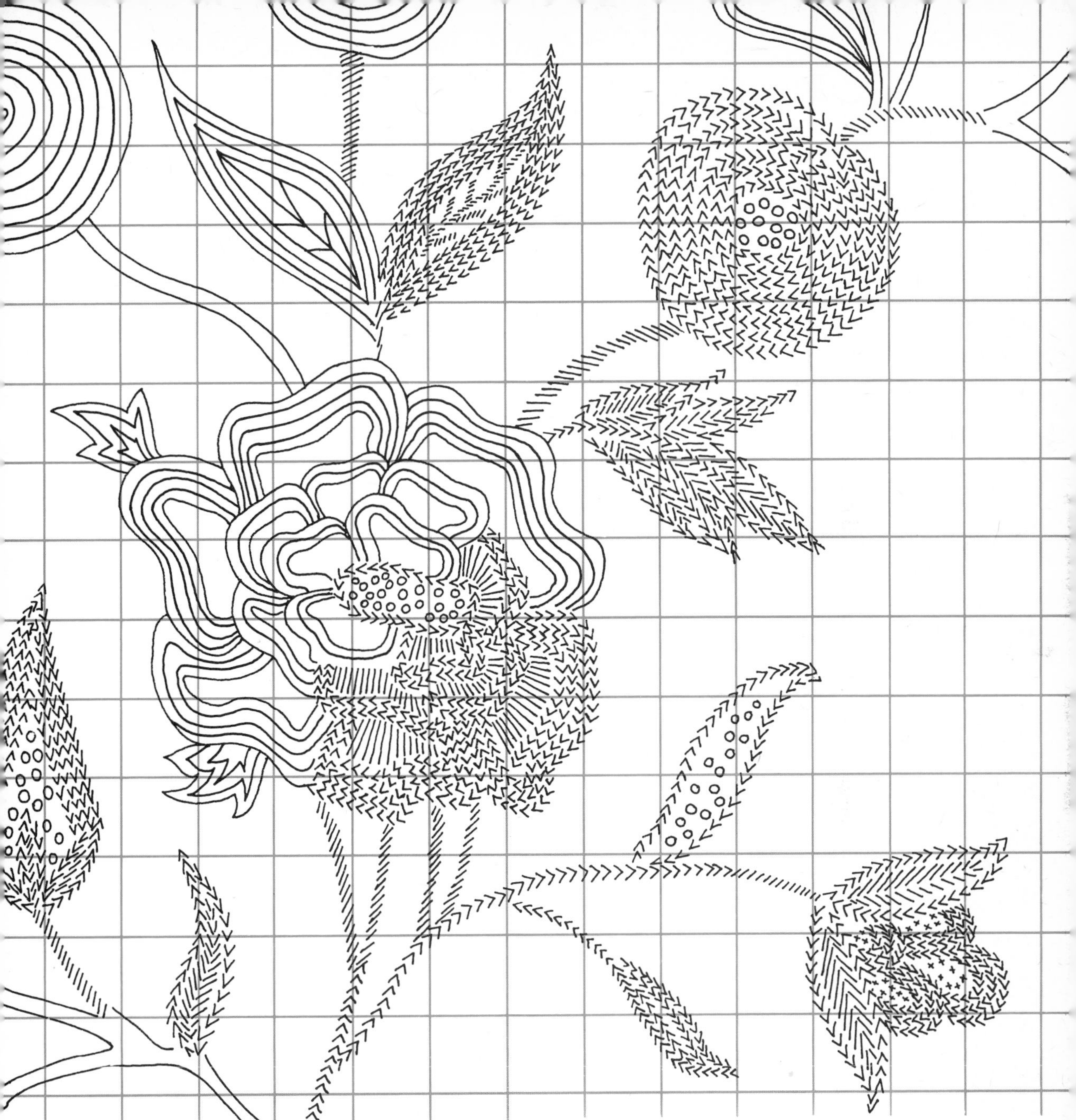

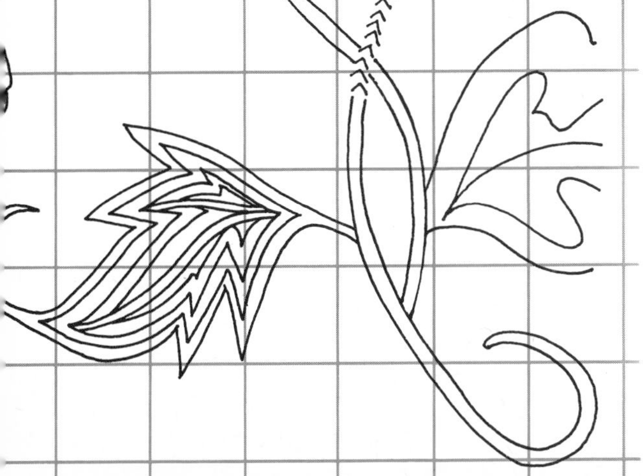

External pocket for a woman; about 1720–60

In the 18th century a woman's wardrobe accessories would have included a selection of external pockets to be worn over dresses. These were usually embroidered, like this fine example in linen with crewel wools. Stitches used here include satin, long and short, chain, outline, and stem, with fillings of French knots and buttonhole stitch in chequered effect.

Courtesy The Museum of Costume, Bath

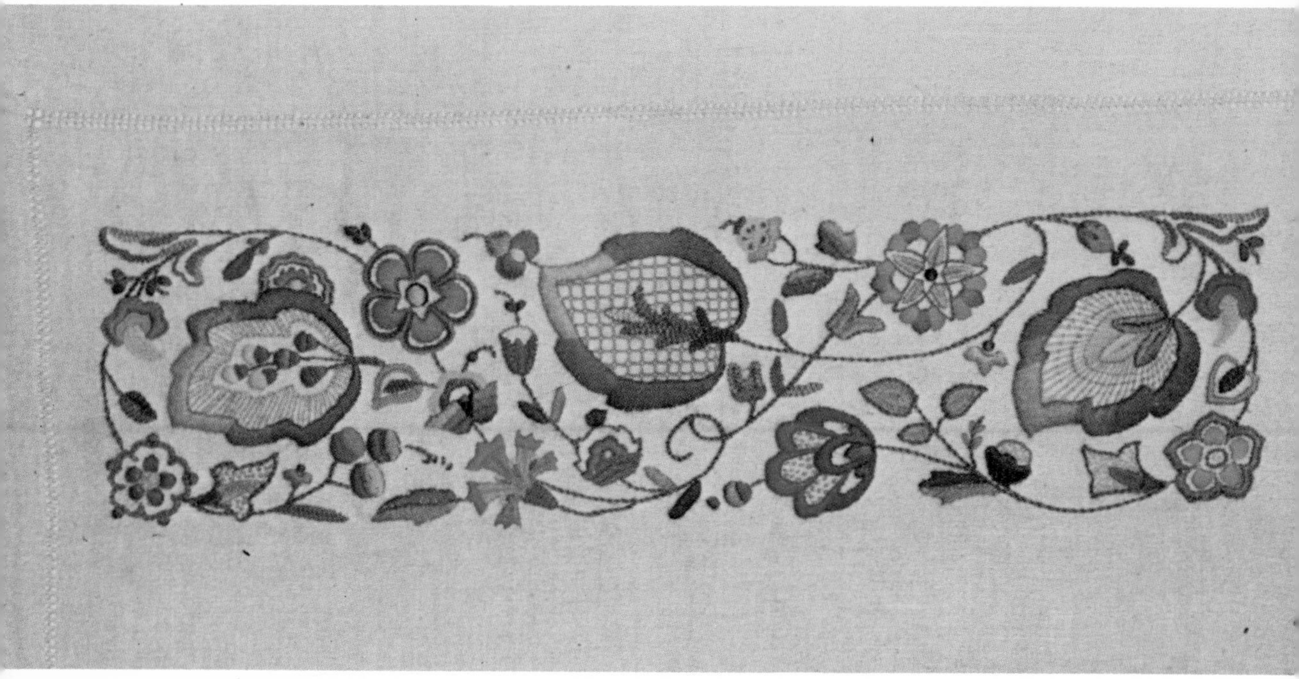

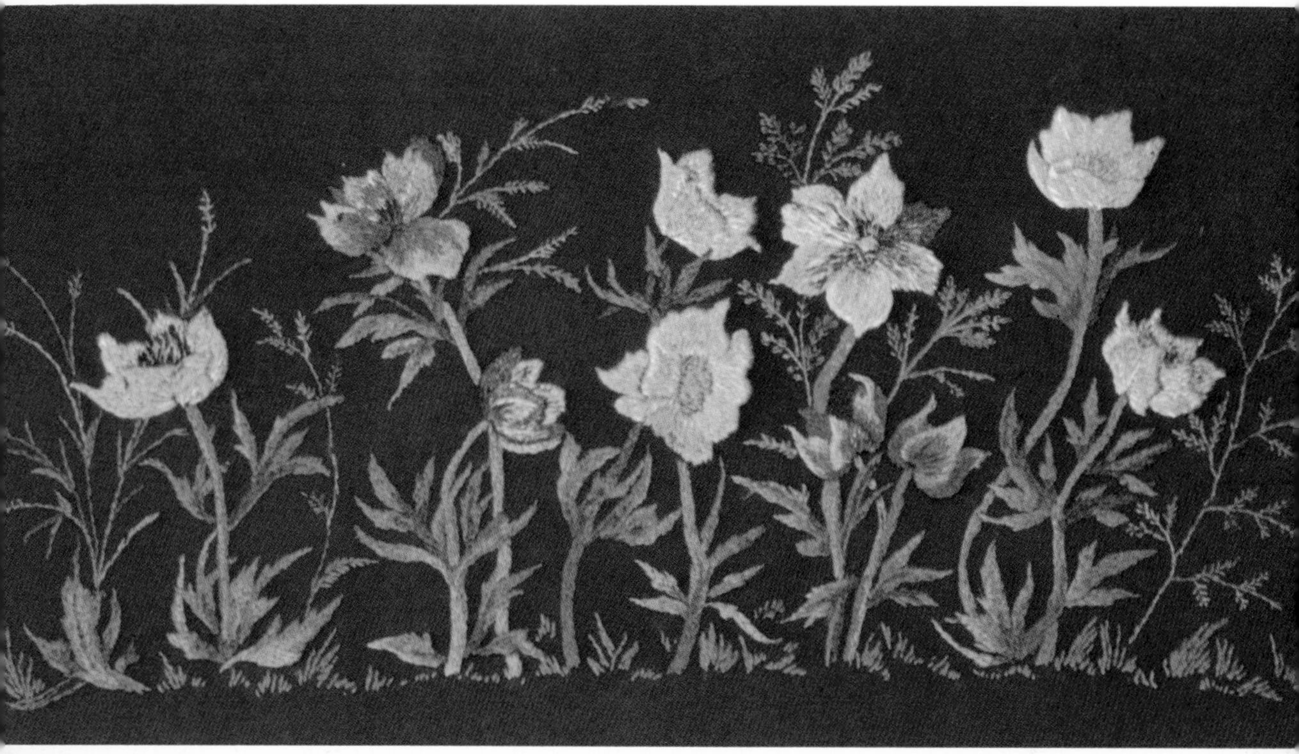

Floral panel in crewel wools on linen, unbleached and hem-stitched; 20th century

A well-balanced and flowing panel, this piece makes a charming and colourful border. The variety of stitches used includes satin, long and short, stem, buttonhole, French knots, herringbone, chain, back stitch, and Cretan stitch, with some couched fillings.

Courtesy The Rachel Kay-Shuttleworth Collection, Gawthorpe Hall, Lancashire

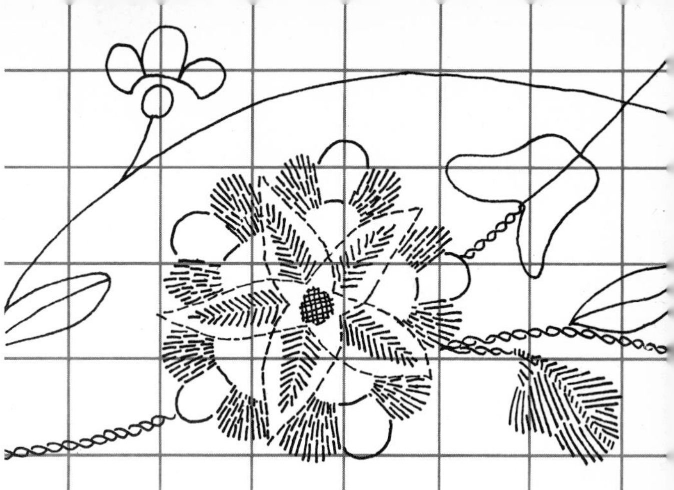

'Anemonies from her garden at San Remo': a cushion cover of serge embroidered in crewel wools (with a small amount of silk); 1902

Part of a suite worked by Mrs Janet E. Kay-Shuttleworth for her brother, the first Lord Shuttleworth, and his wife, this cushion cover with its naturalistic-looking border again shows the use of various colours of wool to achieve tone and realism. The stitches used are long and short, stem, chain, and feather.

Courtesy The Rachel Kay-Shuttleworth Collection, Gawthorpe Hall, Lancashire

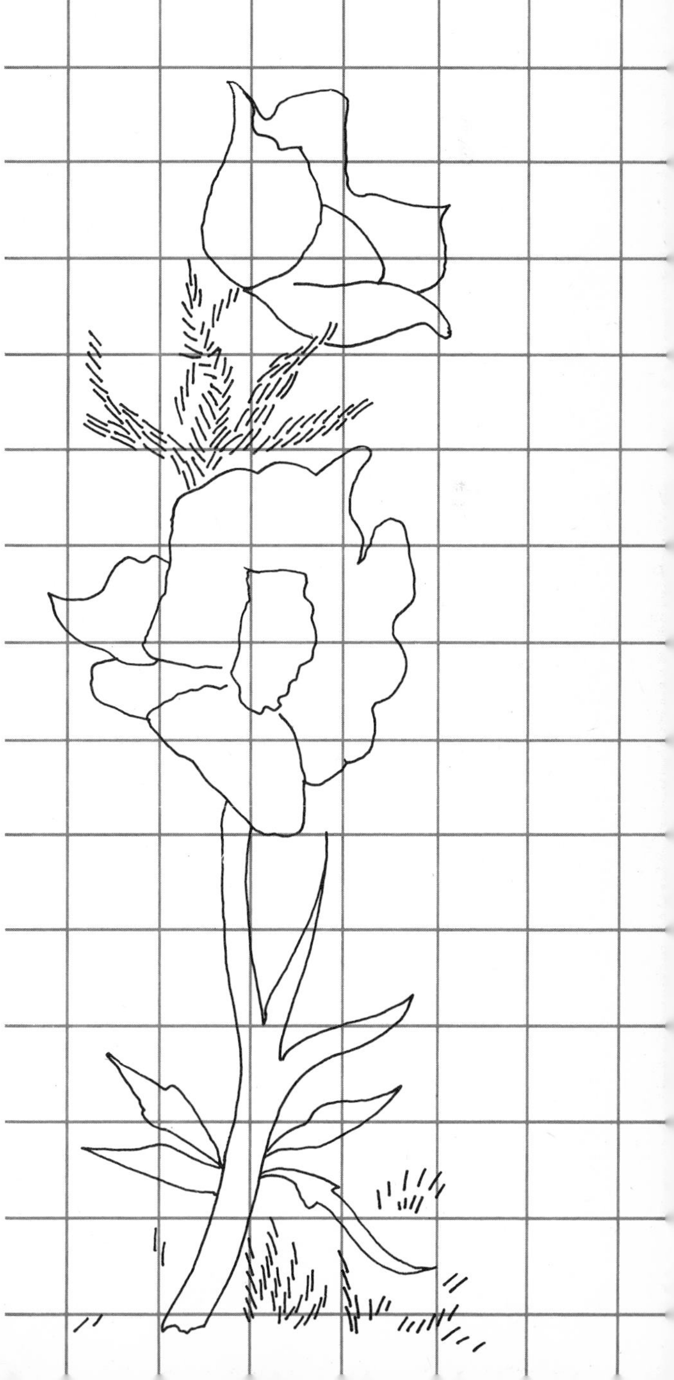

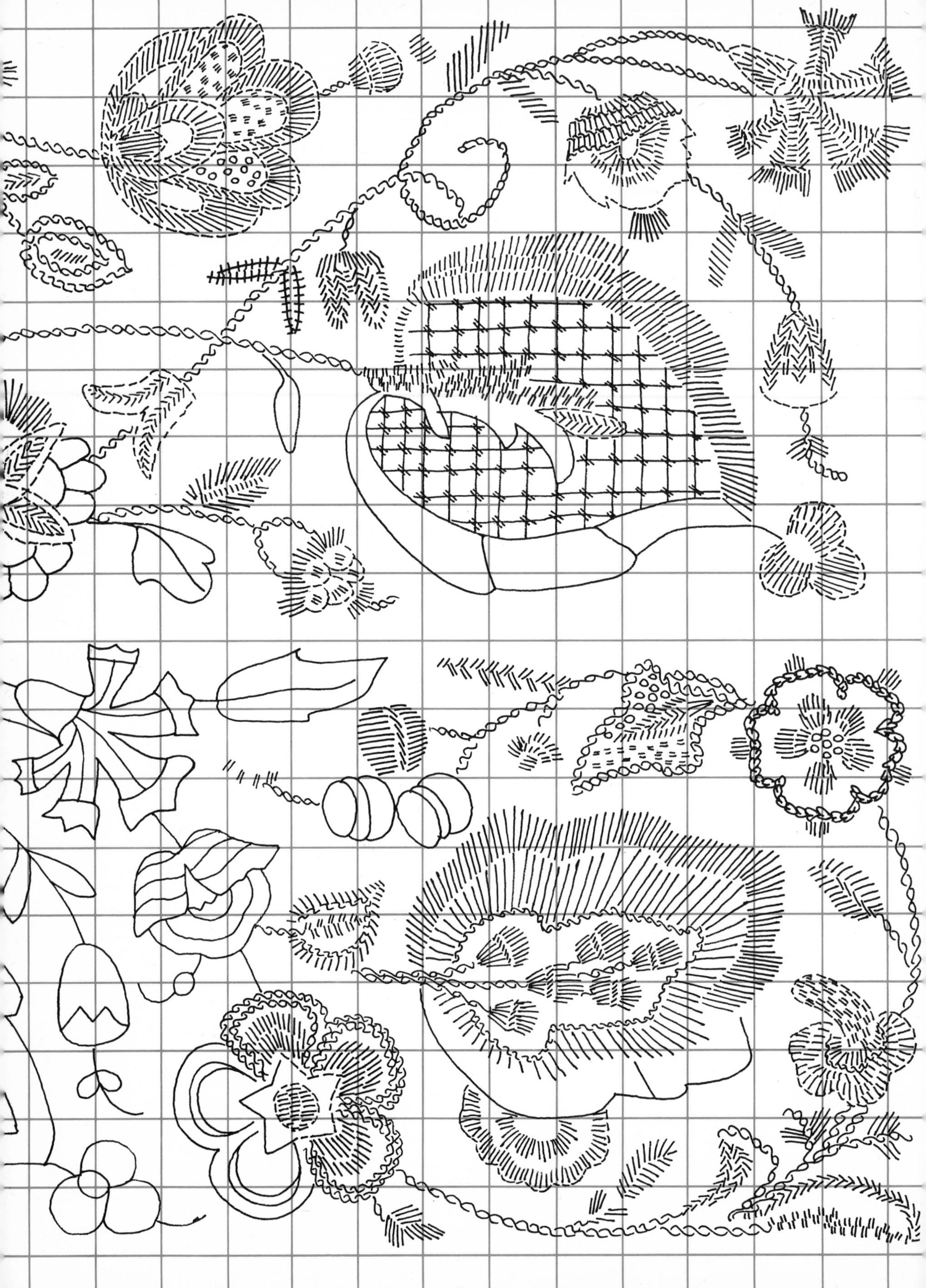

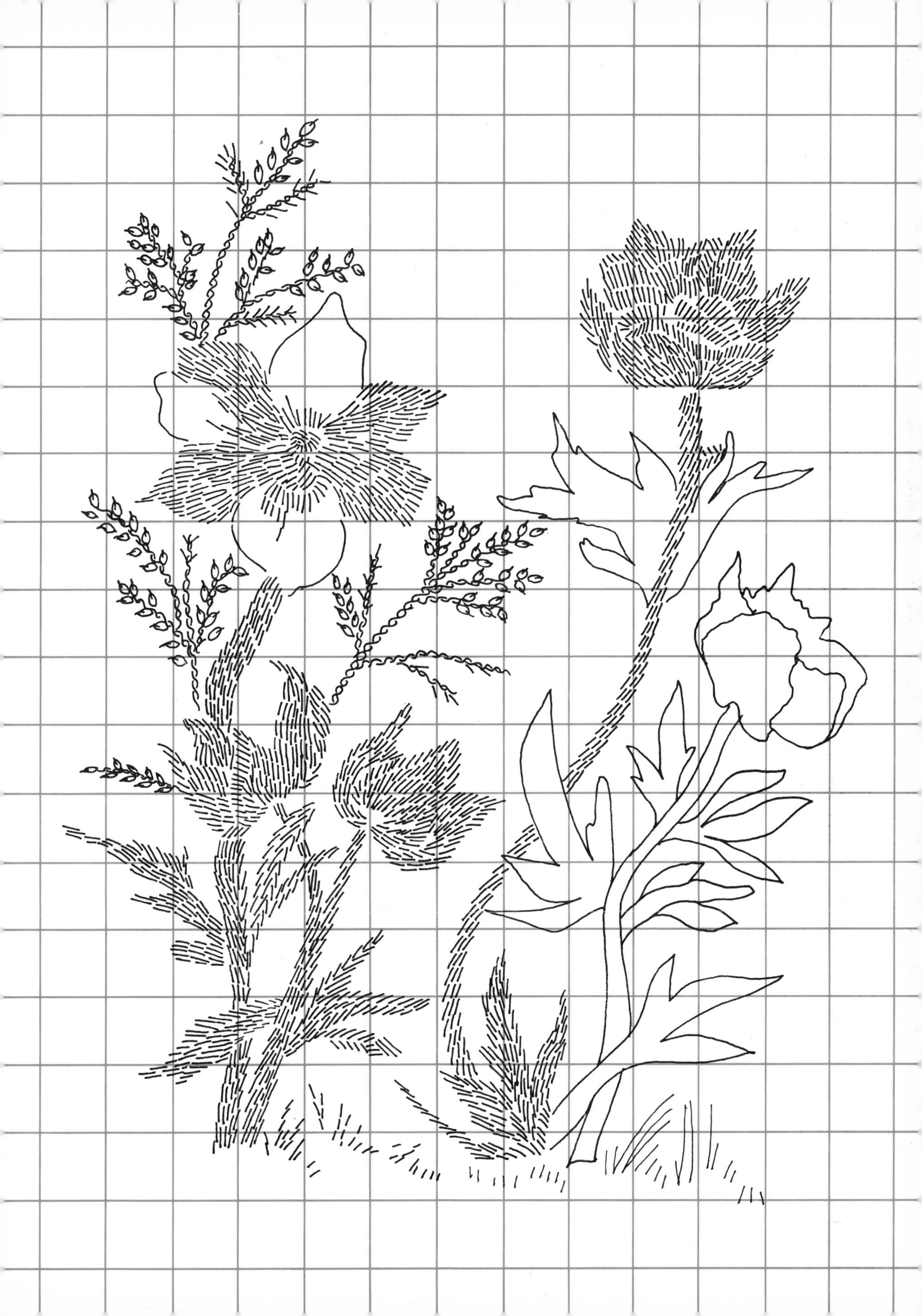

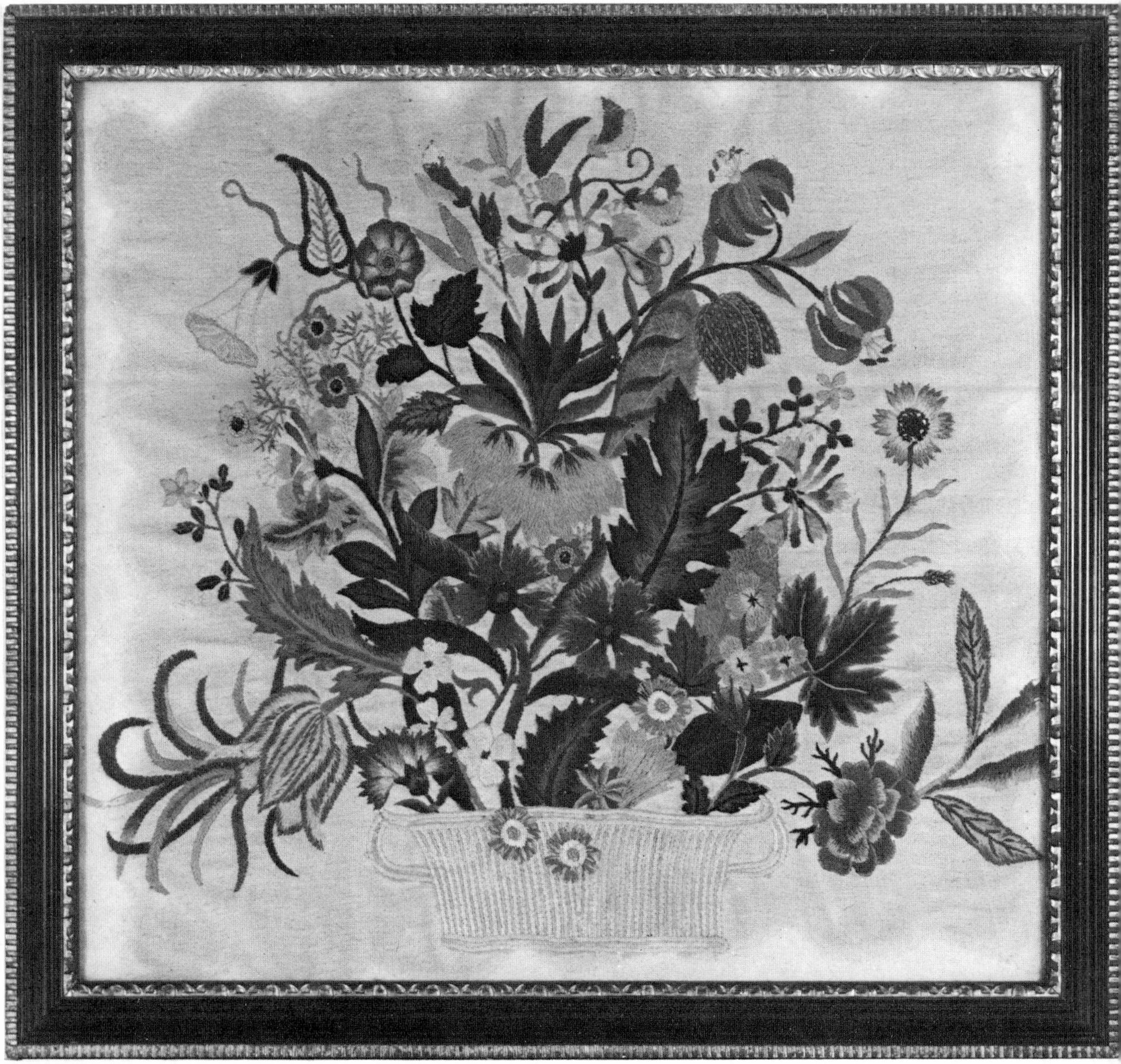

Flowers in a vase or basket; design worked in crewel wools; about 1750

Here a conventional design of large blossoms and big leaves is arranged symmetrically.

Solid flower heads are rendered in shaded satin stitch. Outlines are clear-cut and well defined in outline stitch, emphasizing the depth of tint between the design and the background. A wealth of natural colour is achieved in the working of the flowers. This is enhanced by working the stems and leaves in various tones of green.

Courtesy City Museums, Norwich

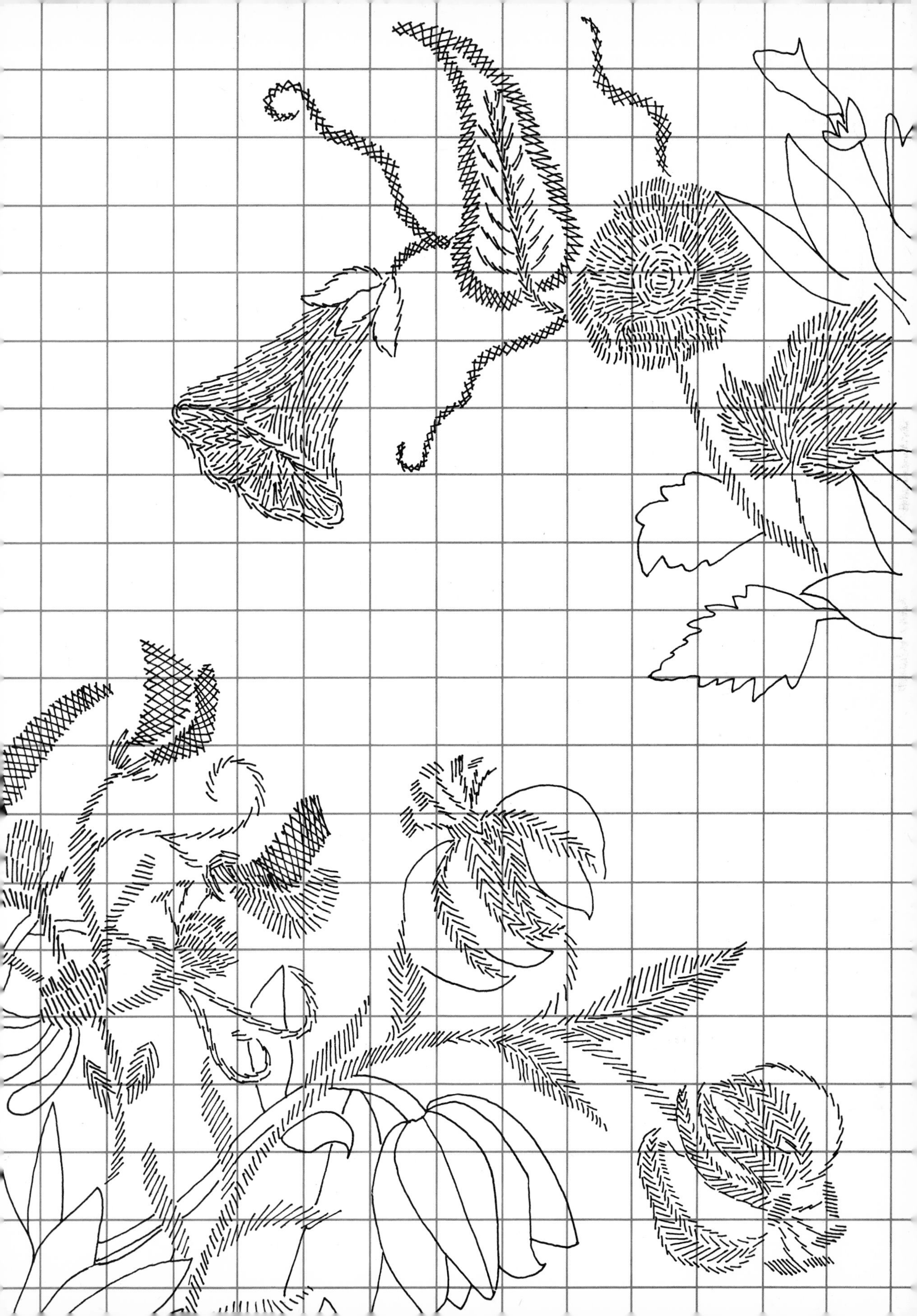

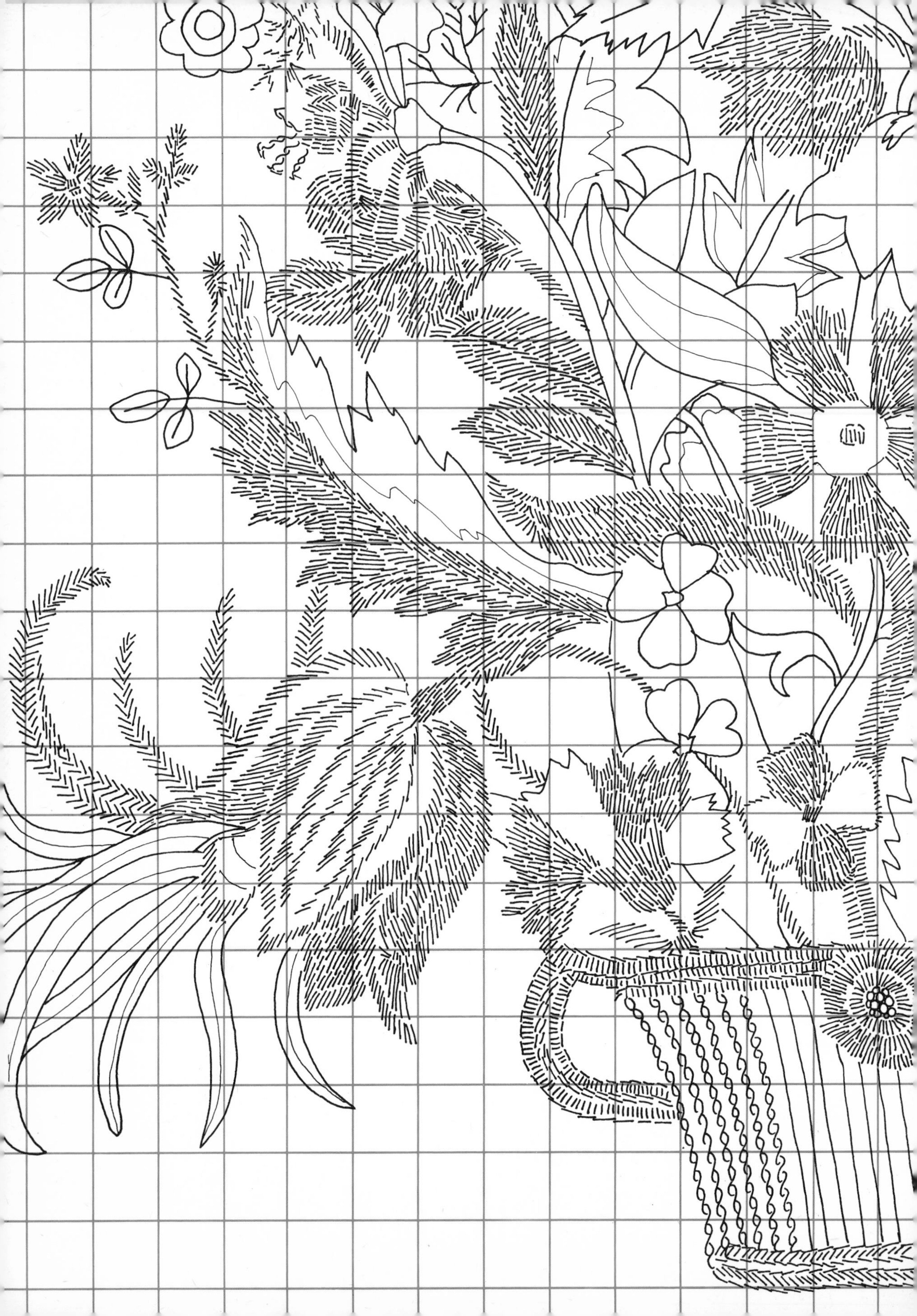

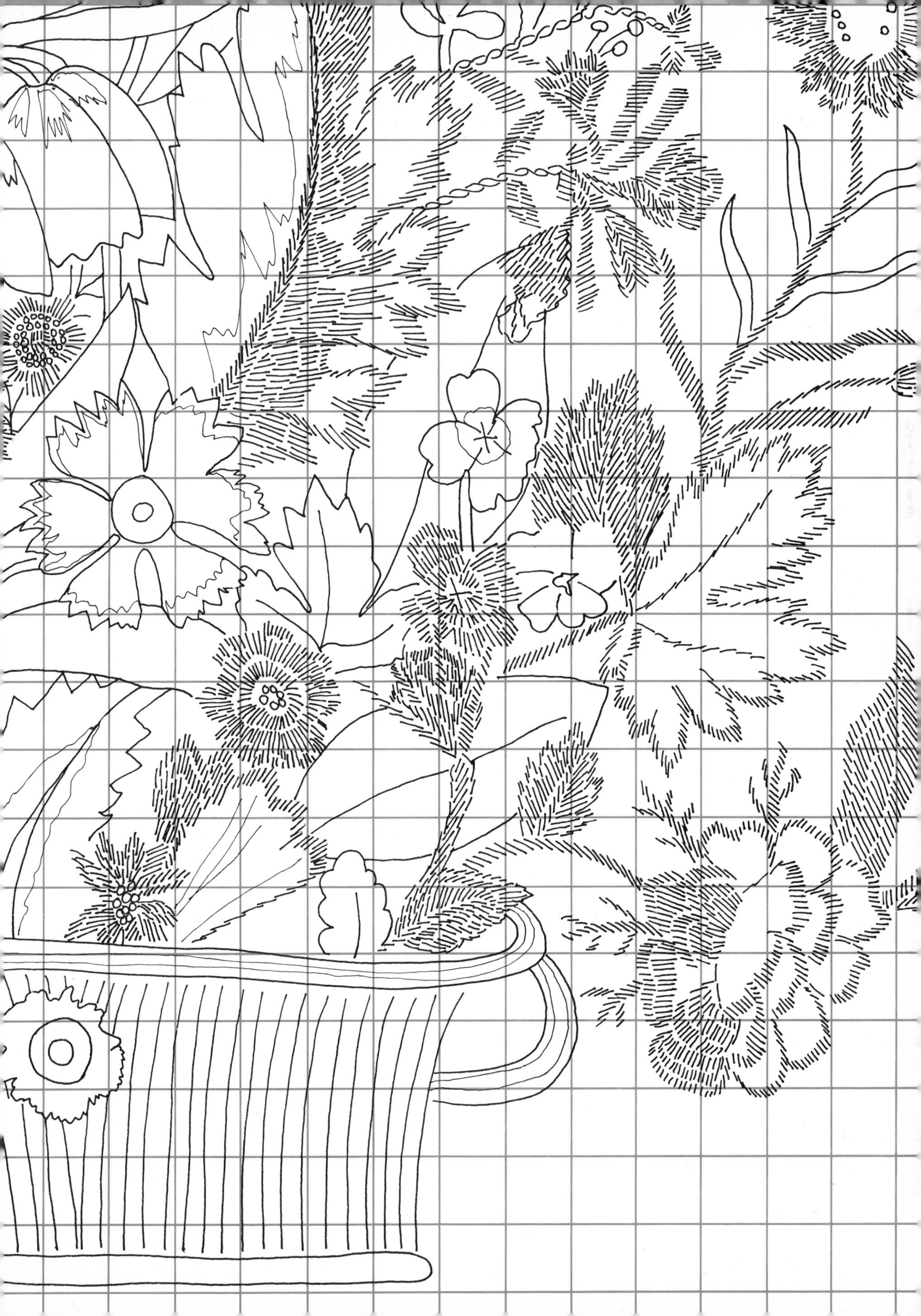

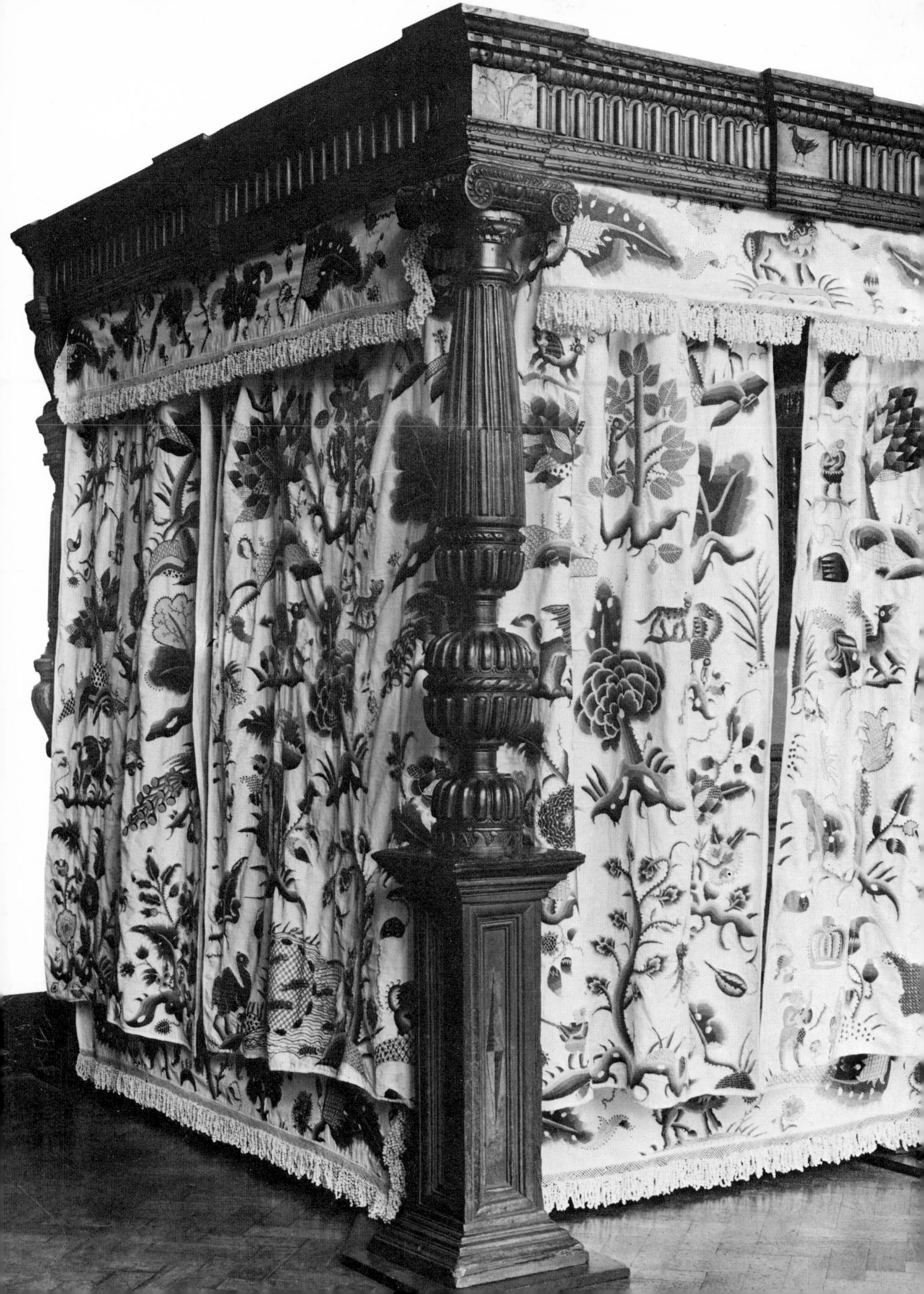

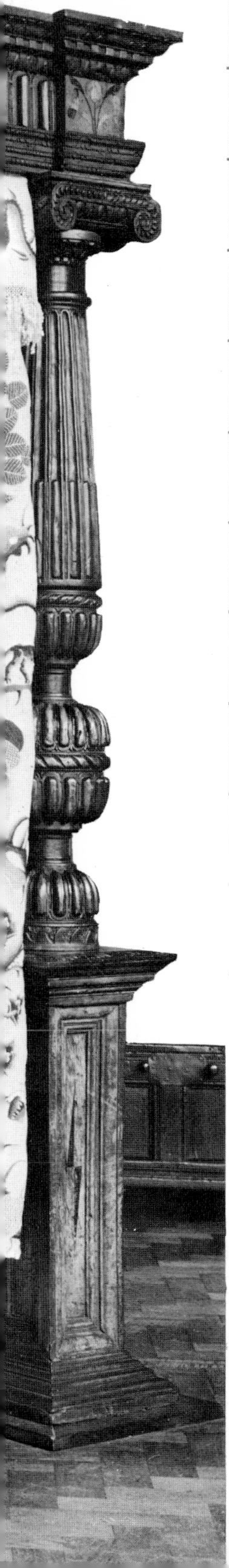

Bed curtains and valances, crewel wools on cotton and linen; signed Abigail Pett, late 17th century

Dominating are the curtains between the bedposts with borders and valances. The surface is covered with sprays of flowers and interspersed are small animals, birds, and insects with human figures as well. The coiling stem pattern is evident.

A medley of flowers in bud and in bloom predominates. The rich variety of stitches used are chosen with the purpose of expressing *form* and the working gives excellent examples of their use, including long and short stitch, split, stem, satin, feather, herringbone, buttonhole, and Roumanian stitches. Fillings show examples of couching, laid work, and cross stitch. A detail is shown on page 108.

Crown copyright, Victoria and Albert Museum, London

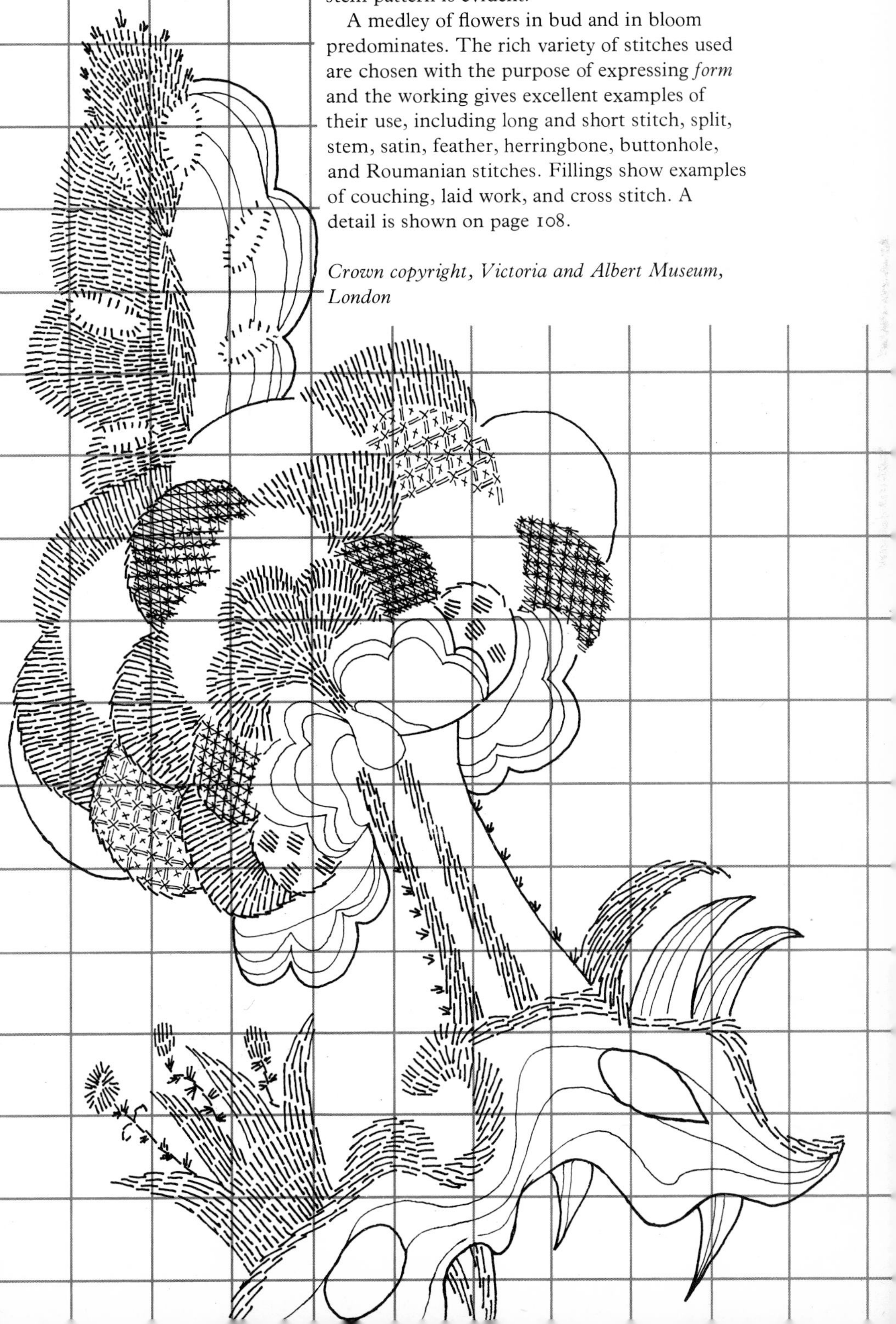

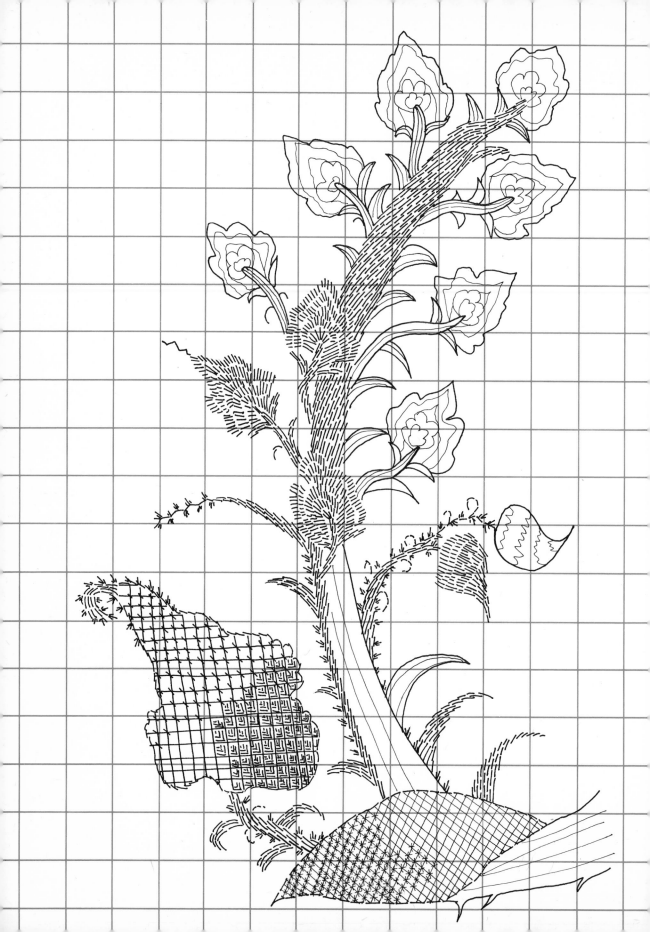

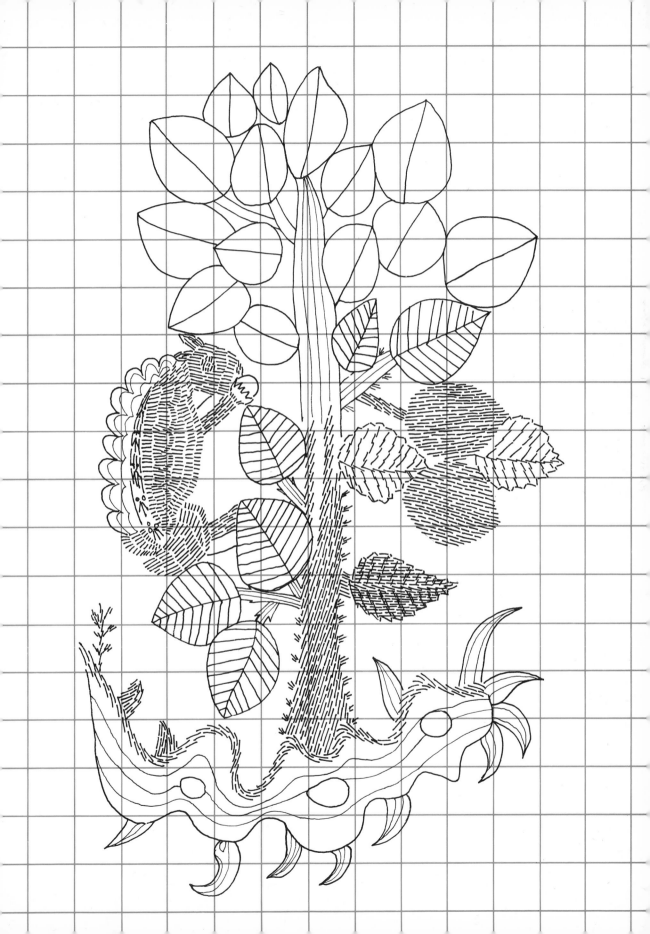

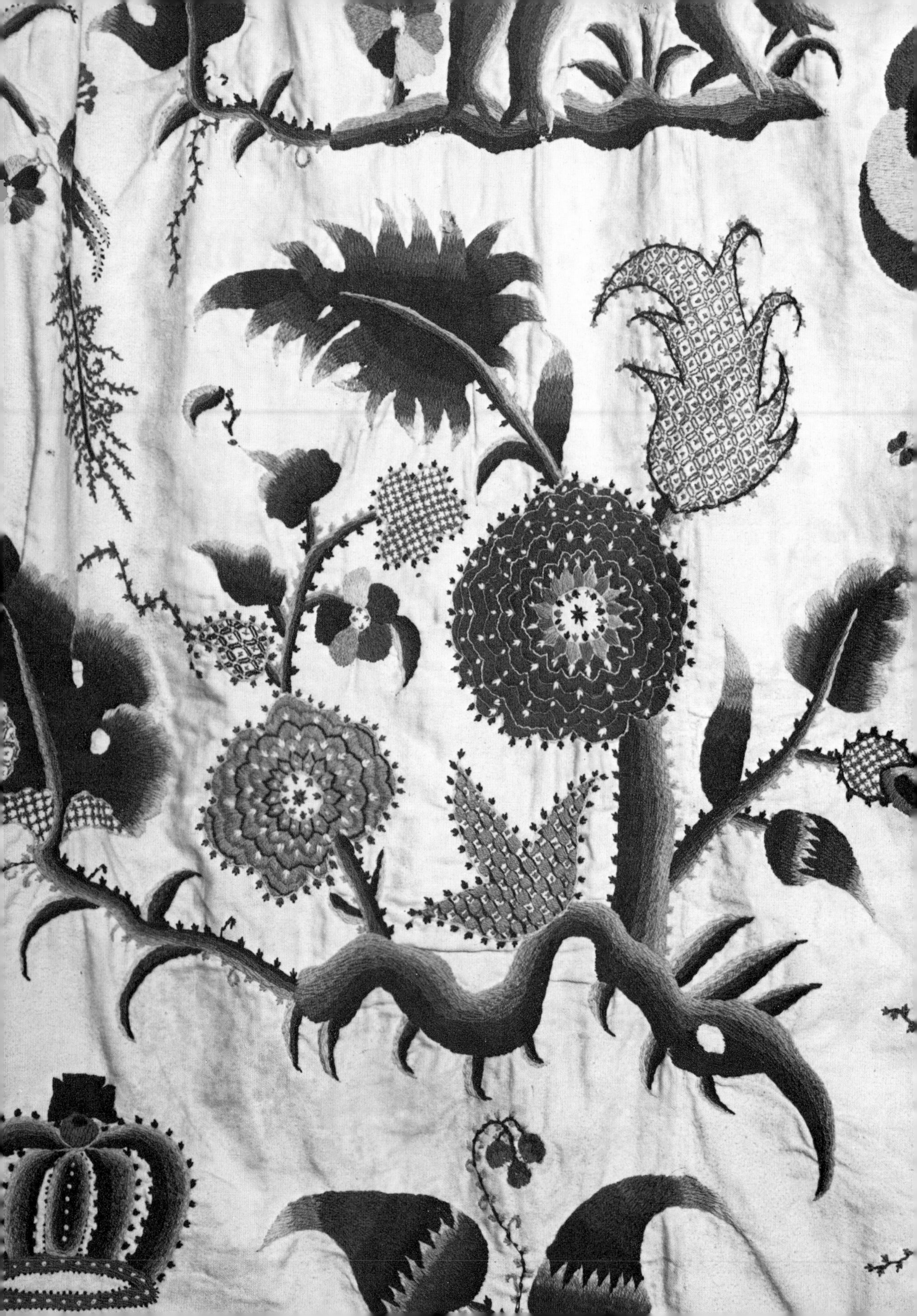

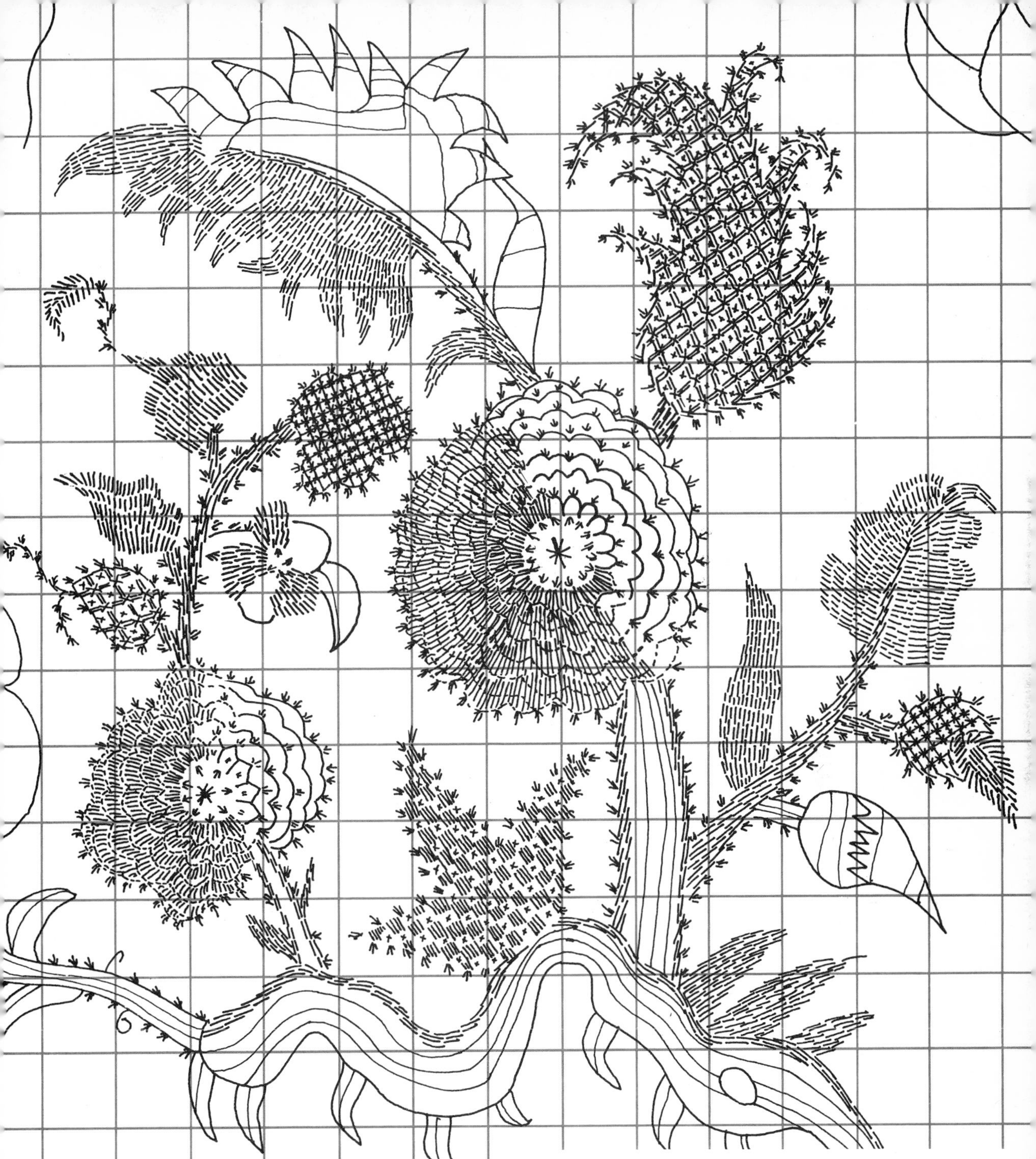
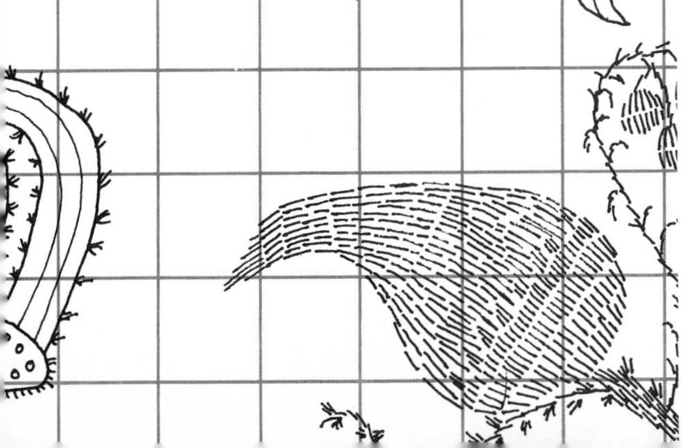

Detail of Abigail Pett bed hanging

The wide tree trunks and several of the larger leaves are in satin stitch, and seeding, couching, and trellis pattern are used for fillings. (See page 104 for the complete work.)

Crown copyright, Victoria and Albert Museum, London

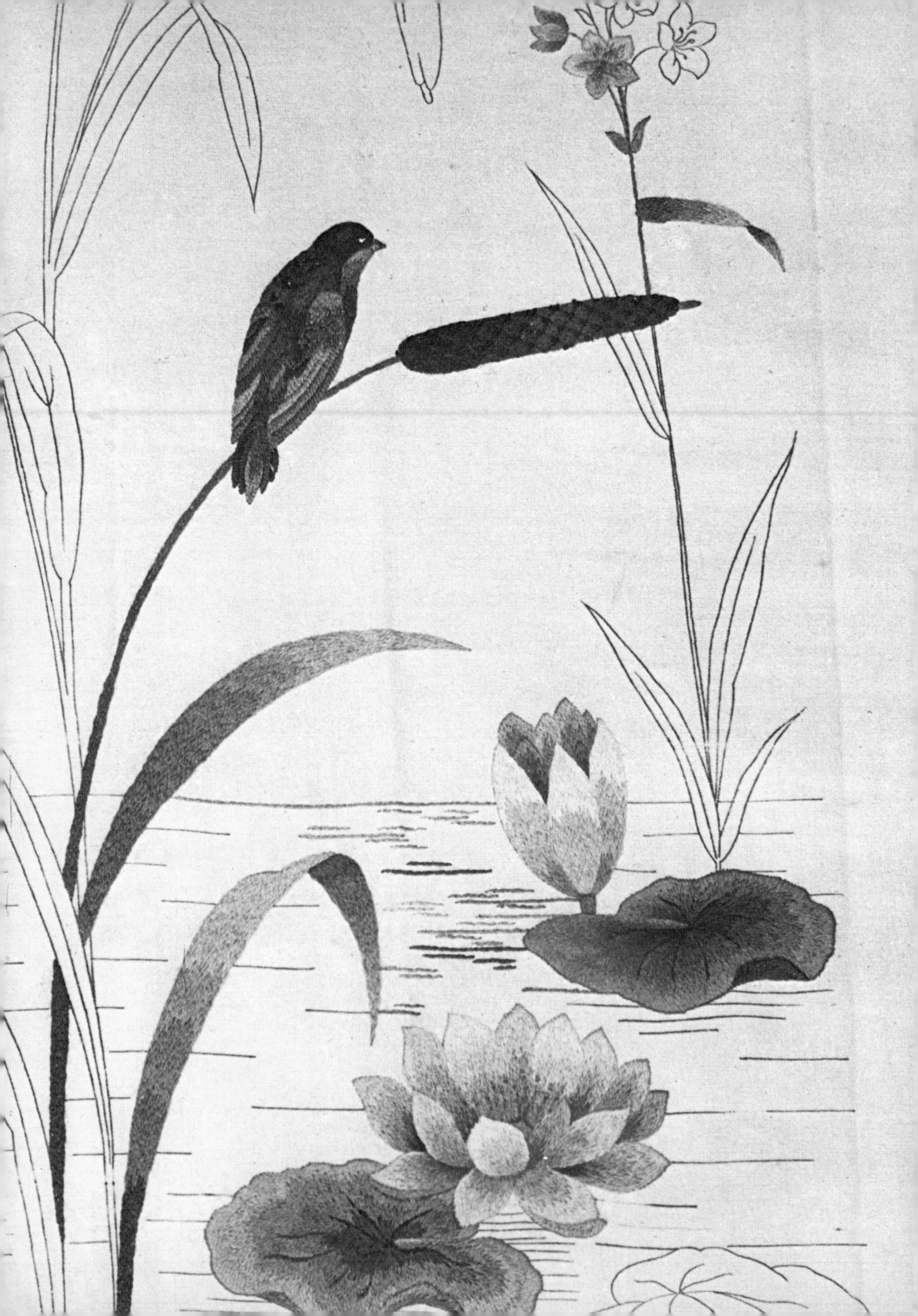

Panel for a screen in crewel wools on linen; about 1890 (unfinished)

In this graceful and pictorial study, birds represent the strong chinoiserie taste of the period and readily lend themselves to needlework.

Natural shading is introduced on the bird design by following in long and short stitch the main lines of the drawing; thus use is made of it to express form. Similarly shading is introduced on the bulrush.

The water-lilies are beautiful in their simplicity and are in strong contrast to the usual medley of embroidered flower heads. The flowers, the long leaves, and the suggestion of water are judiciously embroidered in outline stitch. The design is indicative of a return to sound perspective in embroidery.

Courtesy The Rachel Kay-Shuttleworth Collection, Gawthorpe Hall, Lancashire

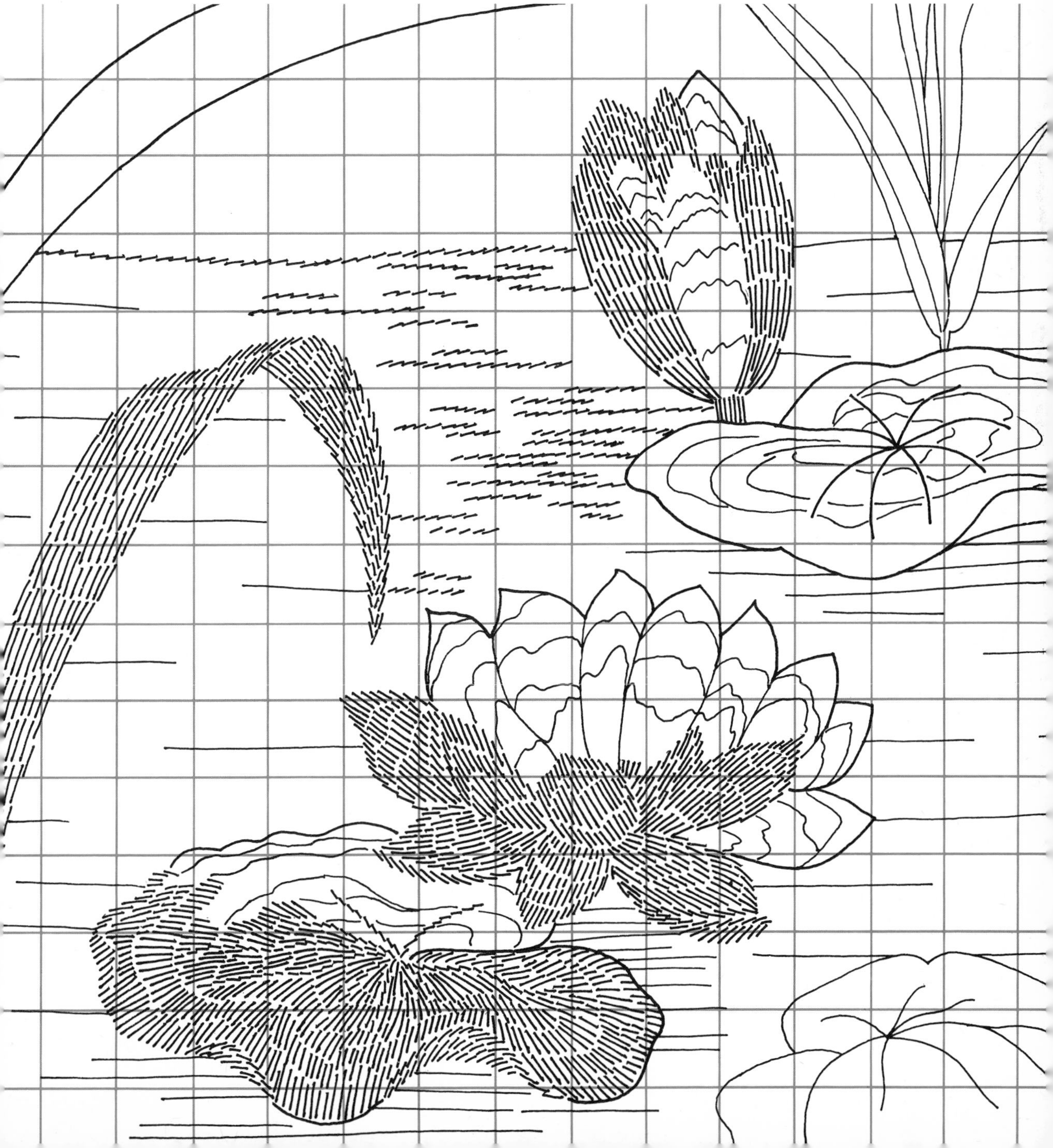

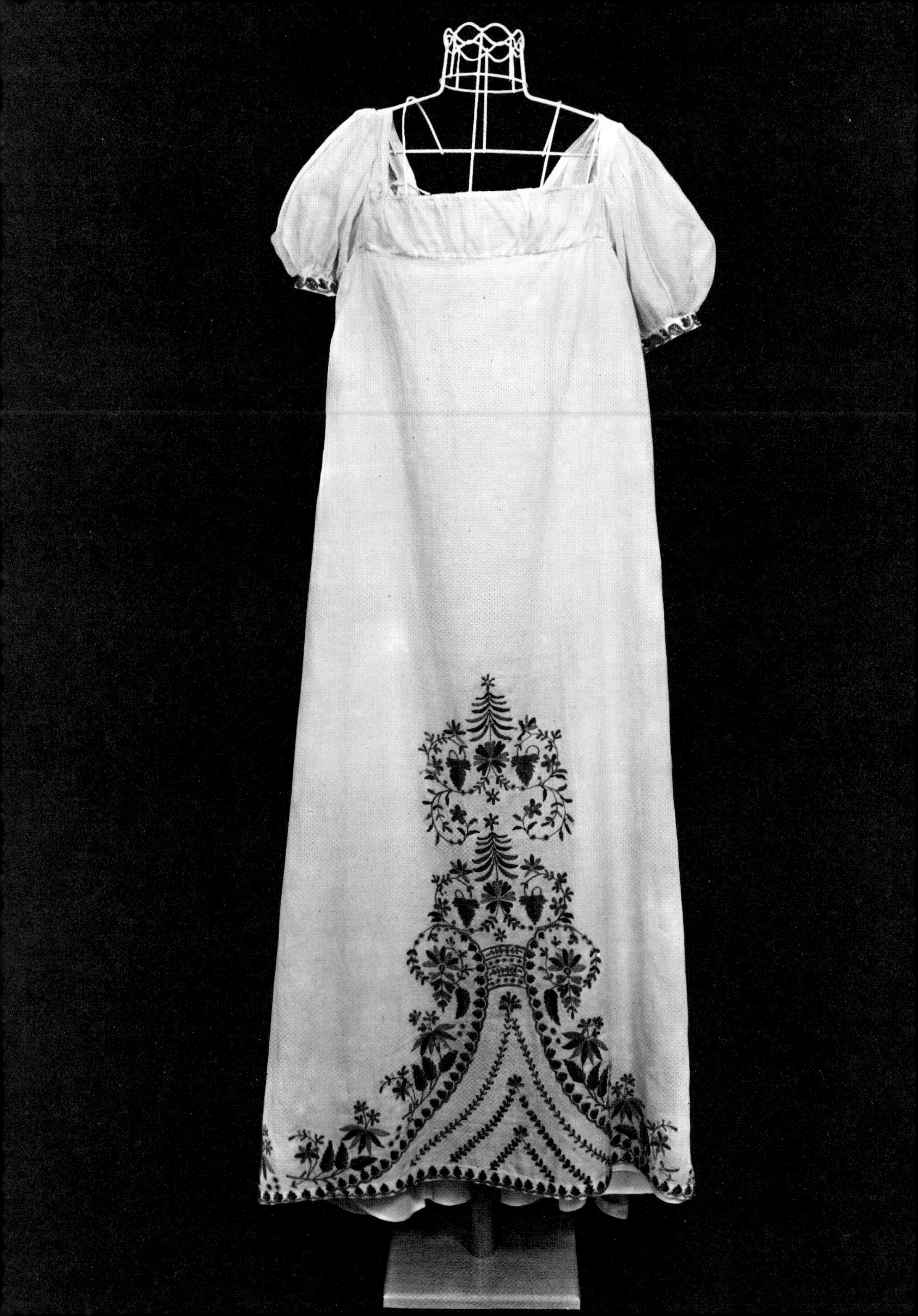

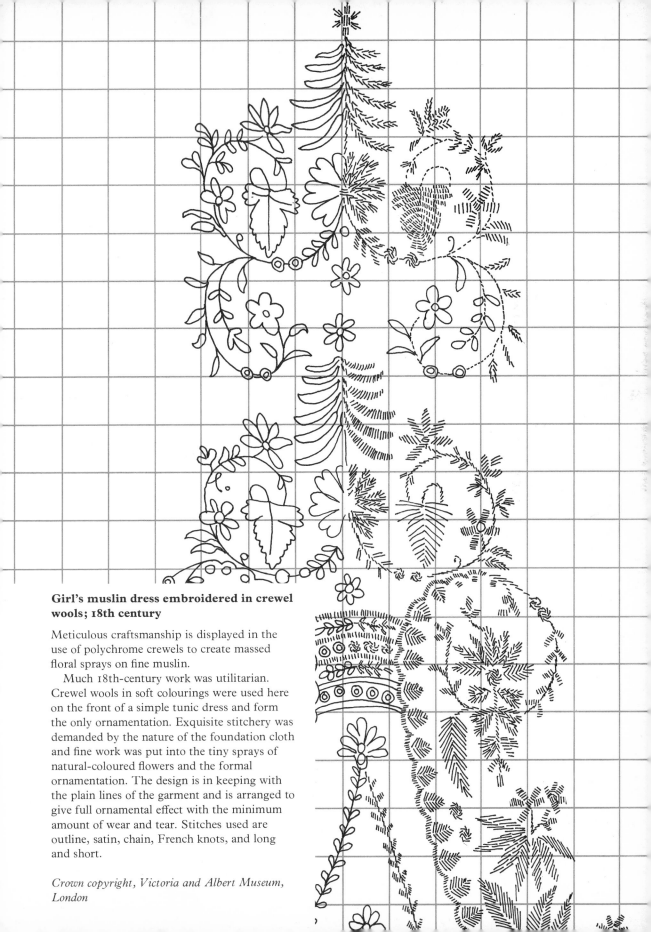

Girl's muslin dress embroidered in crewel wools; 18th century

Meticulous craftsmanship is displayed in the use of polychrome crewels to create massed floral sprays on fine muslin.

Much 18th-century work was utilitarian. Crewel wools in soft colourings were used here on the front of a simple tunic dress and form the only ornamentation. Exquisite stitchery was demanded by the nature of the foundation cloth and fine work was put into the tiny sprays of natural-coloured flowers and the formal ornamentation. The design is in keeping with the plain lines of the garment and is arranged to give full ornamental effect with the minimum amount of wear and tear. Stitches used are outline, satin, chain, French knots, and long and short.

Crown copyright, Victoria and Albert Museum, London

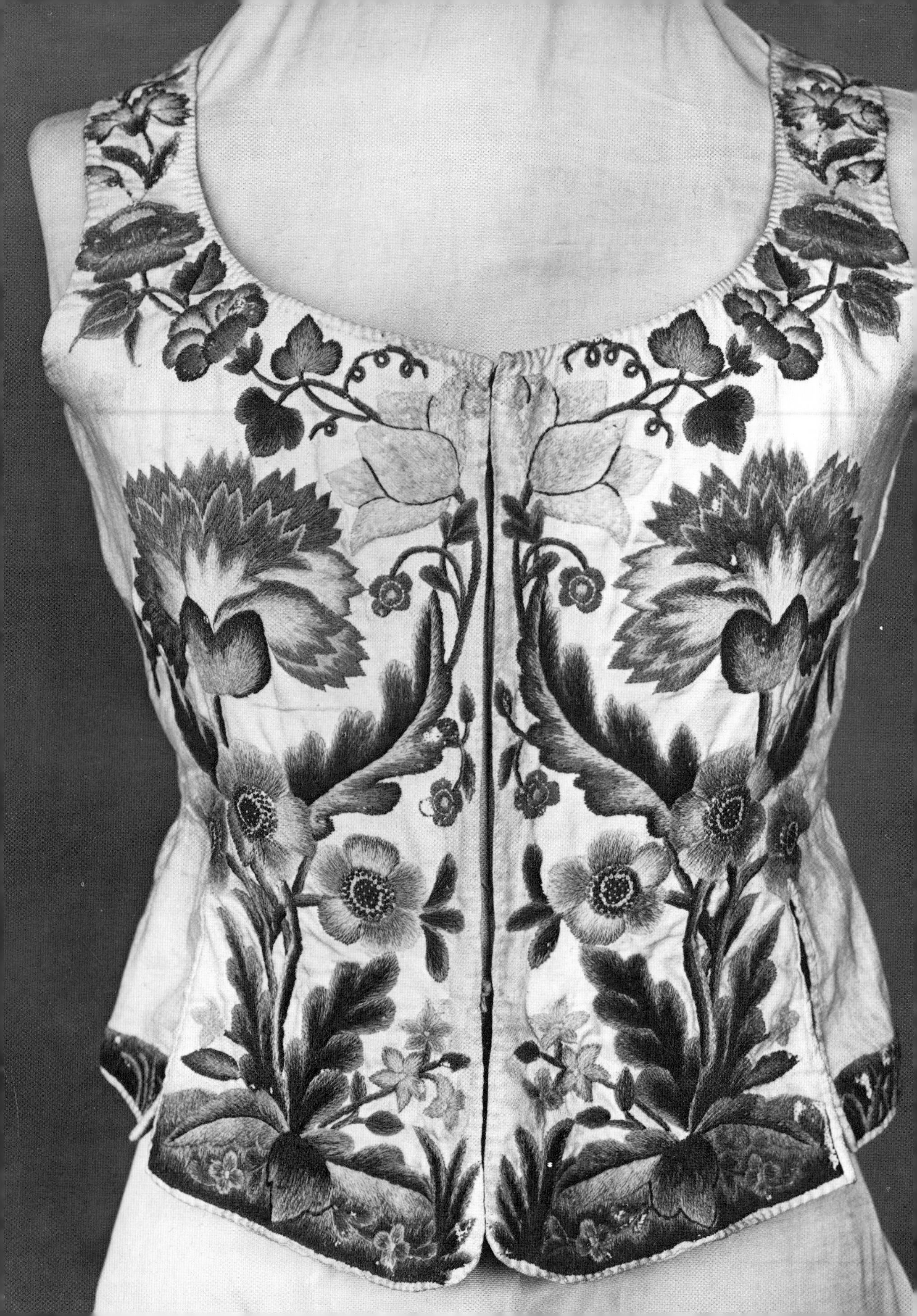

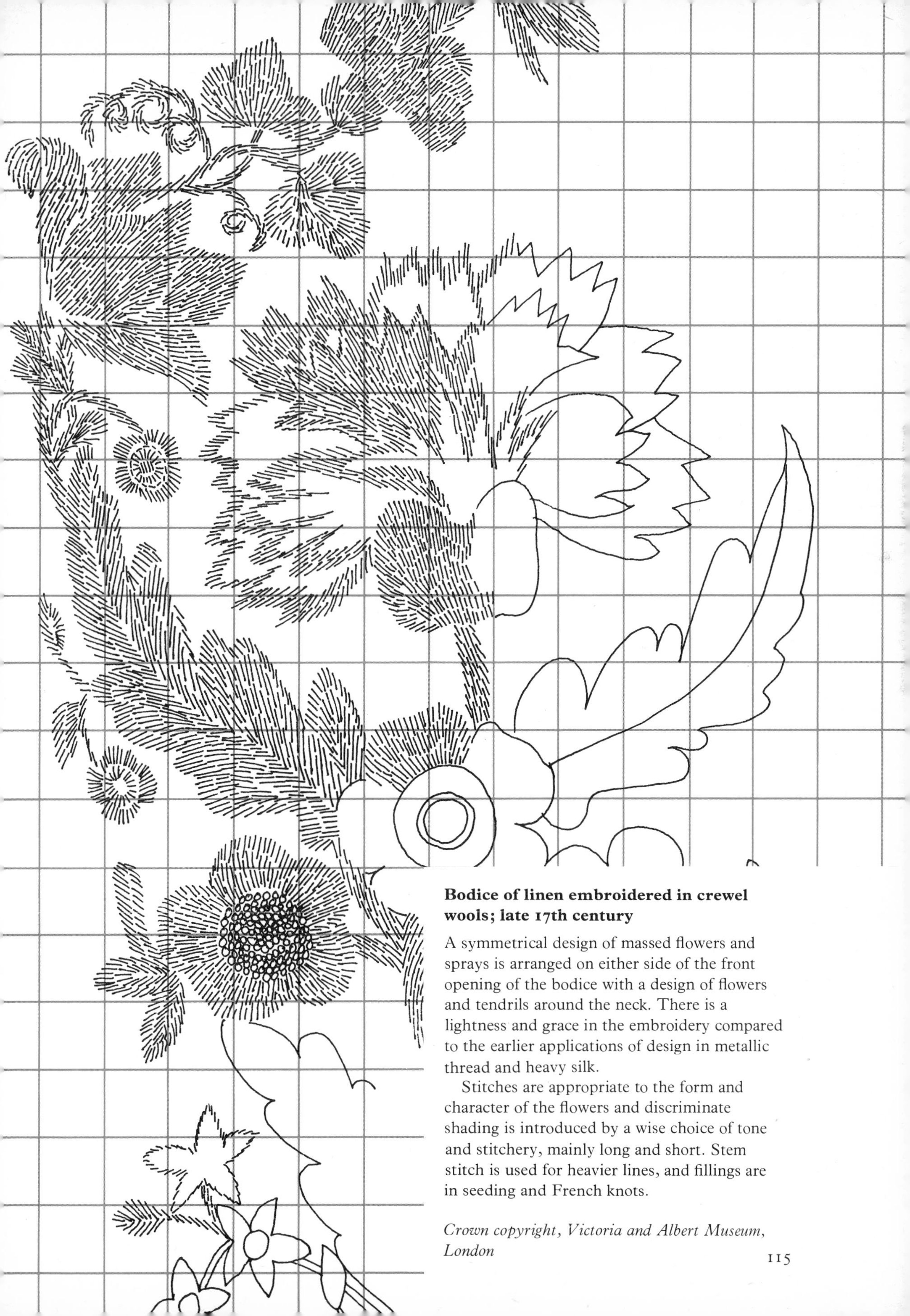

Bodice of linen embroidered in crewel wools; late 17th century

A symmetrical design of massed flowers and sprays is arranged on either side of the front opening of the bodice with a design of flowers and tendrils around the neck. There is a lightness and grace in the embroidery compared to the earlier applications of design in metallic thread and heavy silk.

Stitches are appropriate to the form and character of the flowers and discriminate shading is introduced by a wise choice of tone and stitchery, mainly long and short. Stem stitch is used for heavier lines, and fillings are in seeding and French knots.

Crown copyright, Victoria and Albert Museum, London

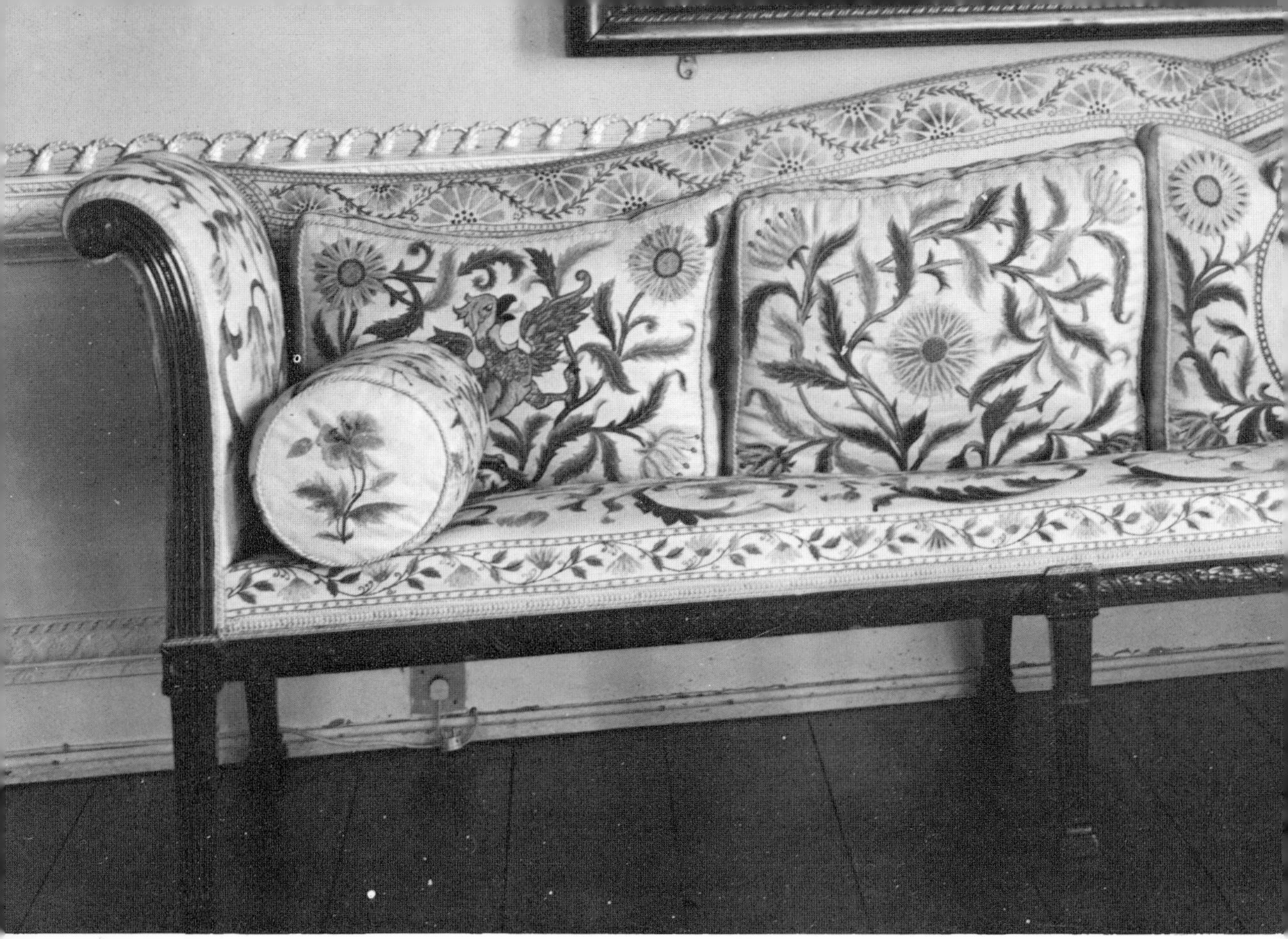

Settee cover; 20th century

This modern interpretation and application of crewel work preserves the best of traditional designs and workmanship. The arrangement in sections to form a continuous panel facilitates embroidering either by an individual or a group. Flower motifs predominate with a central panel bearing a coat of arms.

Satin stitch emphasizes the heavier outlines which include scrolls and coiling stems and is also used for leaves and lettering; long and short stitch has been used to show up shading. The delicate floral border pattern in this specimen is somewhat unusual, introducing lightness into the panel. The cover by its design and its purpose gives an excellent opportunity for the display of a wise colour scheme as well as good needlework. (The ends of the cushions opposite to those shown are the ones illustrated in the drawings.)

Crown copyright, Osterley Park House, London

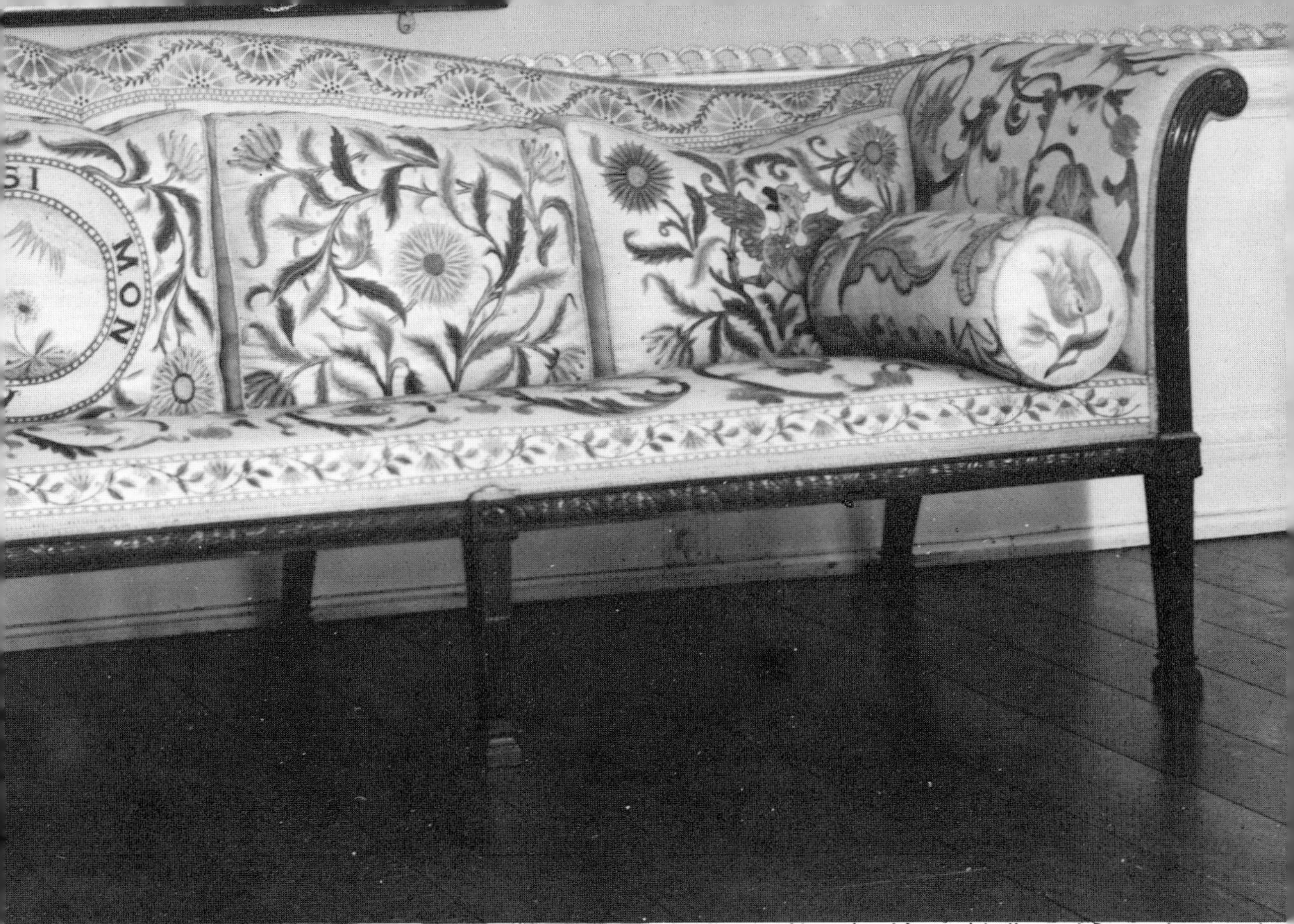
SI
MON

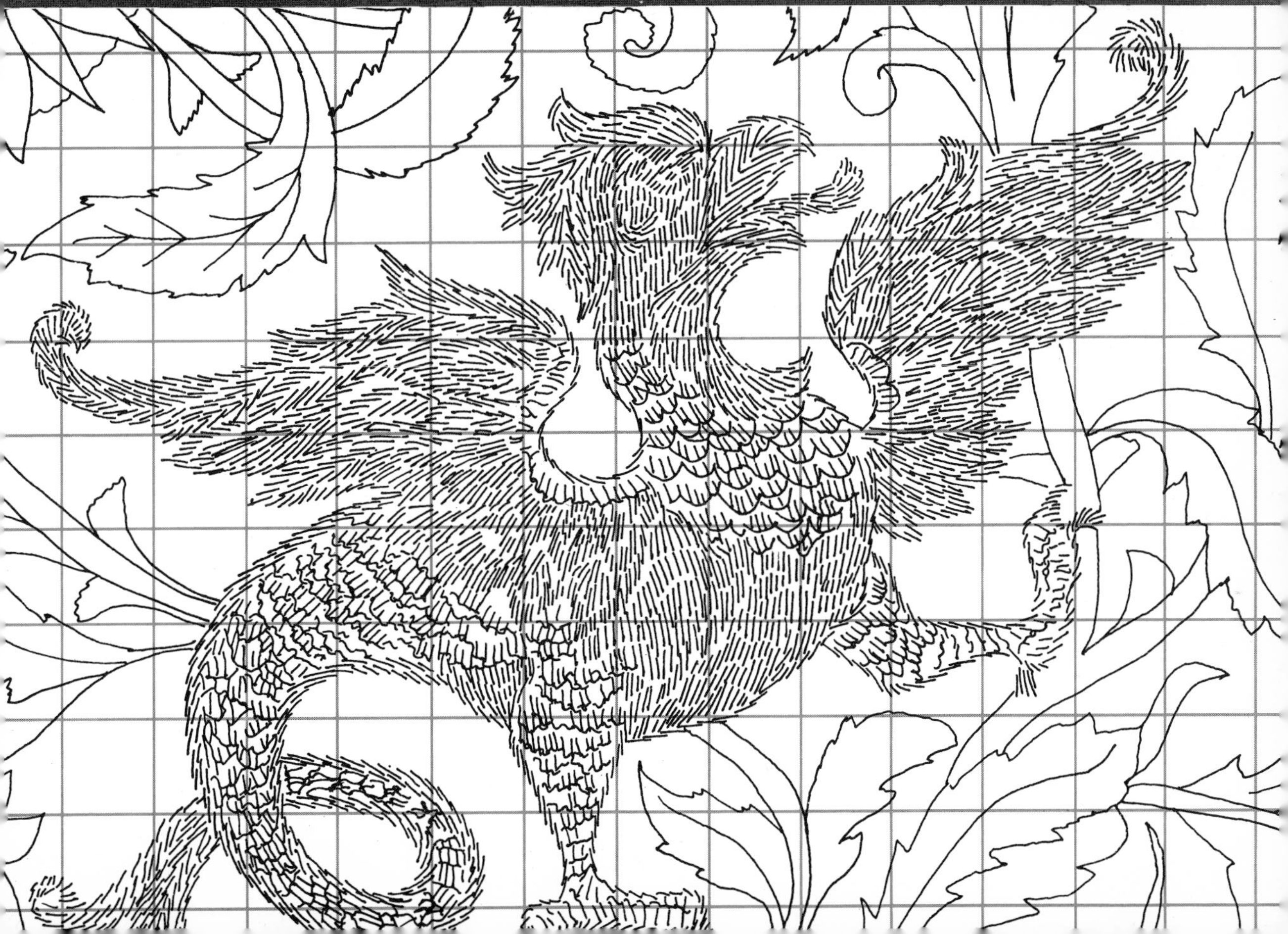

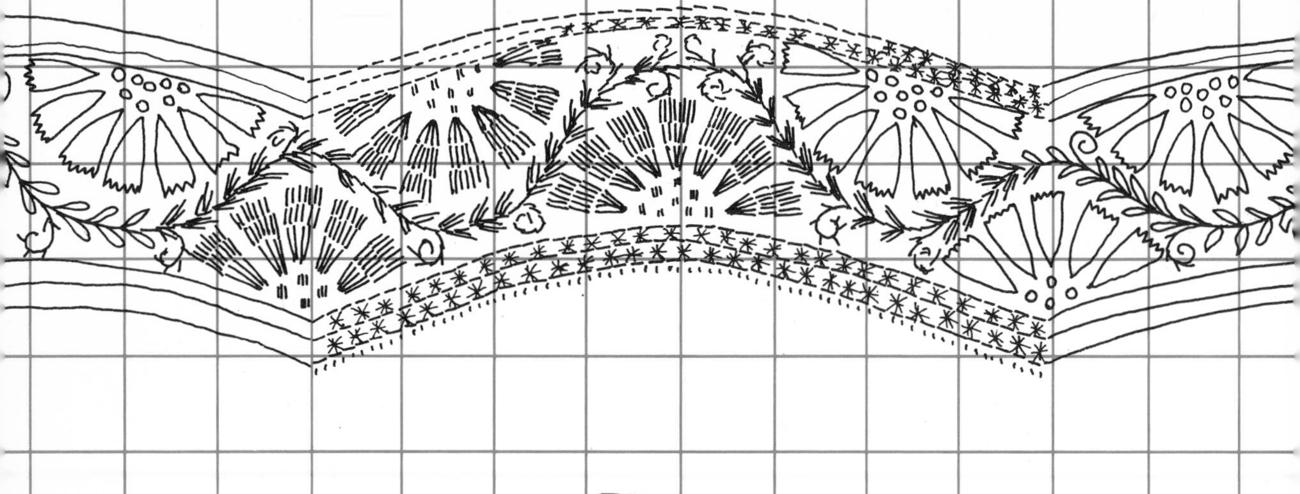

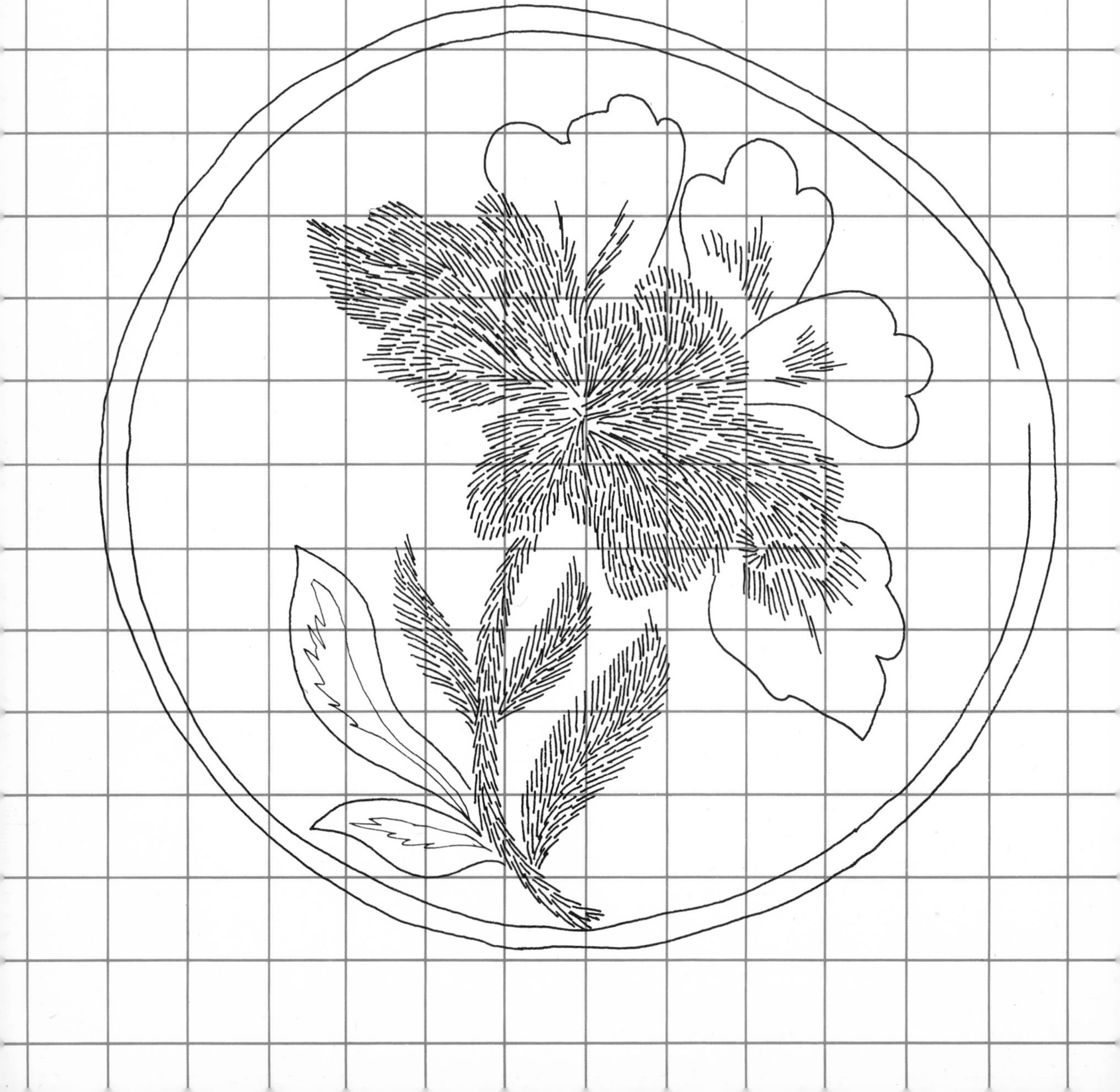

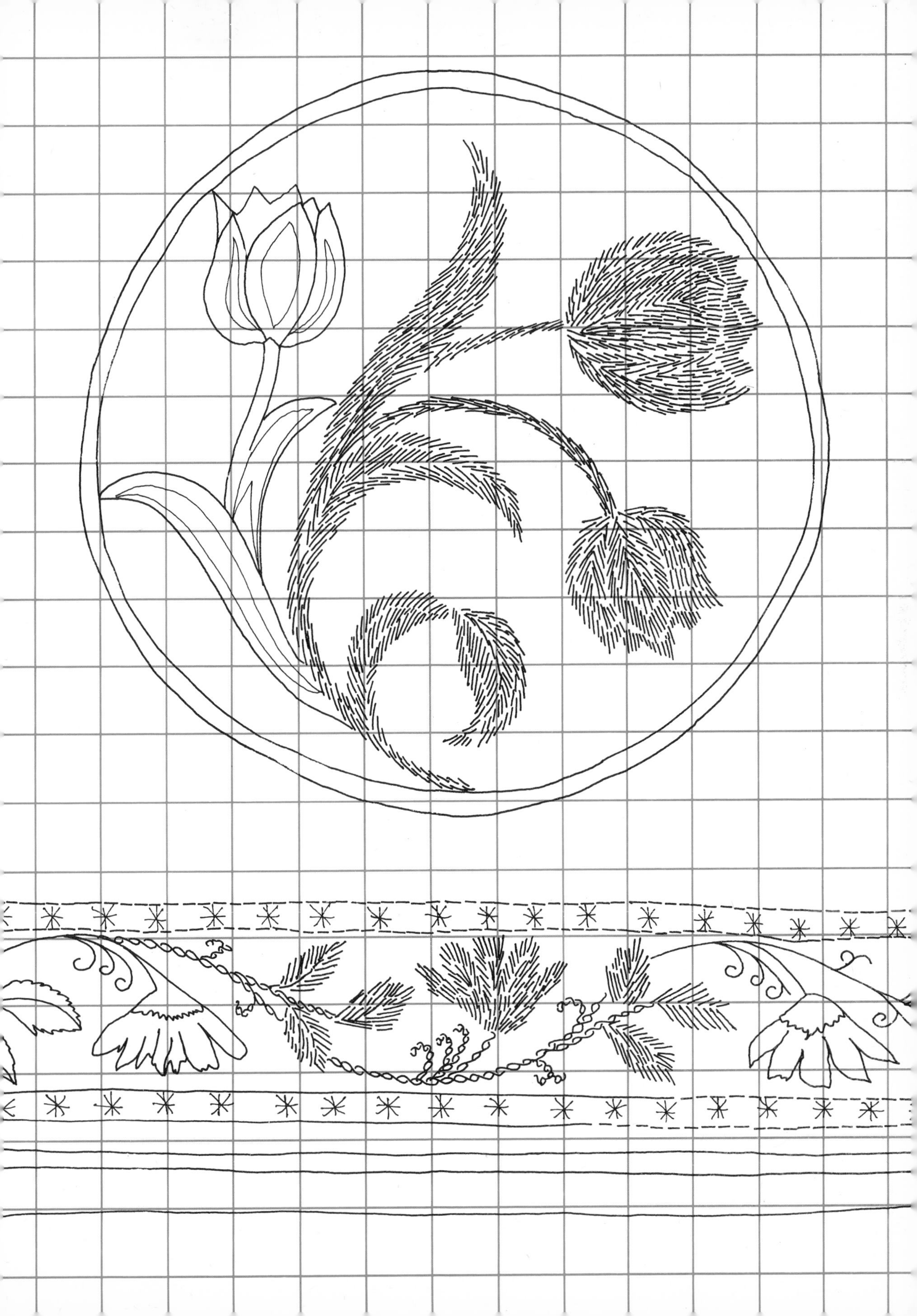

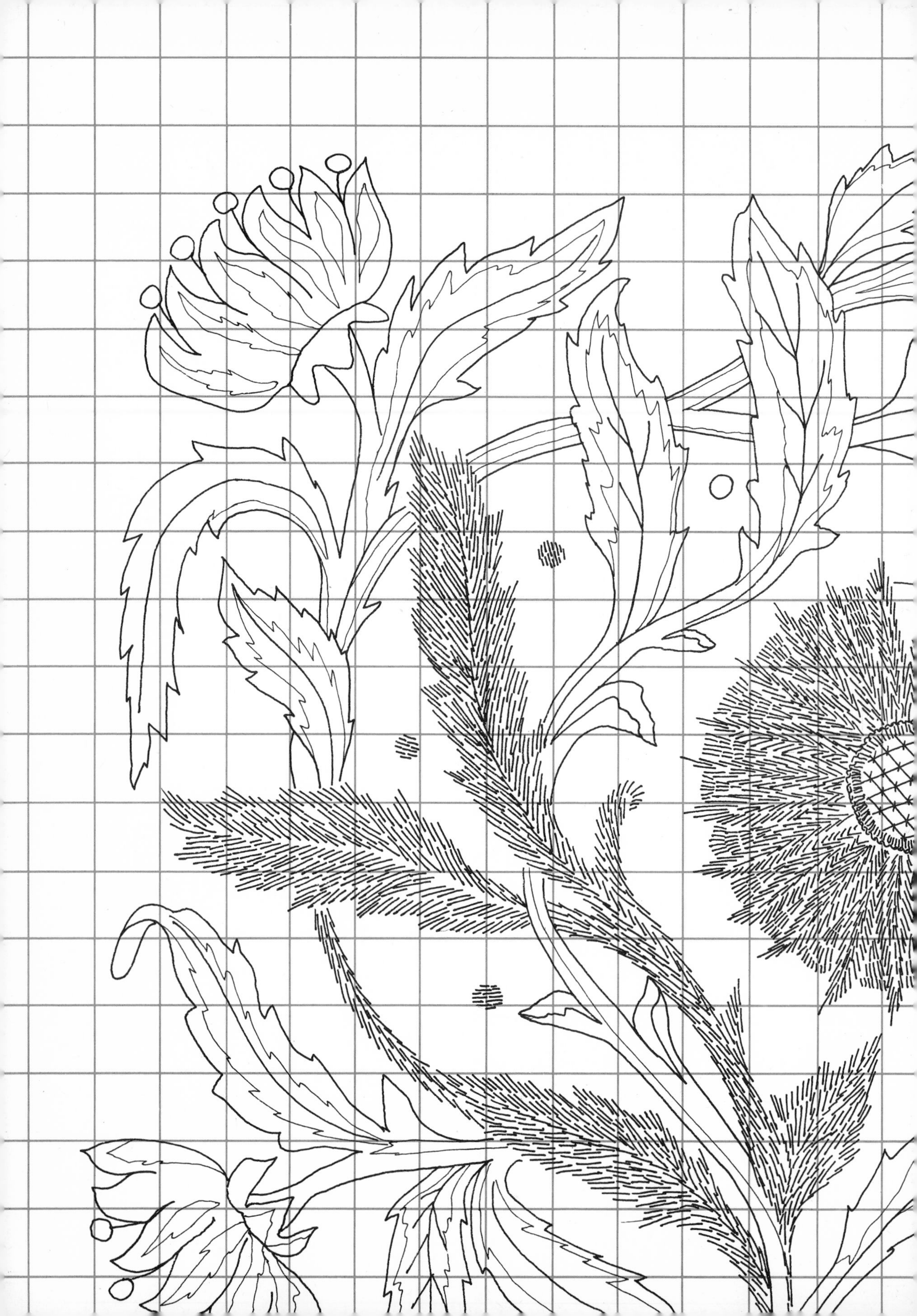

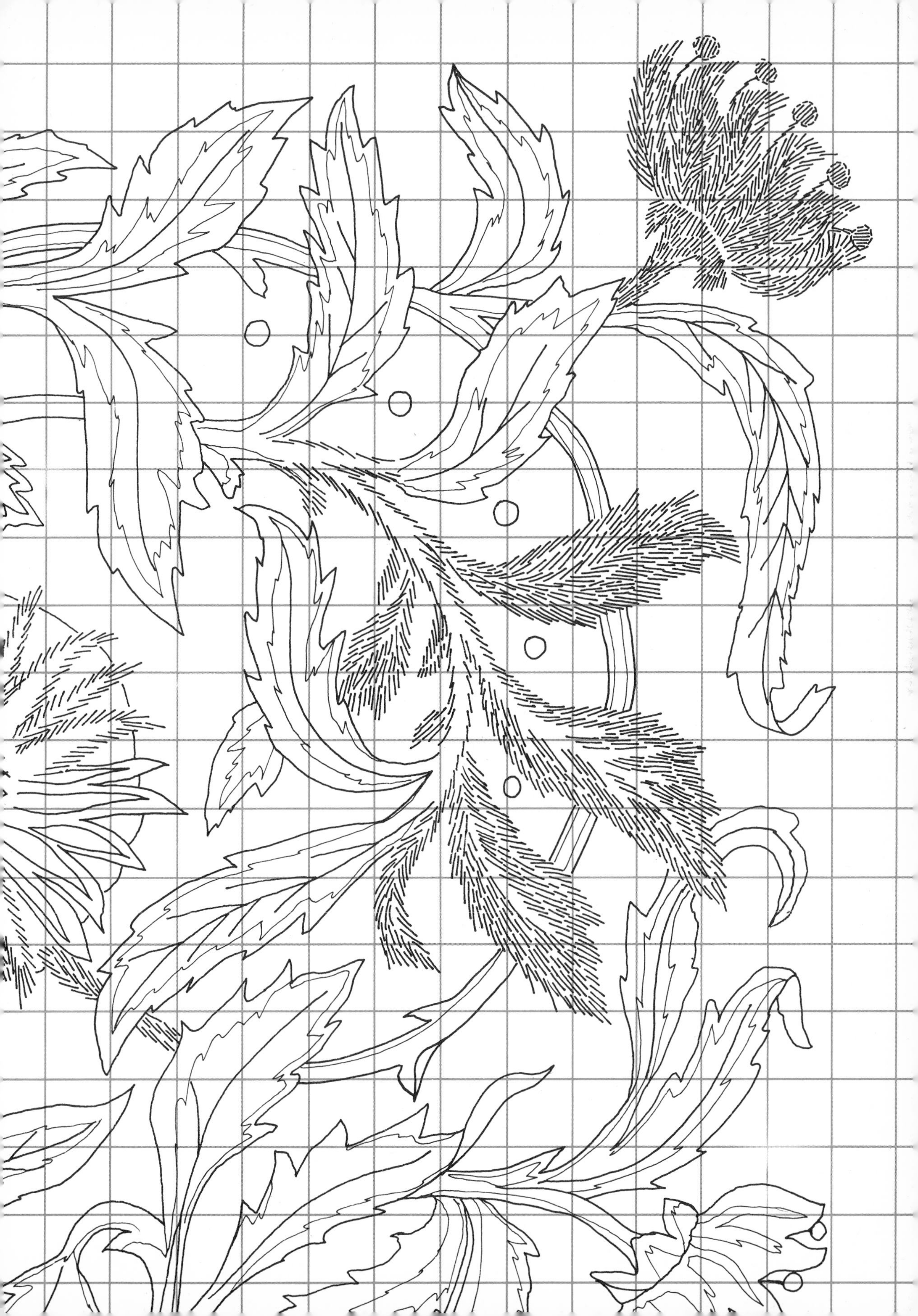

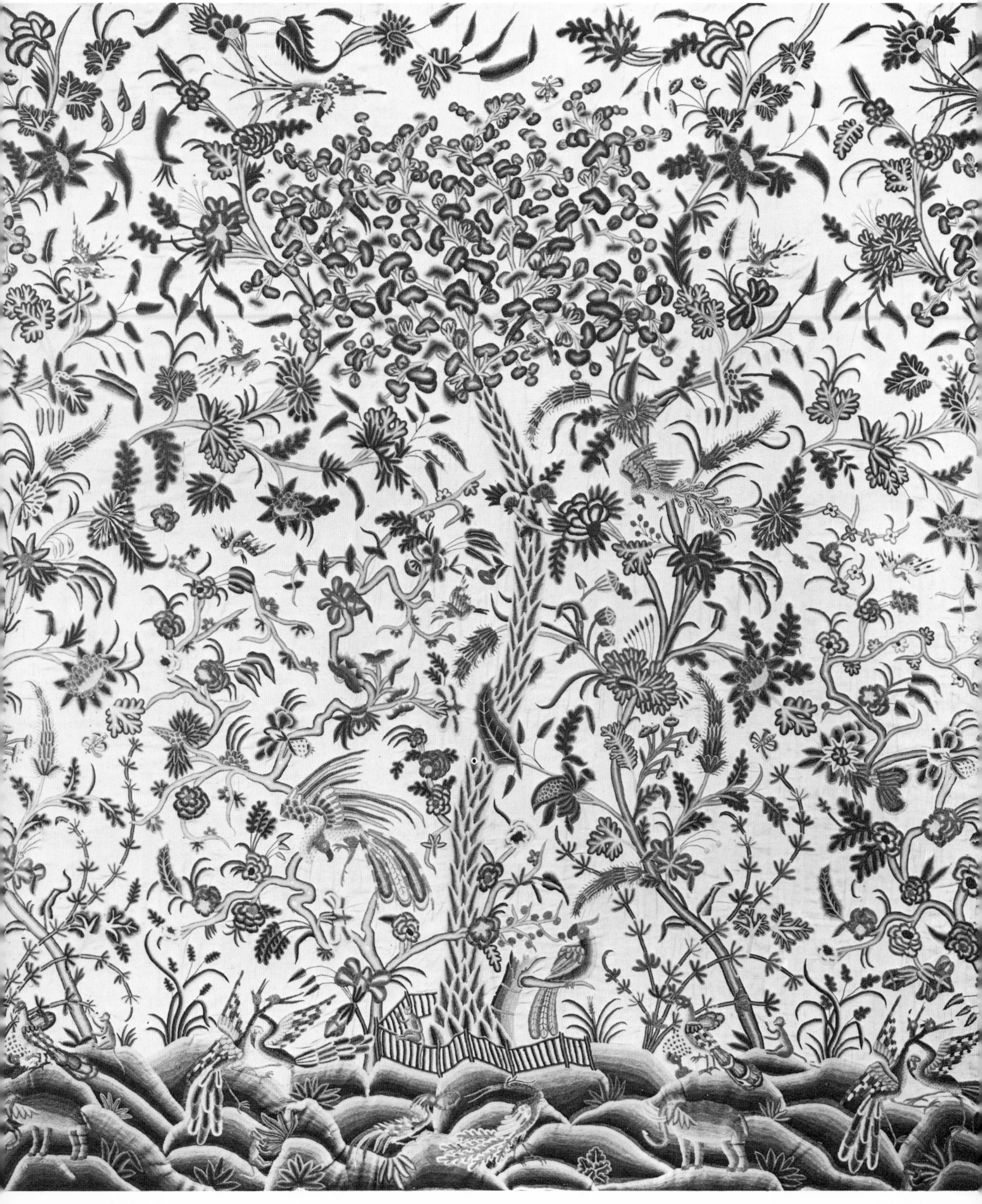

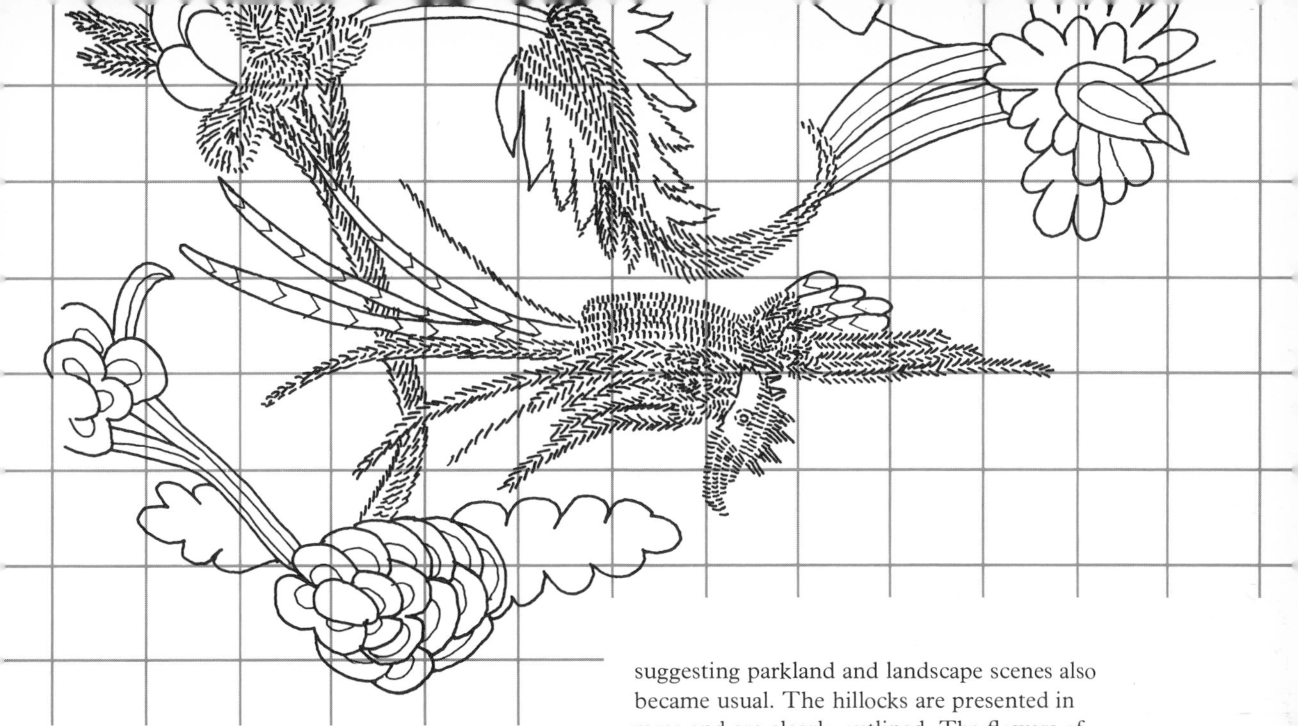

Curtain in crewel wools on cotton and linen; late 17th century

The design is that of a conventional Tree of Life or Paradise Tree and incorporates distinctive Christian and European (especially English and Dutch) influences.

The 'scaled' tree trunk became a usual ornamentation. A fence at the base of the tree suggesting parkland and landscape scenes also became usual. The hillocks are presented in mass and are clearly outlined. The flowers of various kinds and the leaves, many with fronds, call for meticulous attention to detail in stitchery. These in the main are satin, outline, chain, split, stem, herringbone, feather, and French knots, with some use of couching.

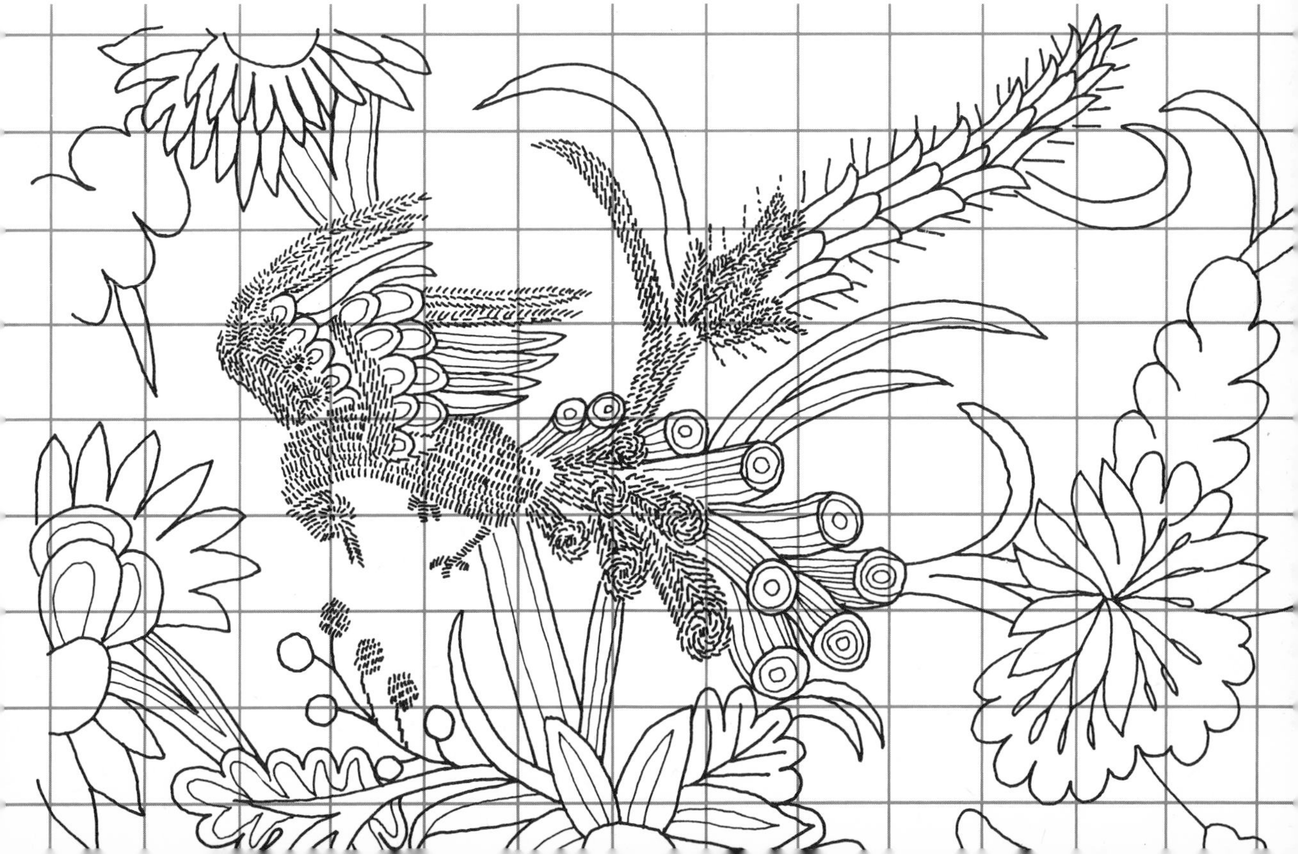

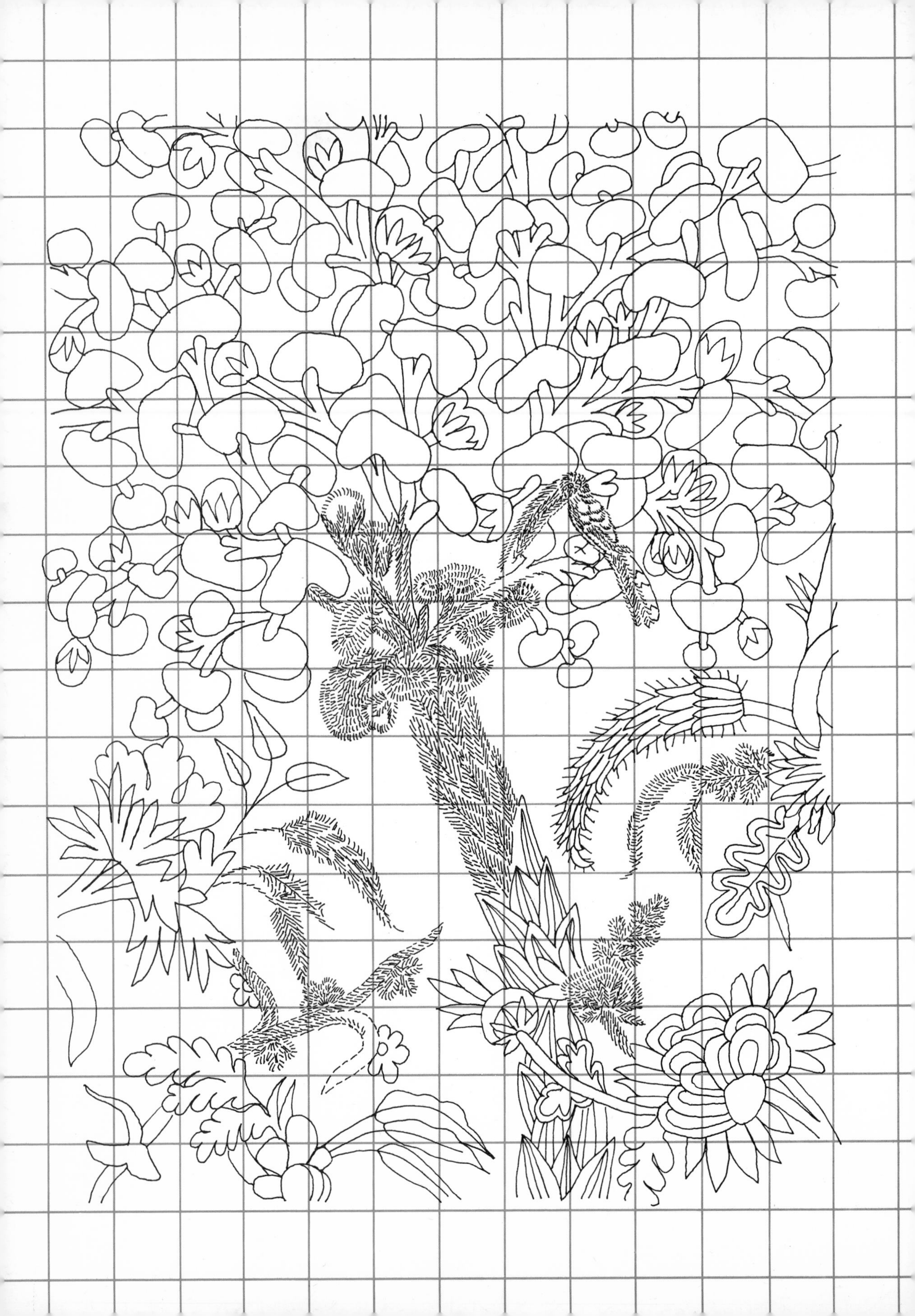

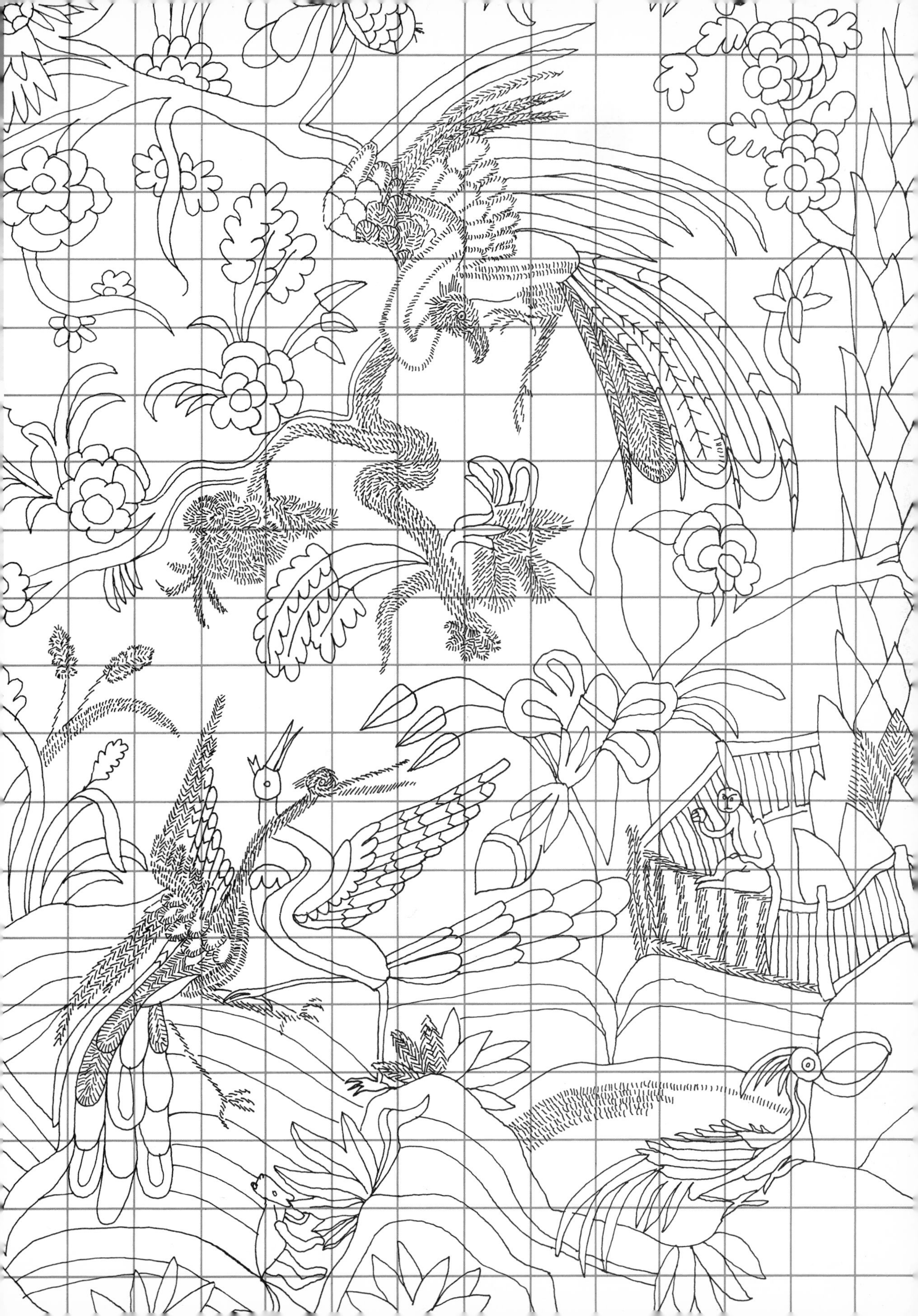

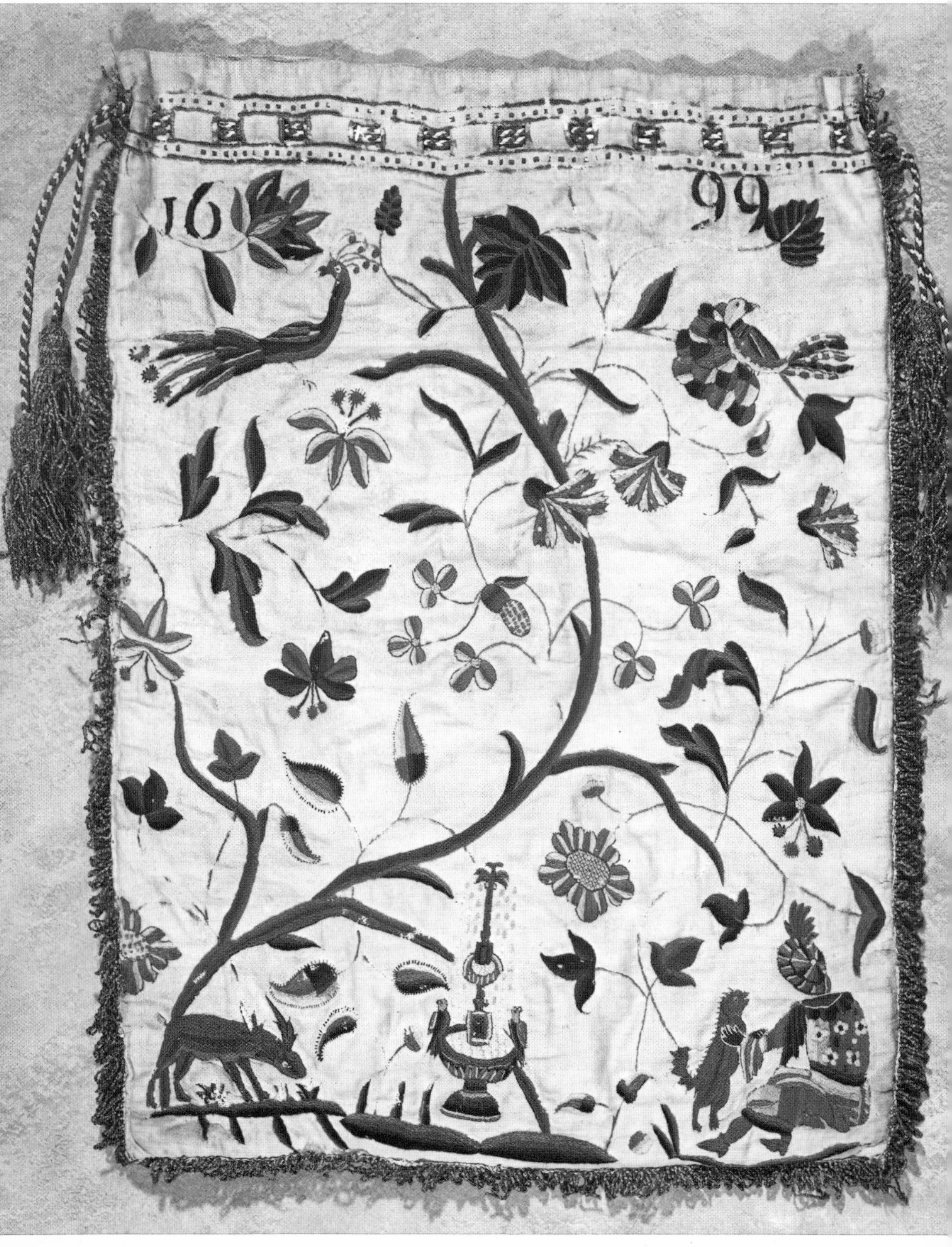
16
99

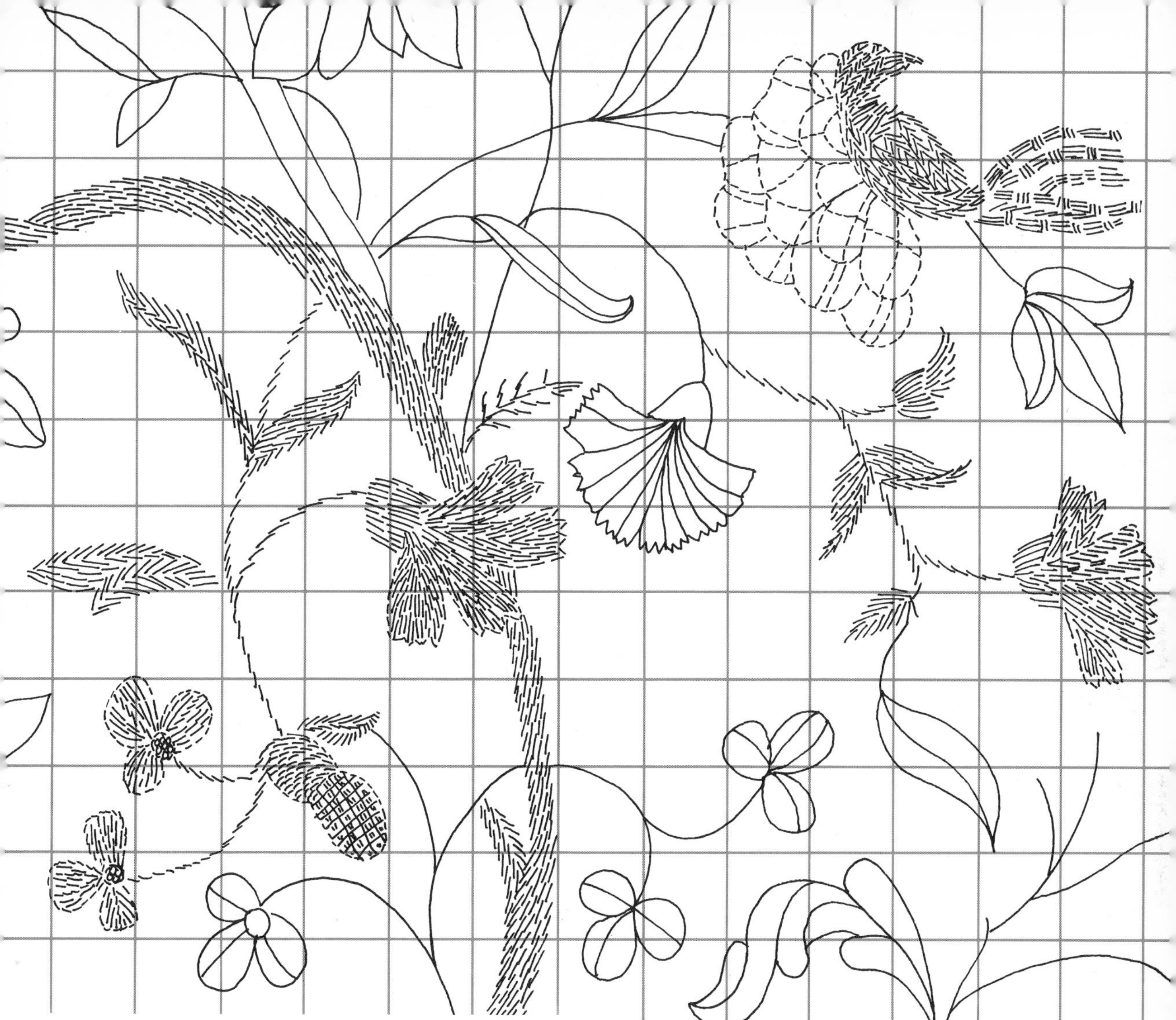

Workbag in multi-coloured crewel wools on twill background; 1699

The traditional Tree of Life is symbolized in the fountain. An all-over design, it derives unity from the serpentine line of the tree branch and from the animals and birds that appear in each corner amid leaves and blossoms. At the top are two meandering lines of parallel chain stitch forming a border.

On the surface of the bag there is a variety of leaves, tendrils, and blossoms worked mainly in satin and long and short stitches, which allow for wide gradations in shading. Outline and chain stitches are also used, and fillings are achieved by seeding and detached chain stitch. Clustered French knots are arranged in some flower and leaf centres.

Courtesy The Museum of Costume, Bath

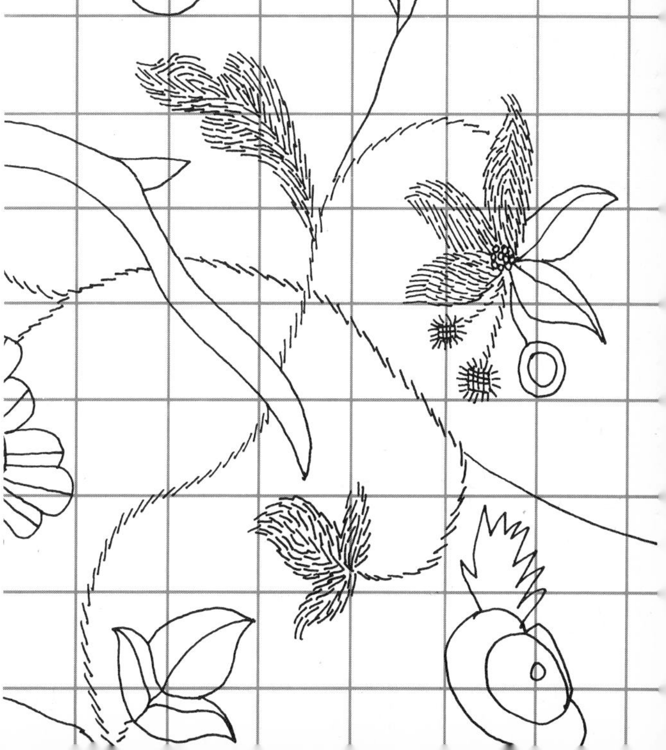

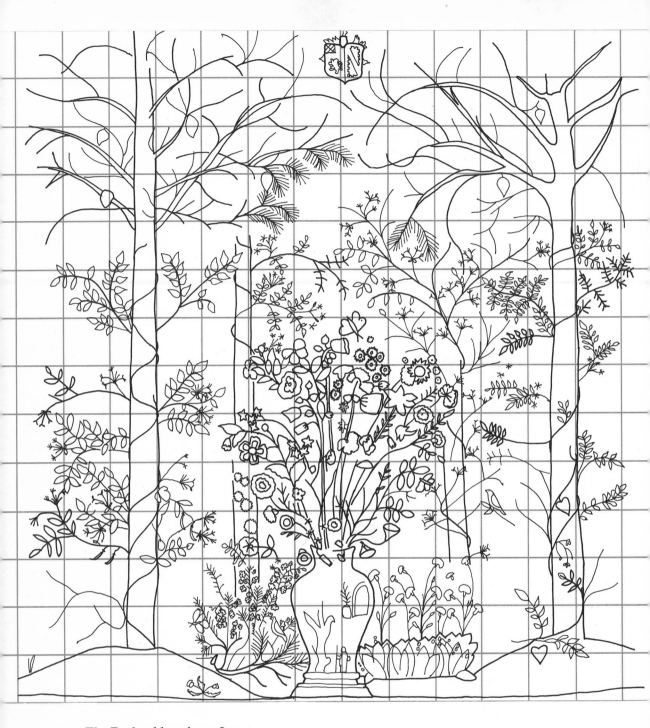

The Bocland hanging; 1825–50

This superb hanging has a backing of worsted embroidered in crewel wools in long and short, stem, and chain stitches, with French knots and couching. At the top are the arms of Bocland impaling an unidentified coat of arms. The hanging is said to have belonged to Major-General Maurice Bocland.

The Tree of Life theme is evident not only in the two embroidered trees but also in the central vase filled to overflowing with beautiful flowers. The vase or fountain motif is regarded as identical in inspiration to the Tree of Life.

Details are shown on pages 131, 134 and 136.

Courtesy Victoria and Albert Museum, London

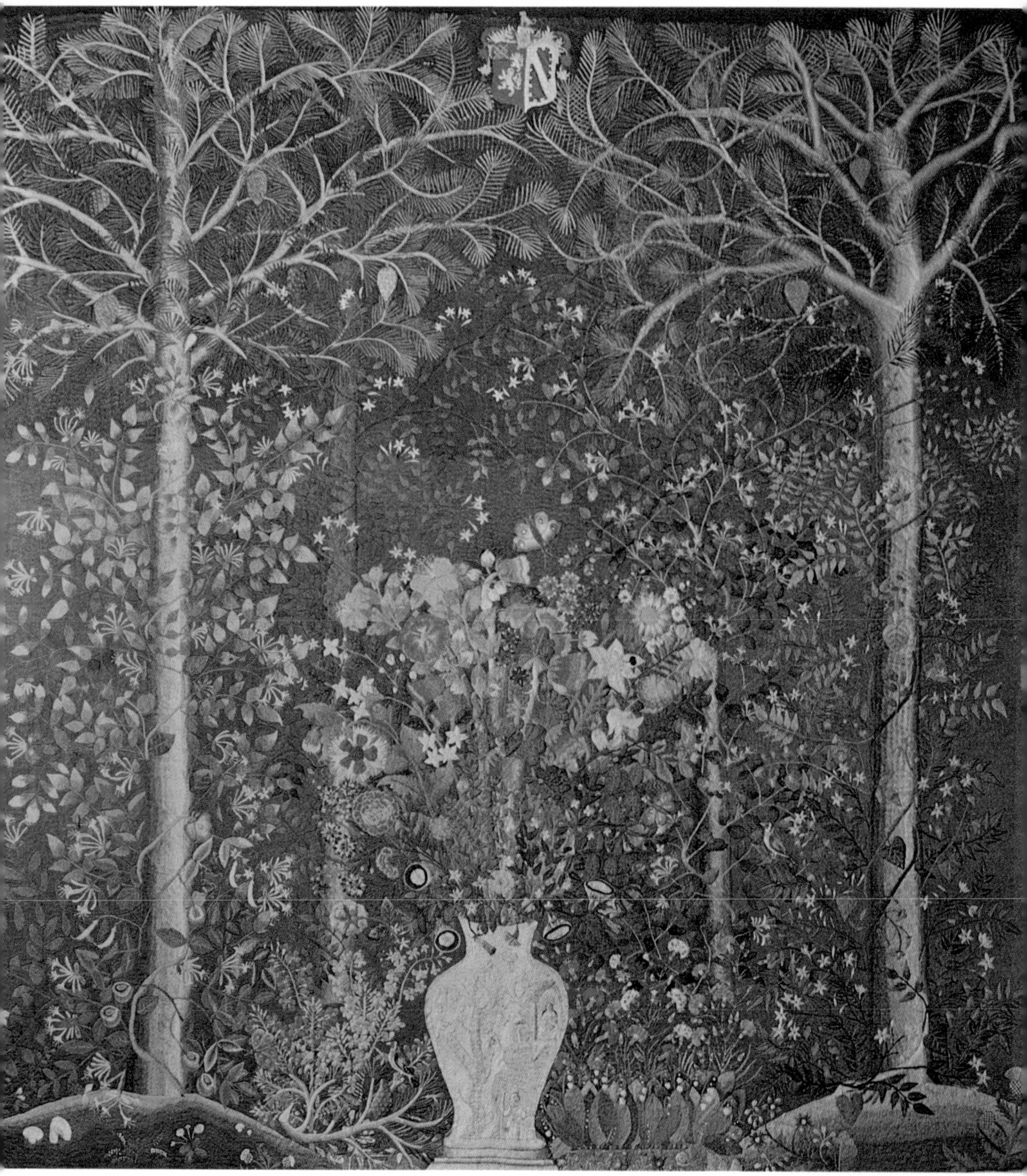

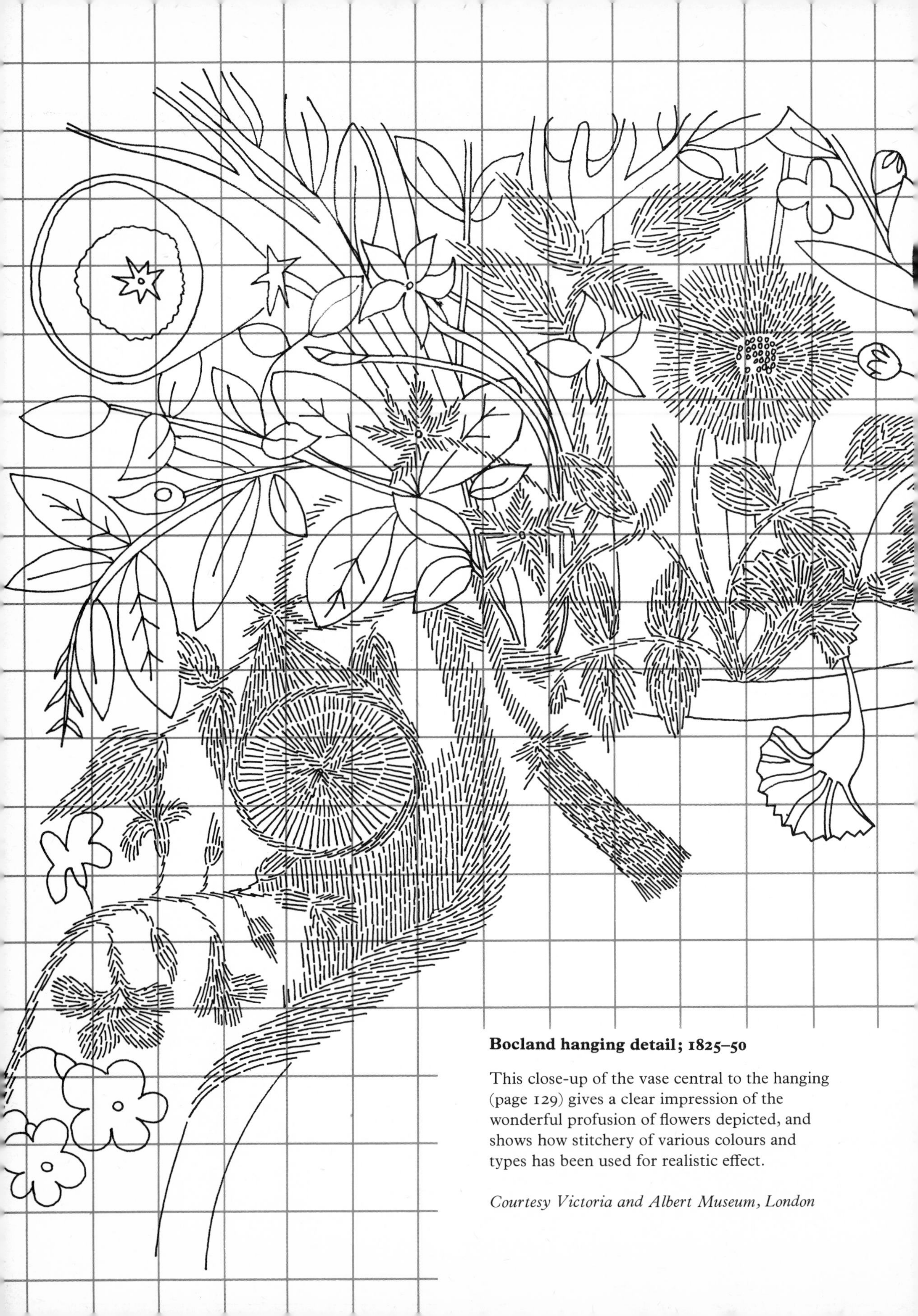

Bocland hanging detail; 1825–50

This close-up of the vase central to the hanging (page 129) gives a clear impression of the wonderful profusion of flowers depicted, and shows how stitchery of various colours and types has been used for realistic effect.

Courtesy Victoria and Albert Museum, London

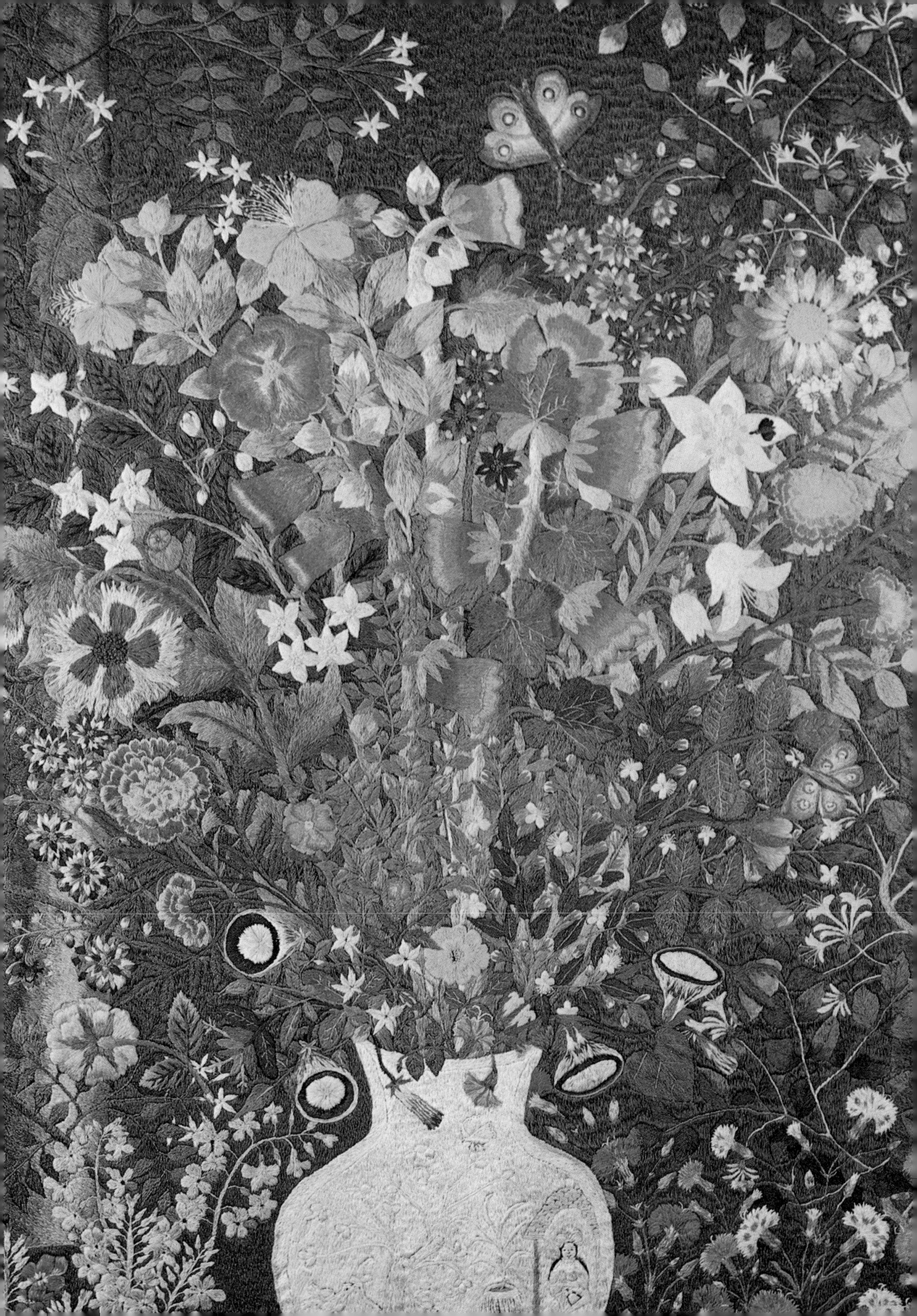

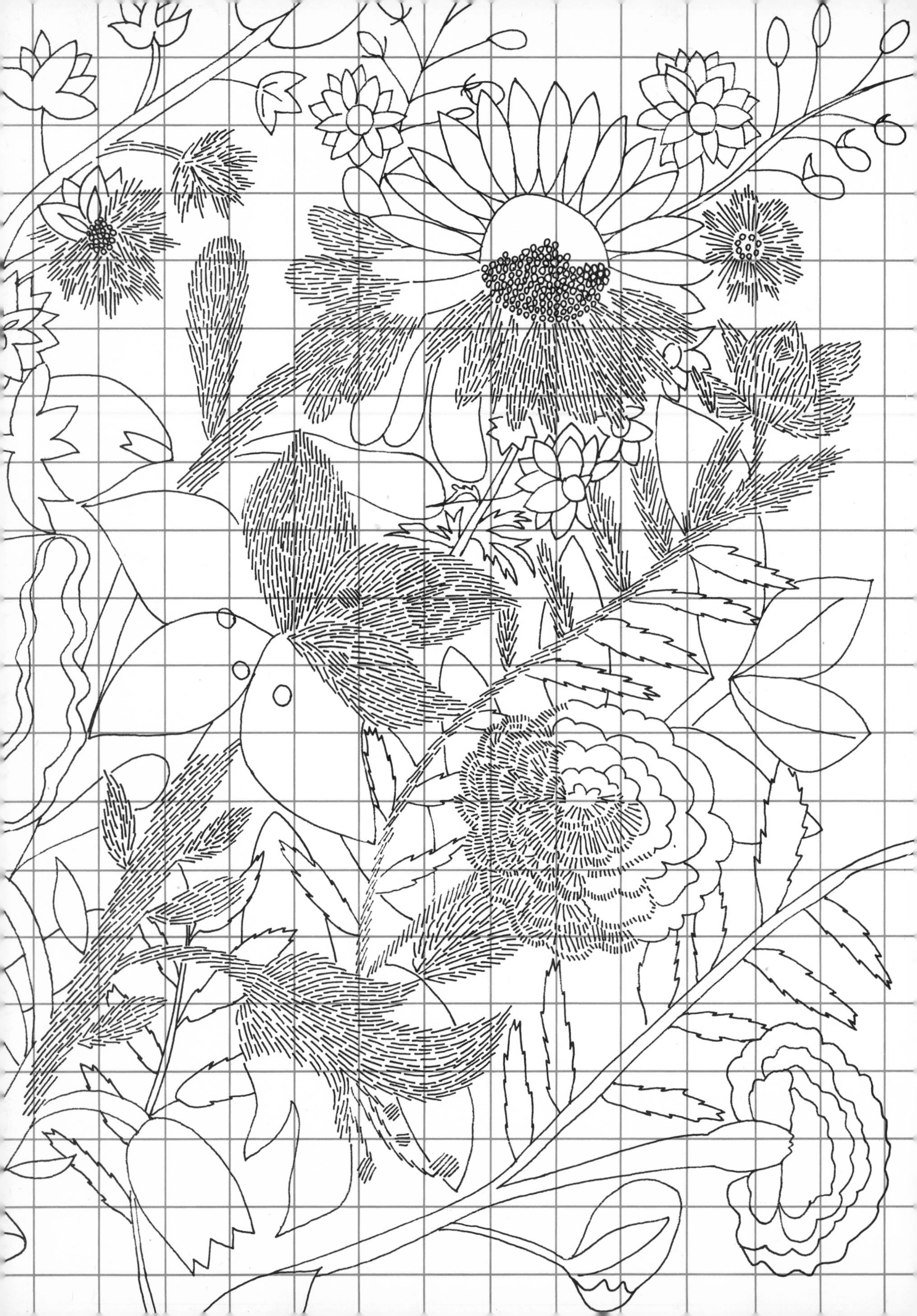

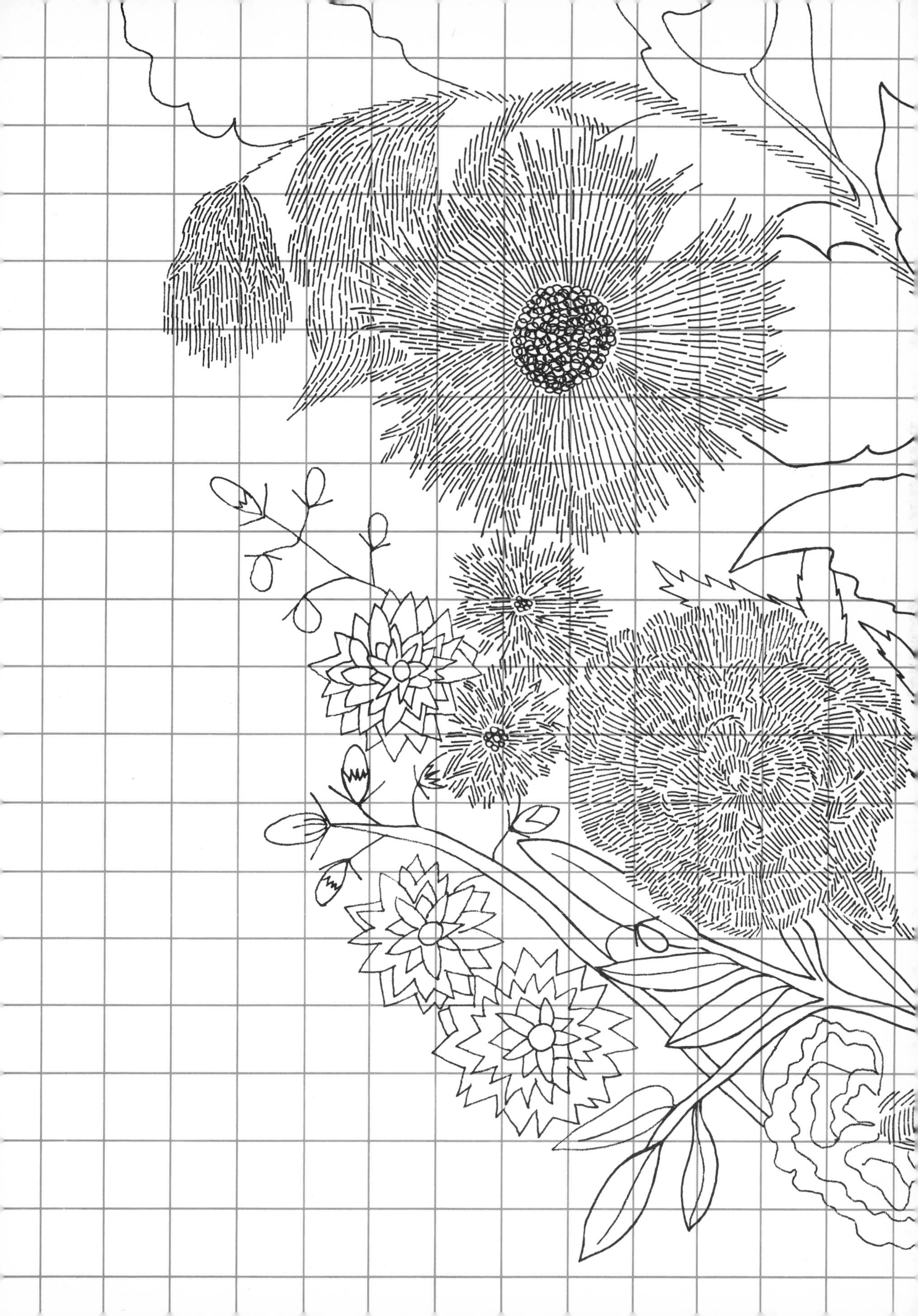

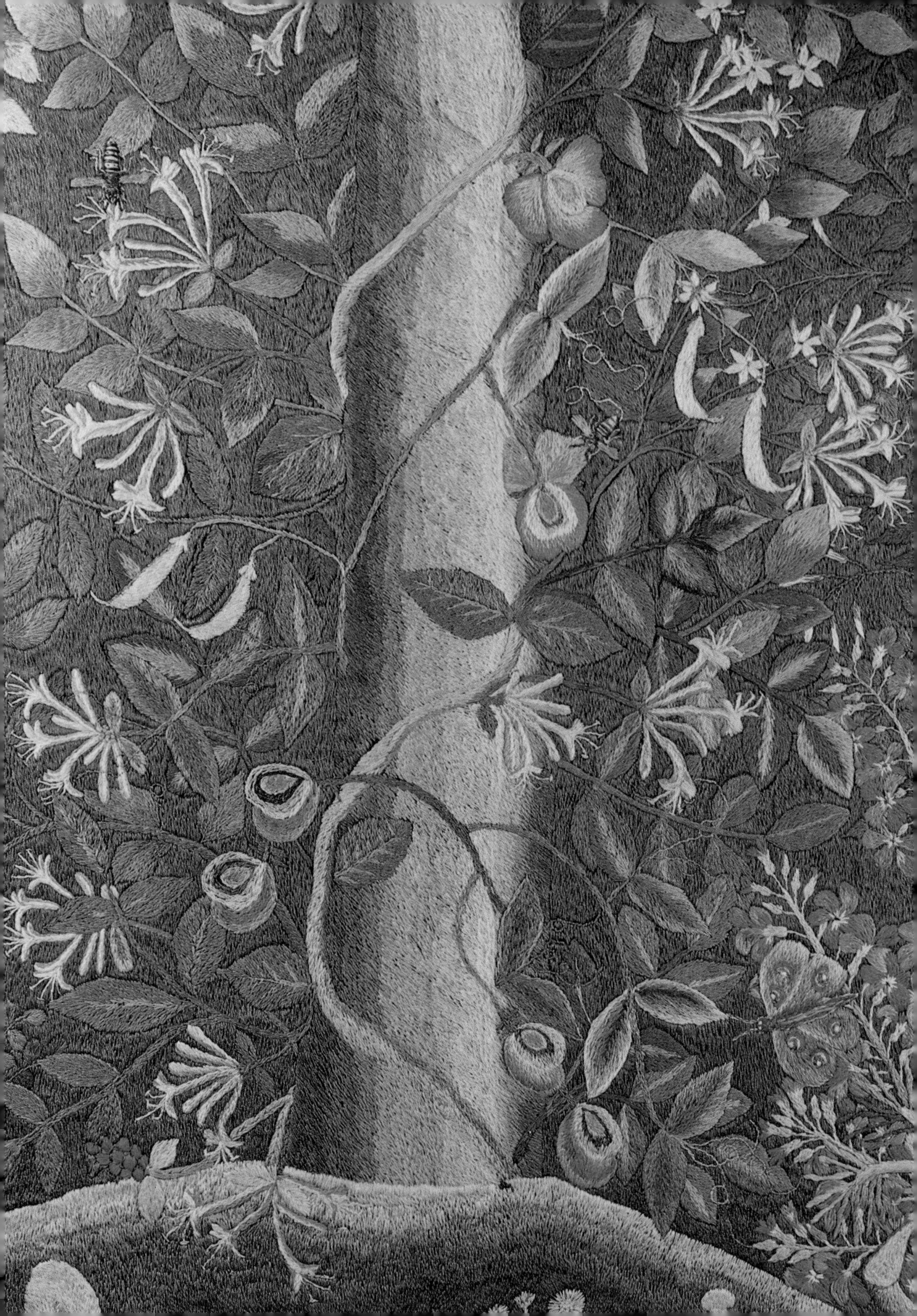

Bocland hanging detail; 1825–50

Here, a detail from the hanging (page 129) shows the popular honeysuckle motif, the vines trailing round the tree trunk. Notice too the tiny bees and the dainty butterfly.

Courtesy Victoria and Albert Museum, London

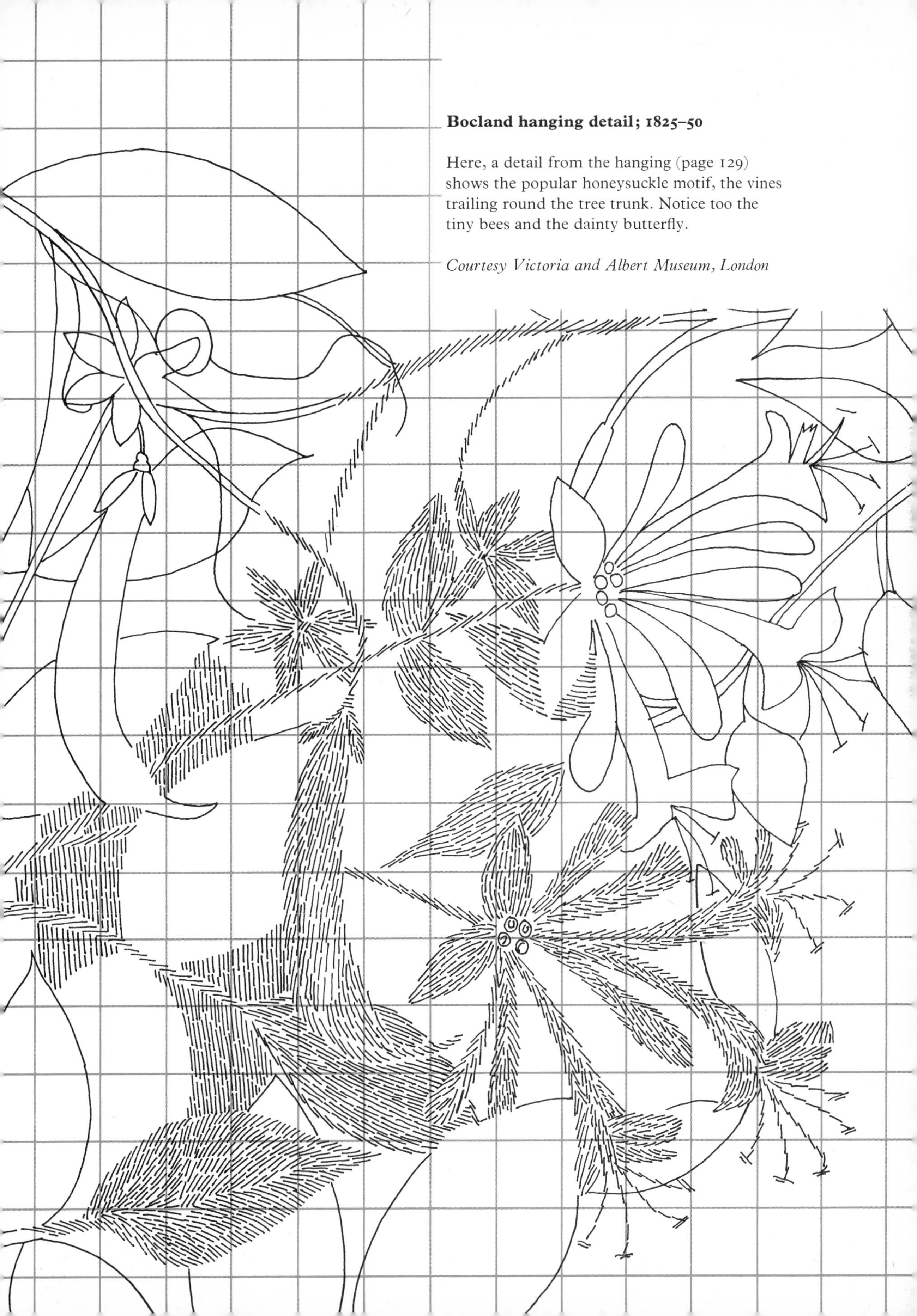

Bocland hanging detail; 1825–50

This detail from the hanging (page 129) is a
very alert-looking bird, and a butterfly of the
same colour as the preceding.

Courtesy Victoria and Albert Museum, London

136

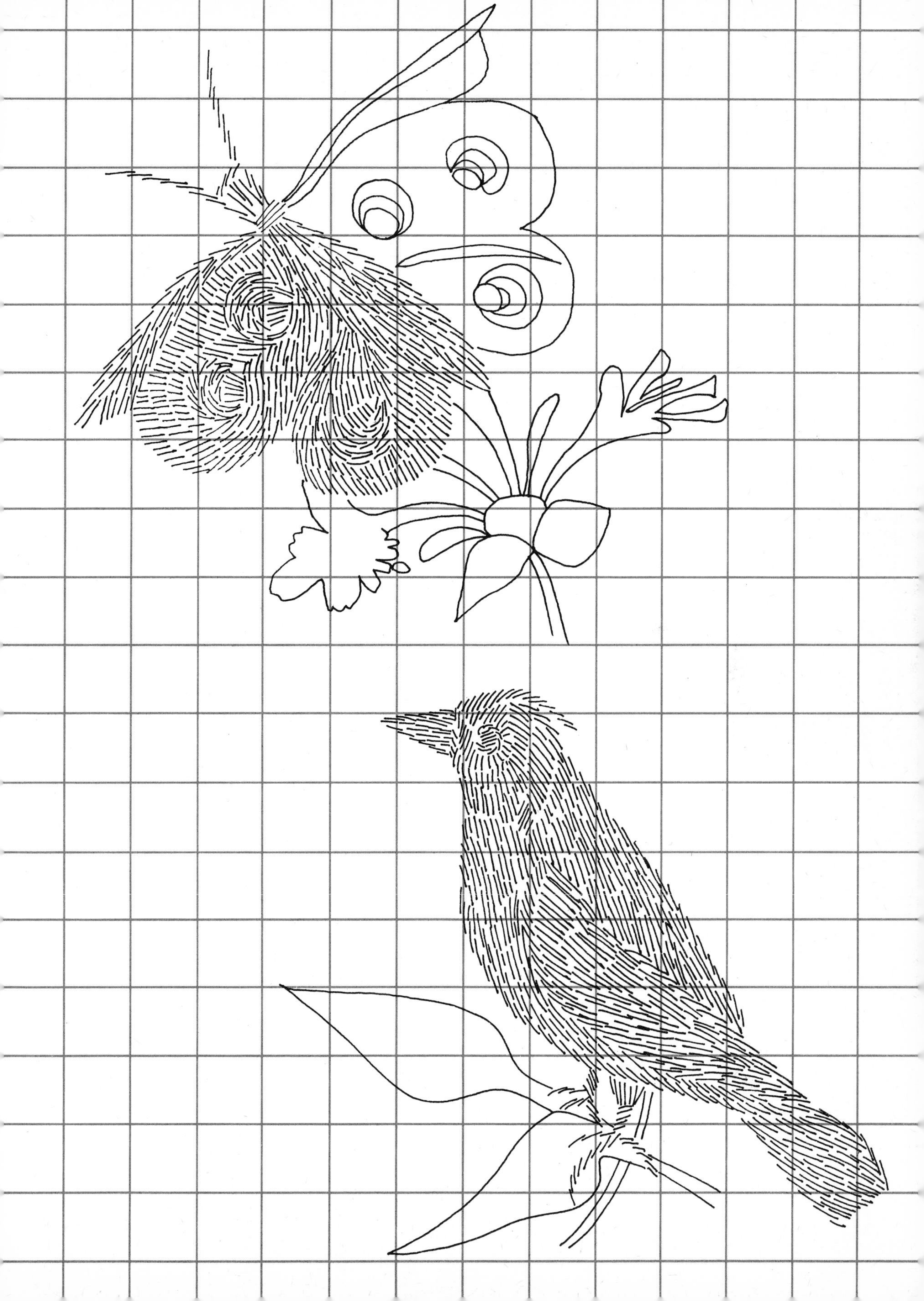

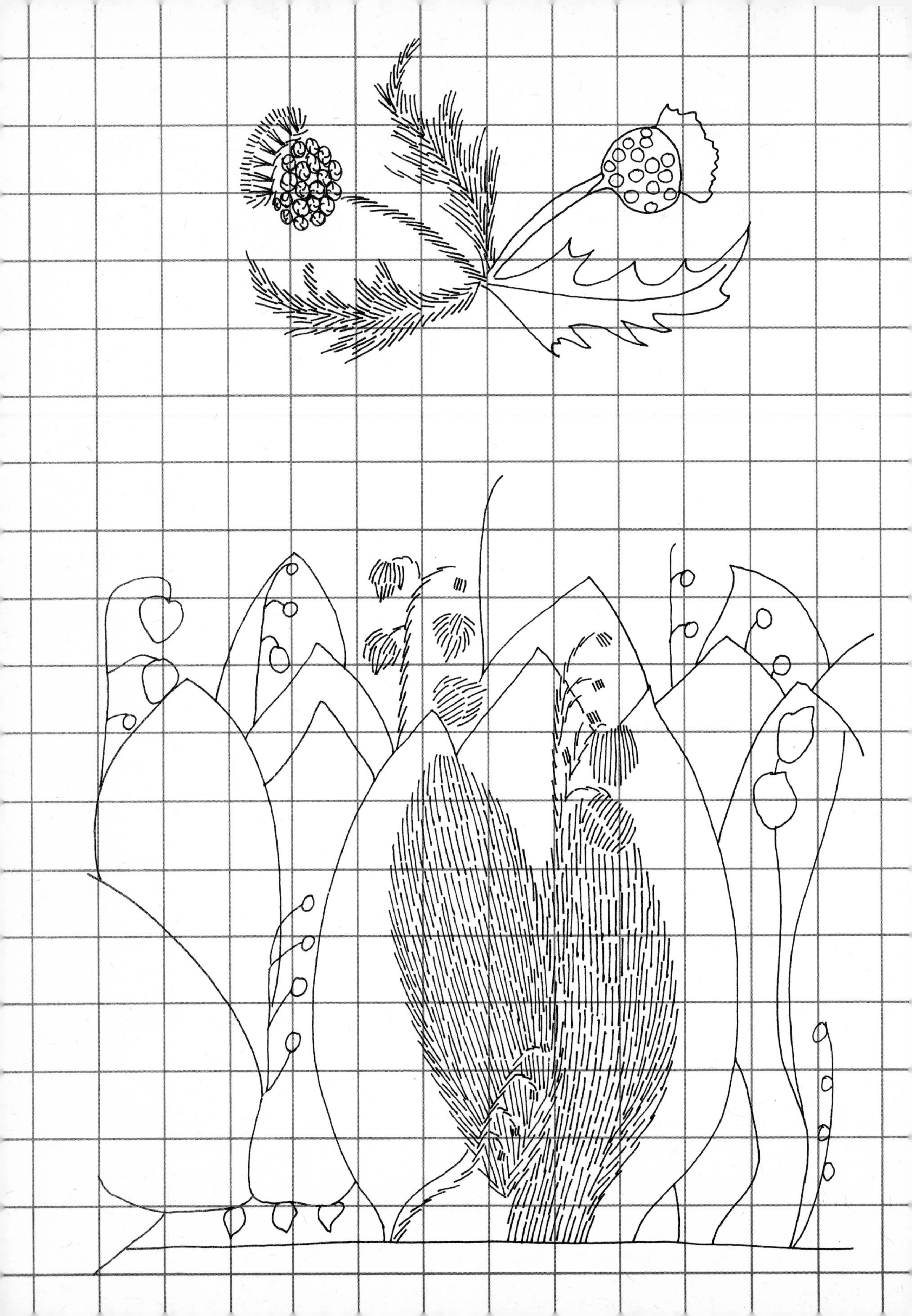

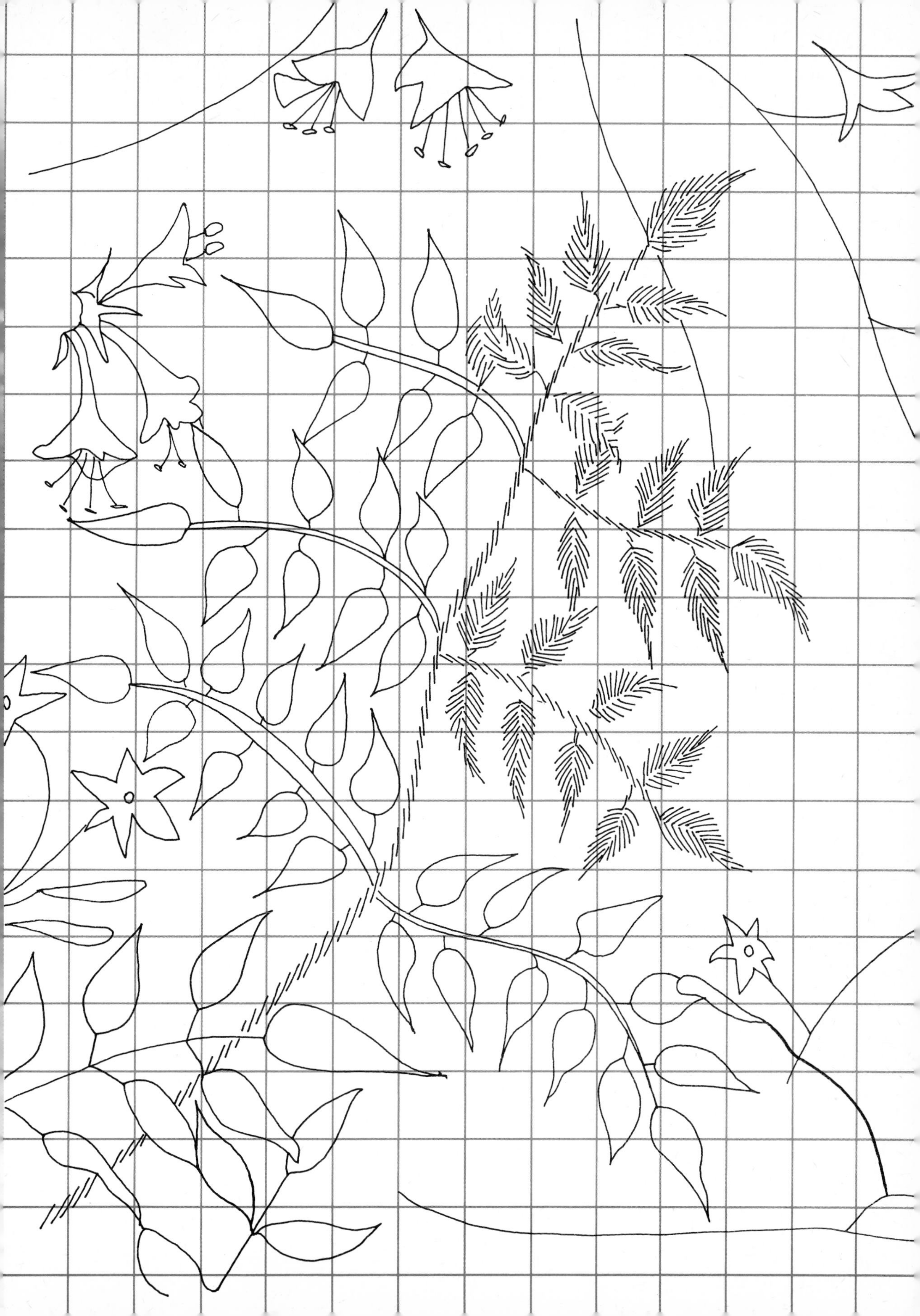

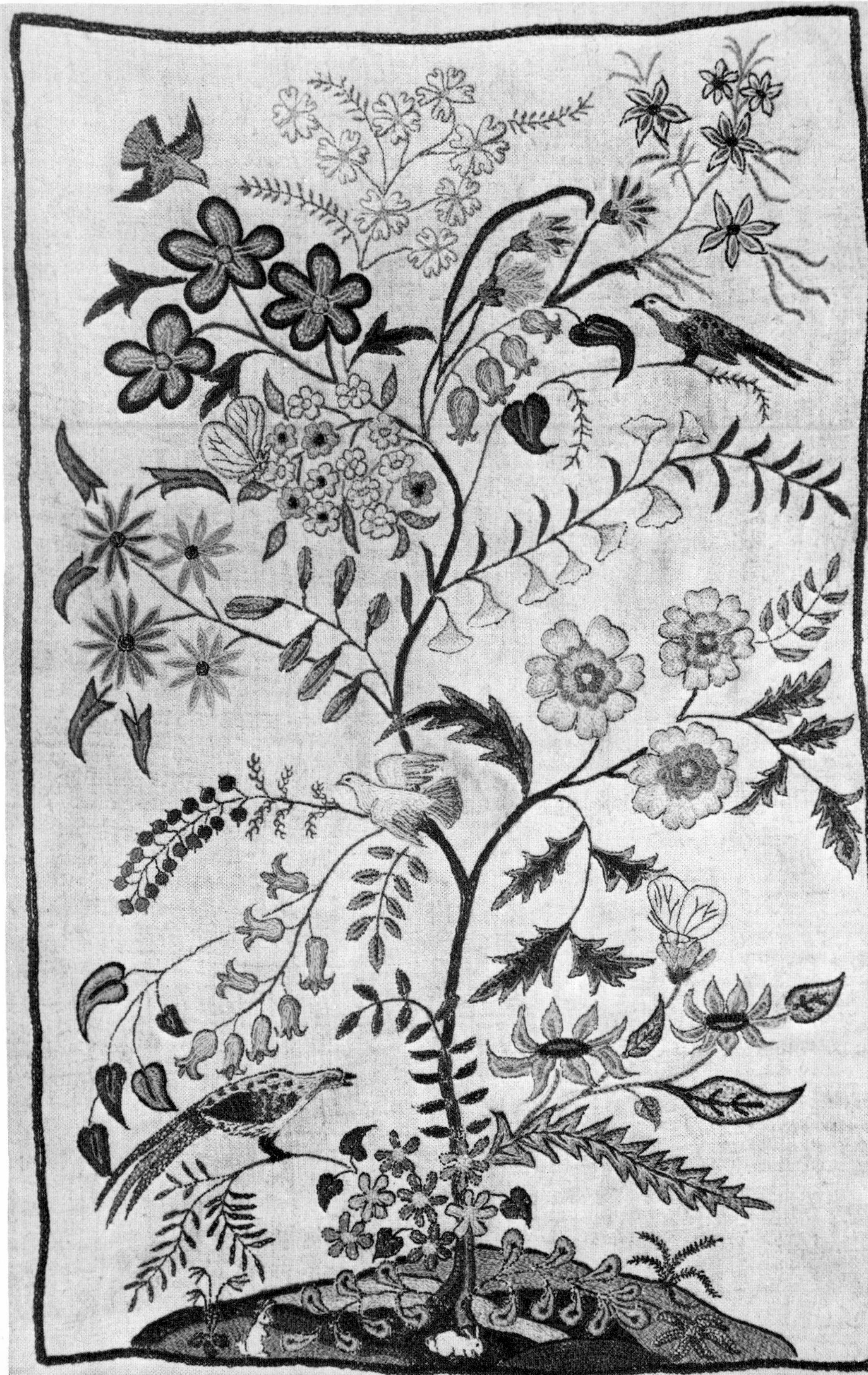

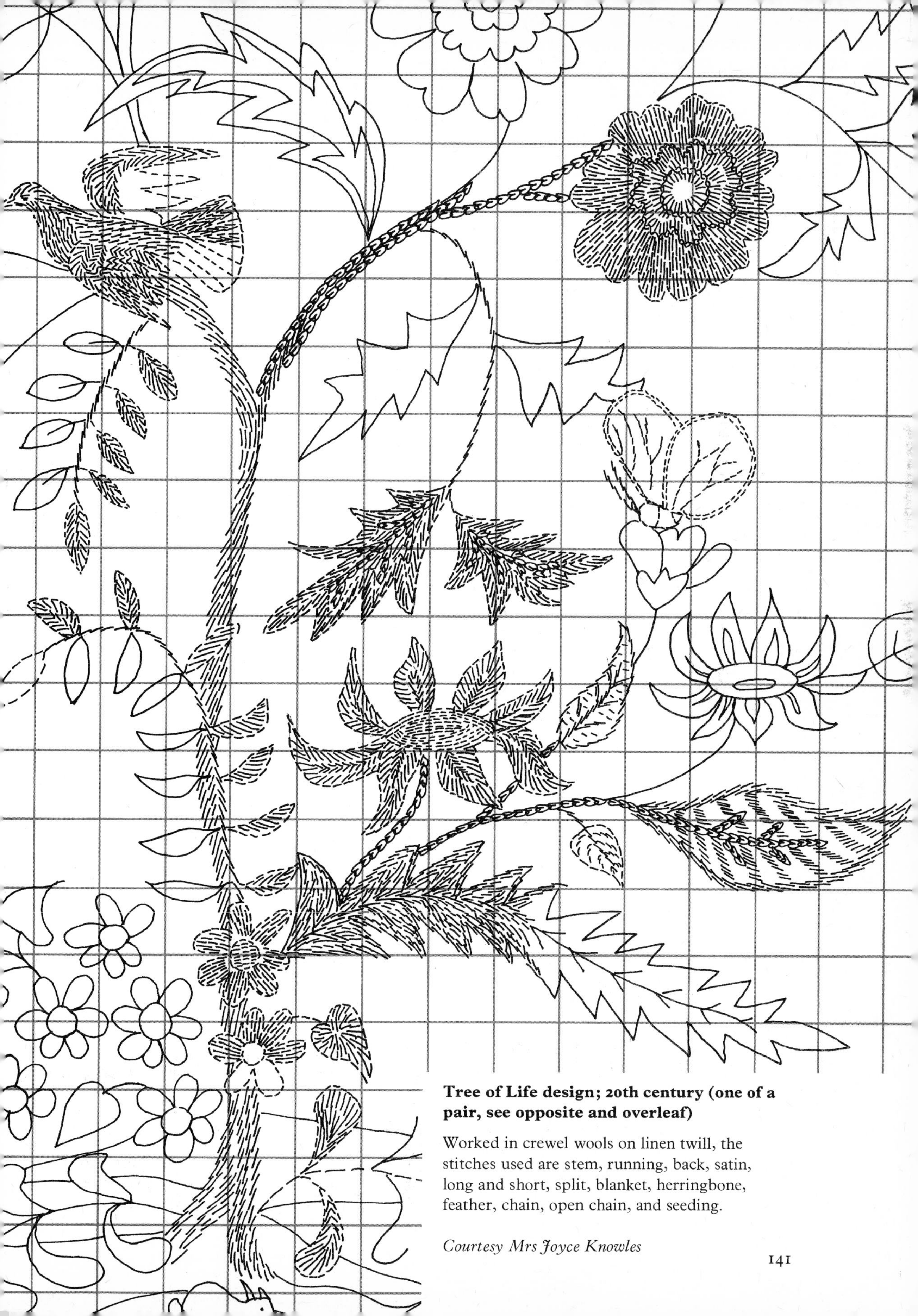

Tree of Life design; 20th century (one of a pair, see opposite and overleaf)

Worked in crewel wools on linen twill, the stitches used are stem, running, back, satin, long and short, split, blanket, herringbone, feather, chain, open chain, and seeding.

Courtesy Mrs Joyce Knowles

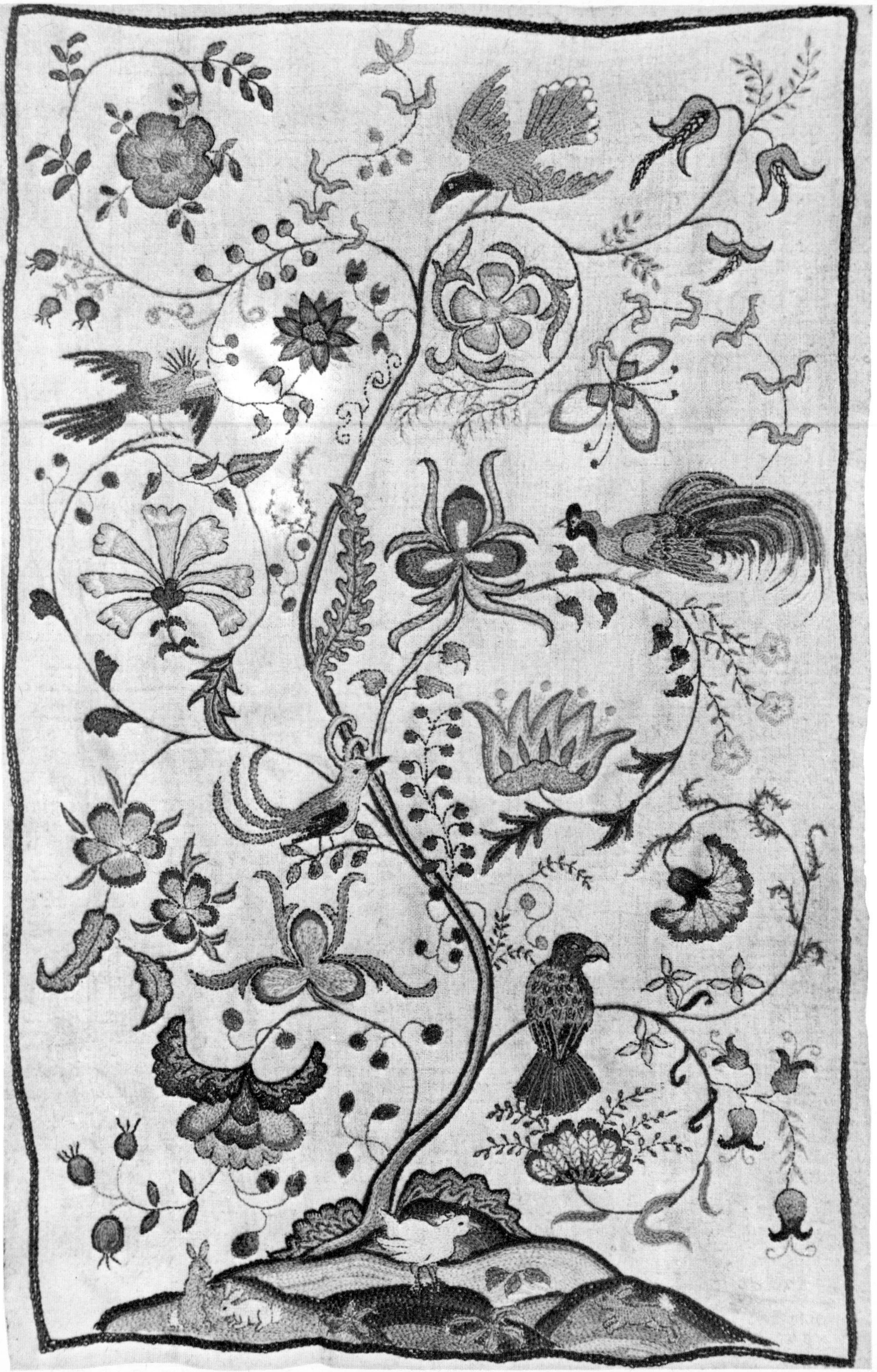

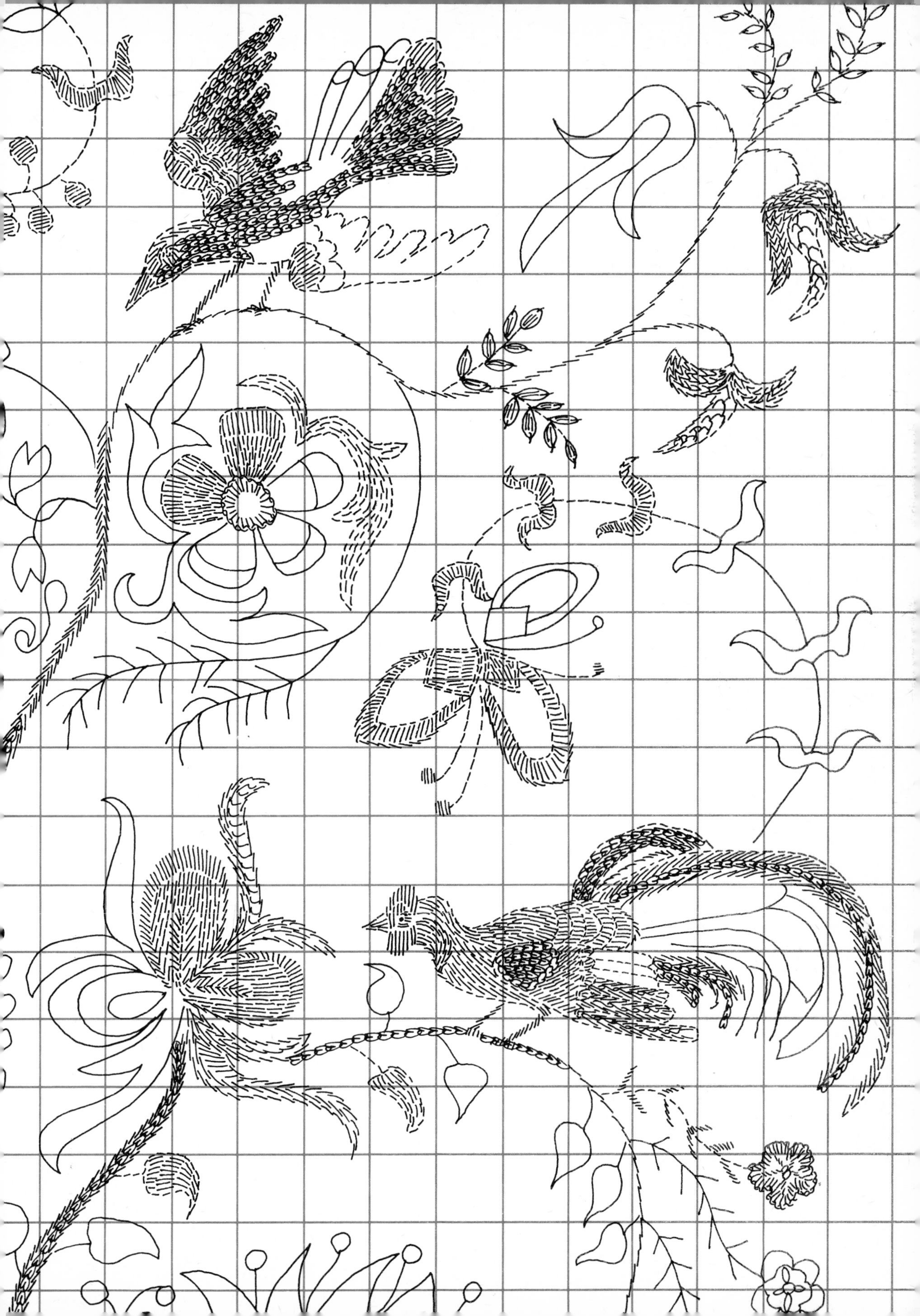

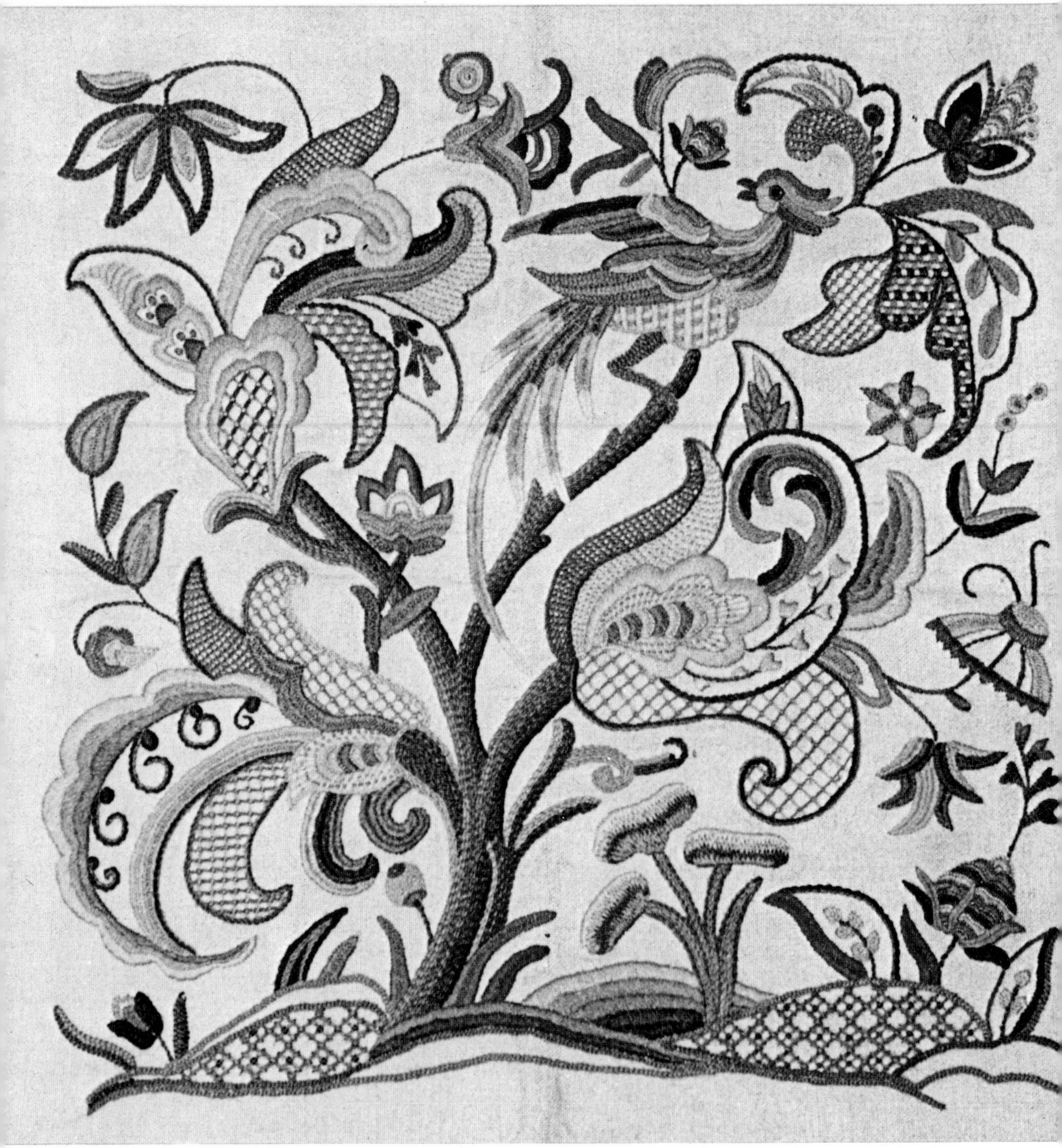

Cushion or chair cover; early 20th century

This is a conventional design of decided character and distinctive quality. The Tree of Life is worked in broad satin stitch and it supports wide leaves and large blossoms, which give an opportunity for a variety of stitches suitable for portraying line. Stitches include long and short, outline, trellis, satin, and chain, and filling stitches. Massed satin stitch is used to depict one hillock at the base of the design with the other two in a form of trellis-type couching.

Courtesy The Rachel Kay-Shuttleworth Collection, Gawthorpe Hall, Lancashire

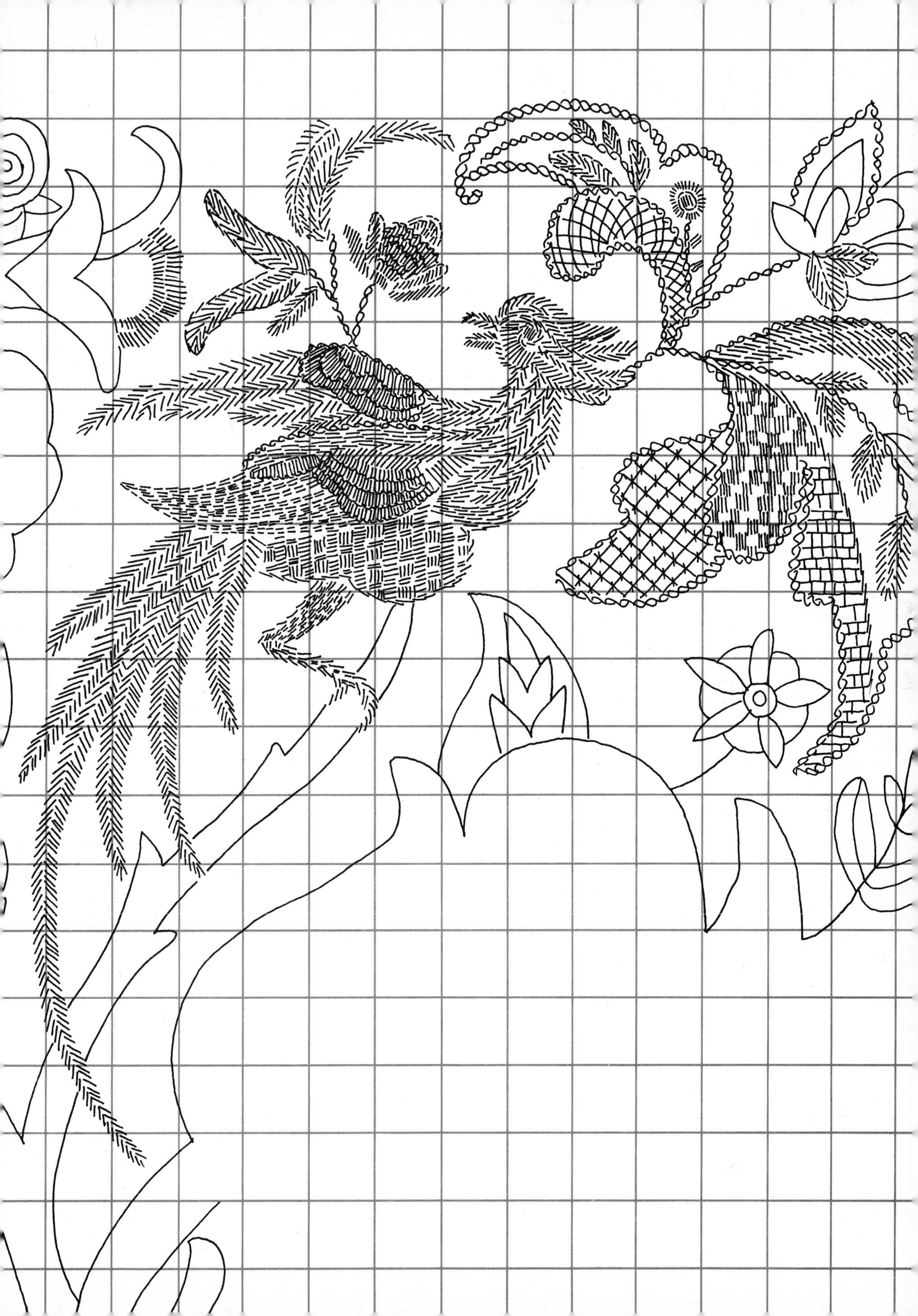

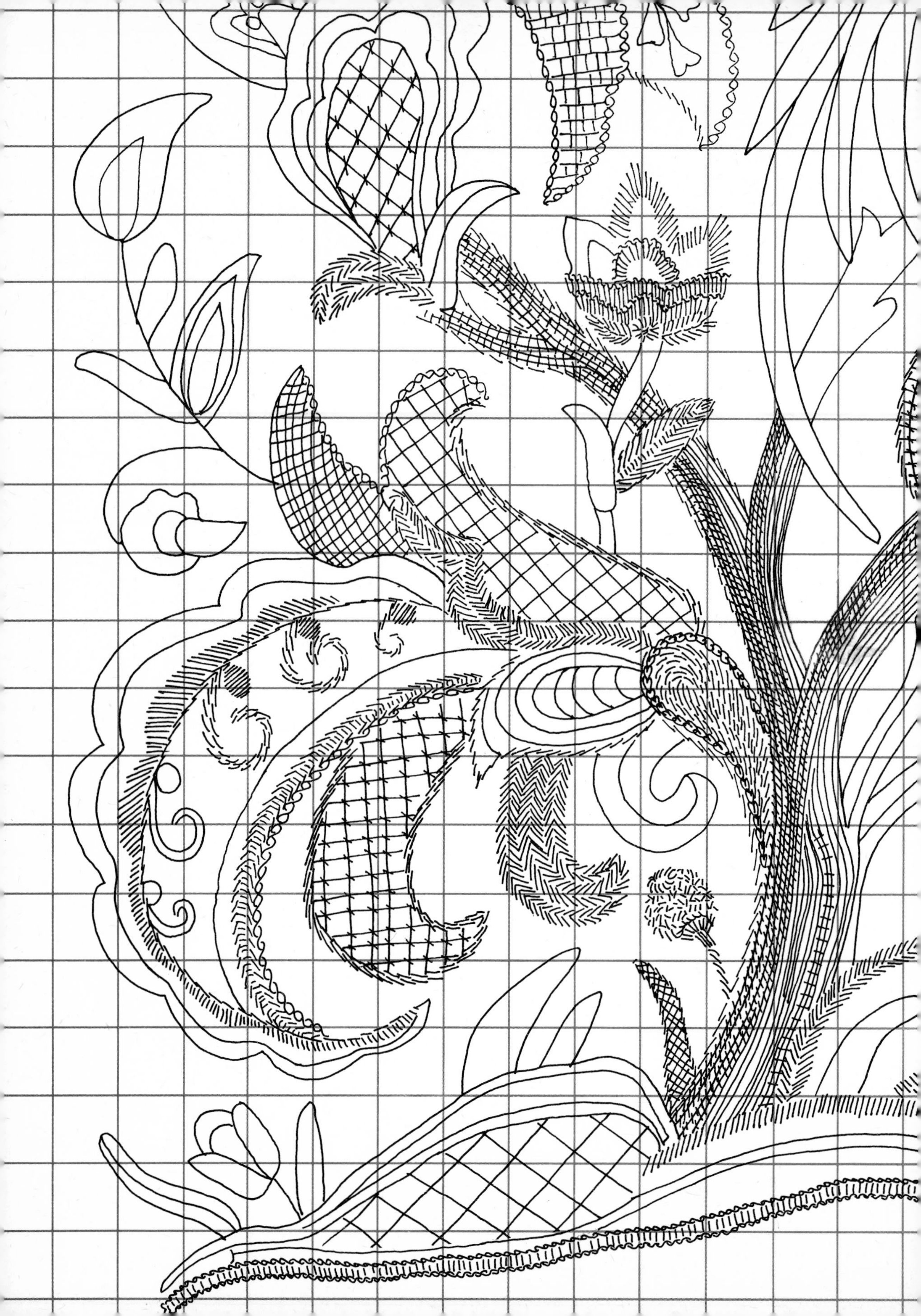

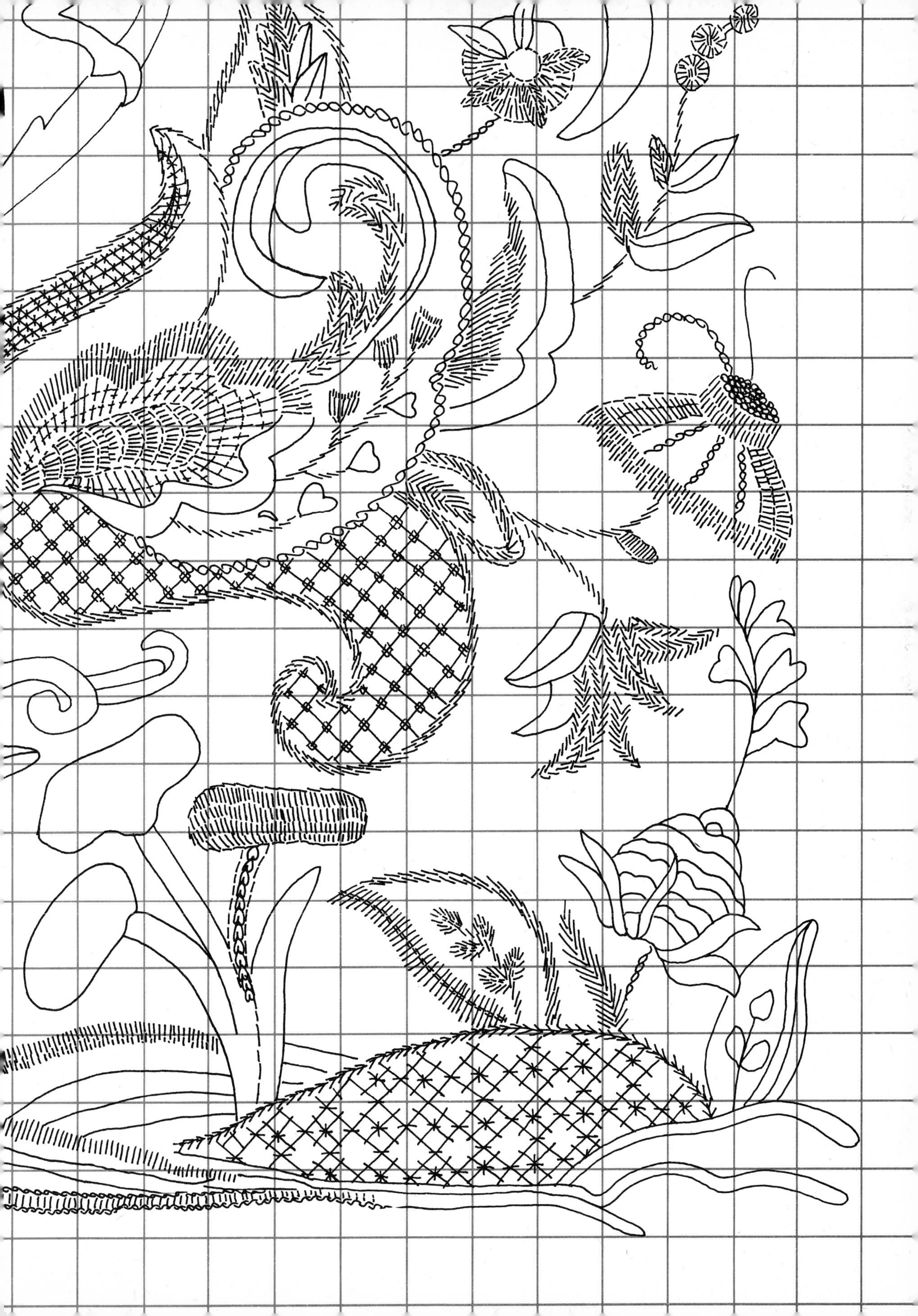

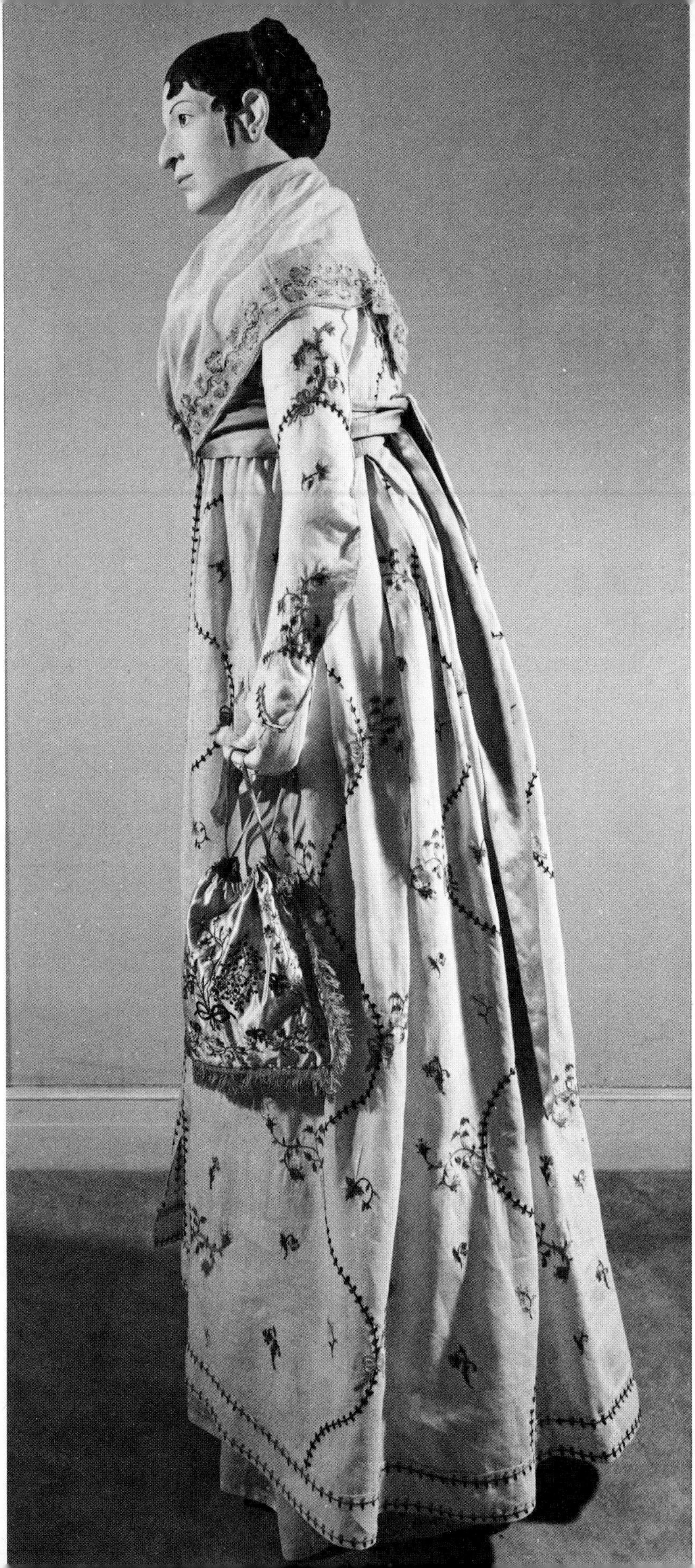

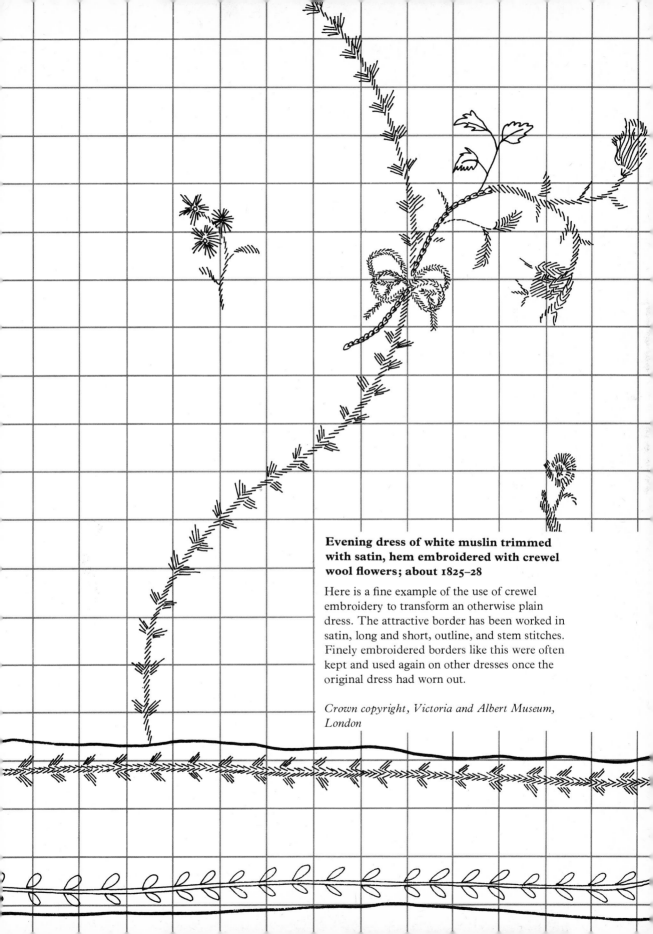

**Evening dress of white muslin trimmed
with satin, hem embroidered with crewel
wool flowers; about 1825–28**

Here is a fine example of the use of crewel
embroidery to transform an otherwise plain
dress. The attractive border has been worked in
satin, long and short, outline, and stem stitches.
Finely embroidered borders like this were often
kept and used again on other dresses once the
original dress had worn out.

*Crown copyright, Victoria and Albert Museum,
London*

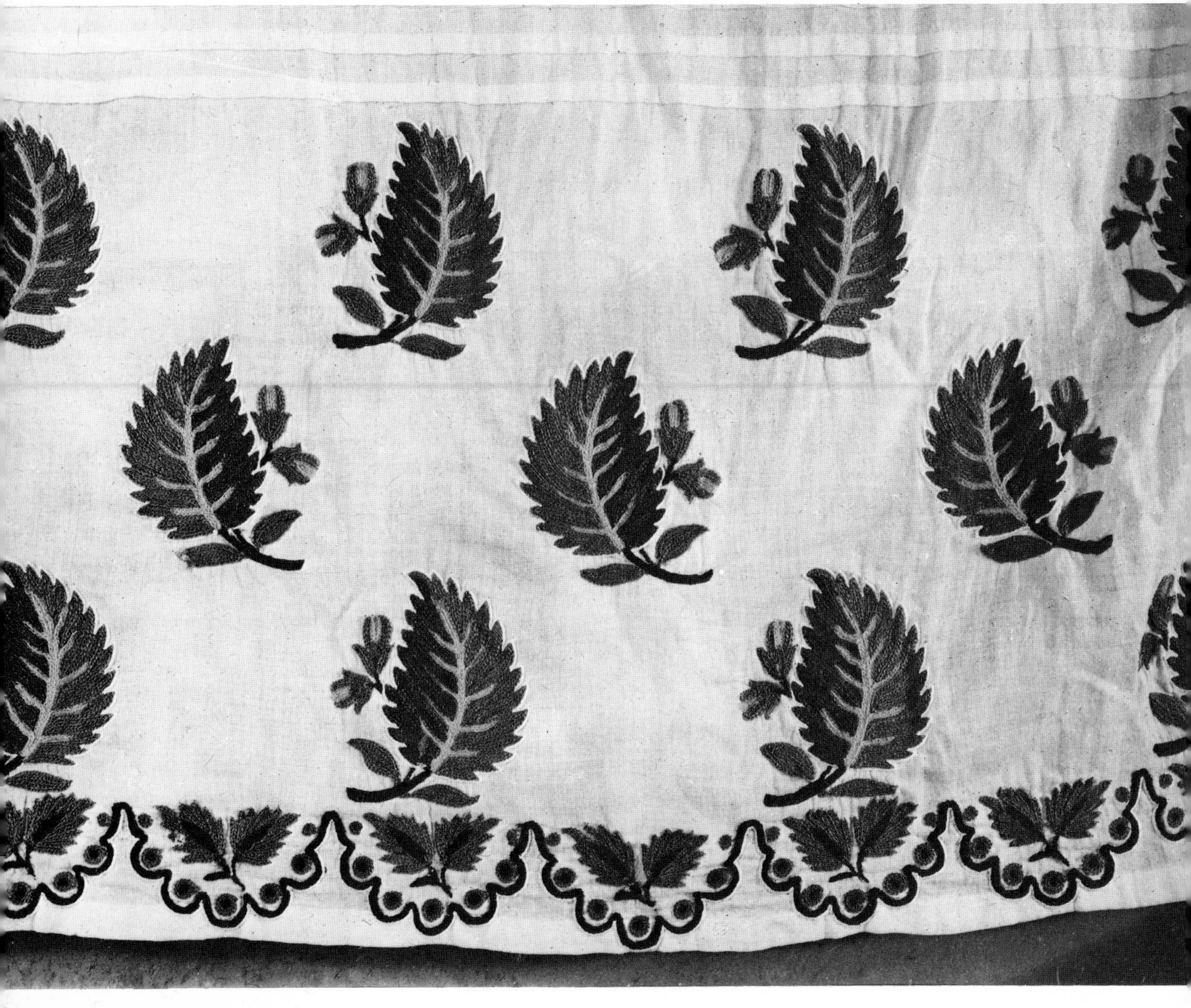

Detail of dress embroidered round the hem with crewel wools; about 1816–18

This dress in white cambric has been embroidered round the hem in a design of leaves and scallops in shades of green and plum. It is a fine piece of crewel embroidery and uses chain stitch.

Courtesy City Museums, Norwich

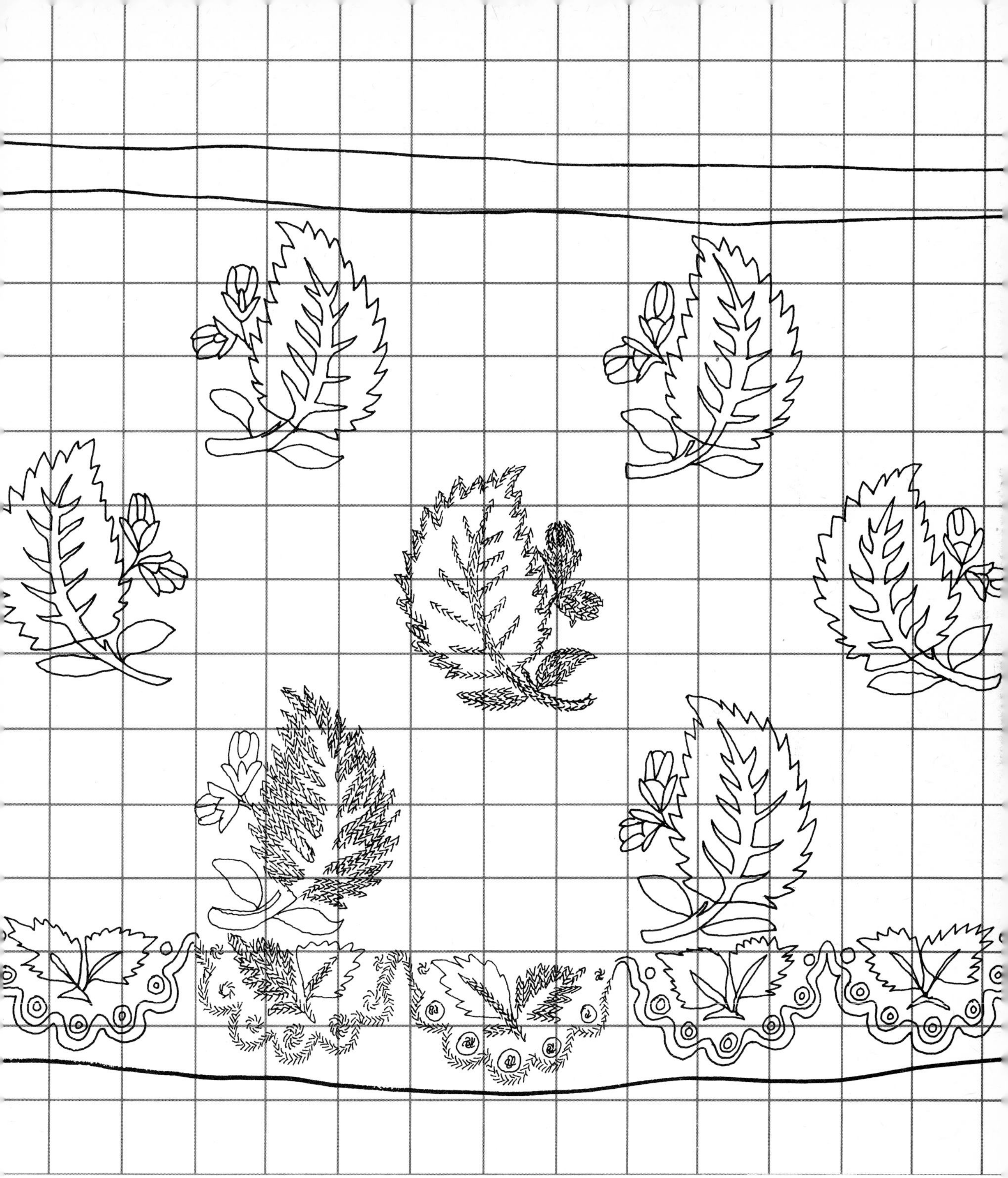

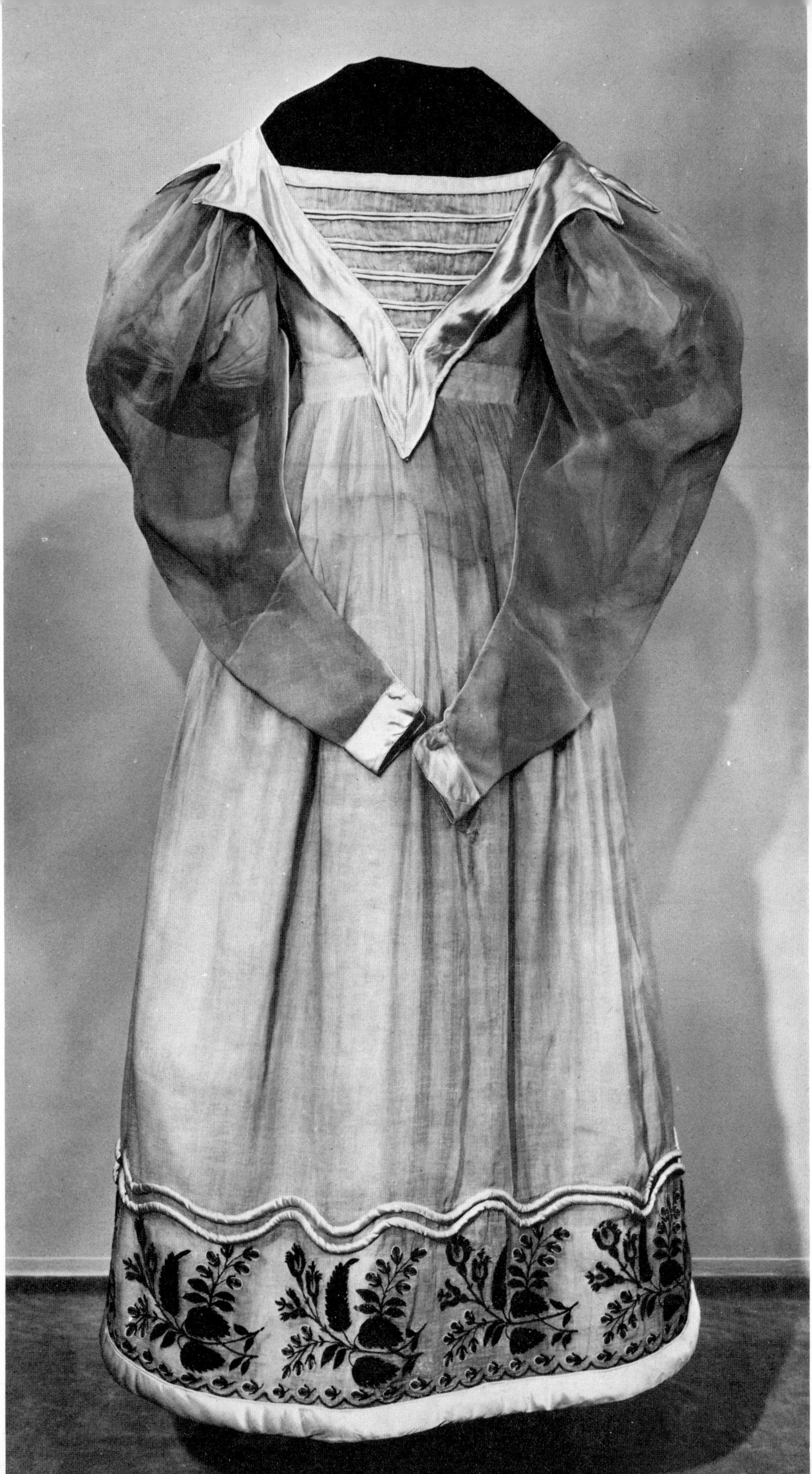

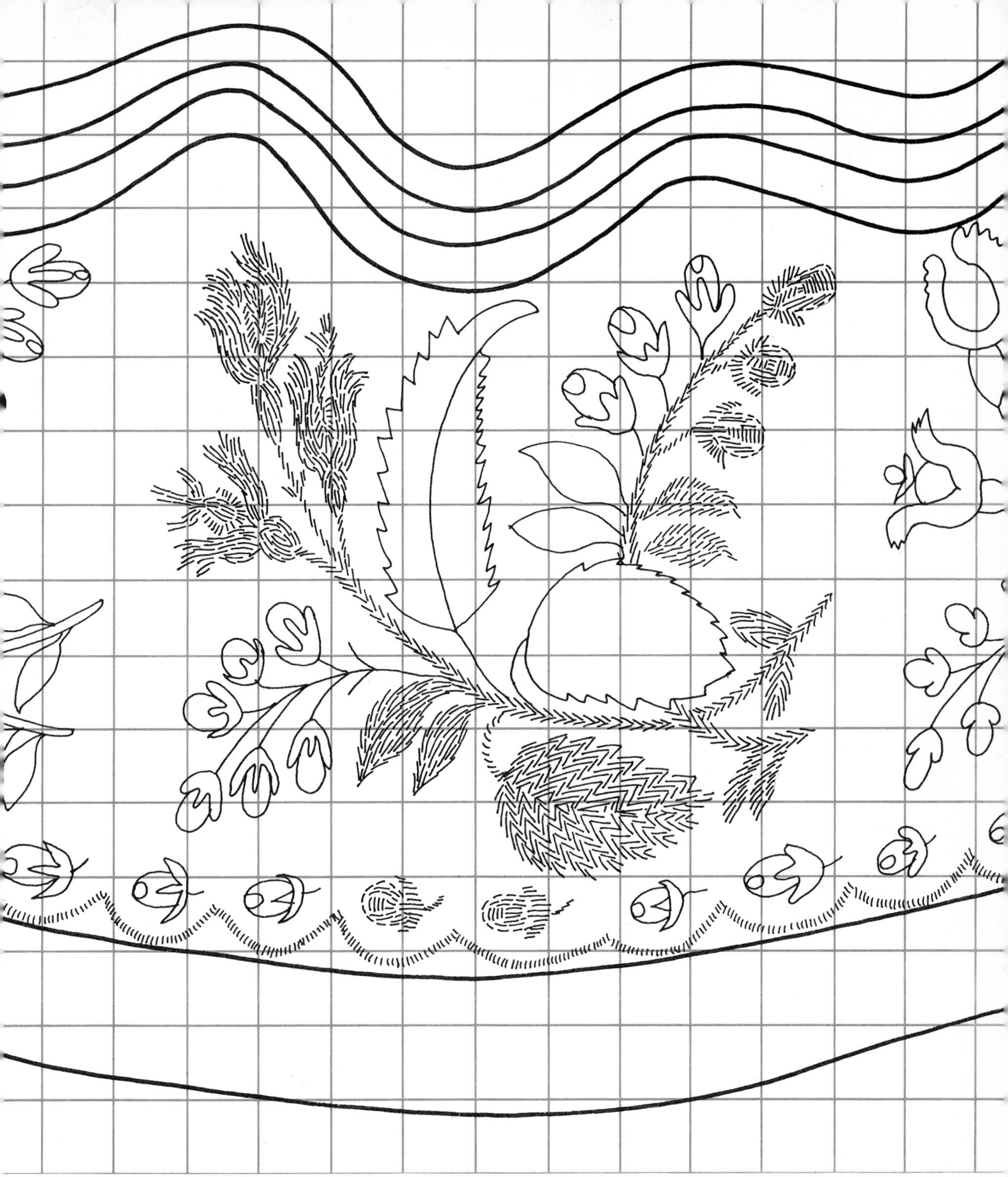

Informal muslin dress with detail of floral pattern embroidered in crewel wools; 1790s

The pattern of dainty floral sprays is unified by the trailing leafy stems evenly spaced on the skirt of the dress and again around the hem. Stitches include chain, stem, outline, satin, and long and short.

Courtesy The Museum of Costume, Bath

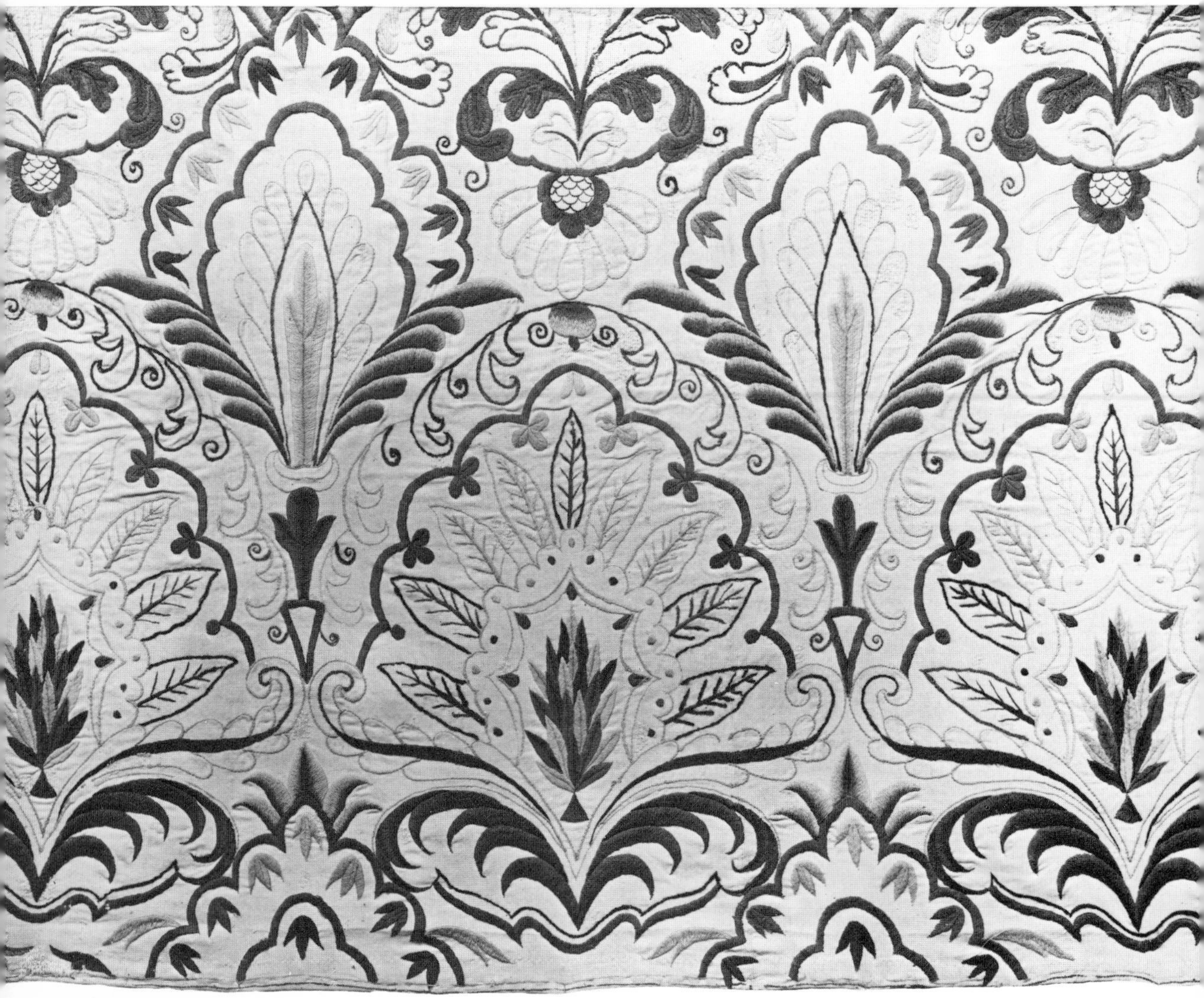

Curtain embroidered in crewel wools on cotton and linen twill; late 17th century

Characteristic of 17th-century design are the well-defined scalloped motifs covering the background material almost entirely. A repeat pattern of leaves and sprays, it is suitable for display on a large curtain. There is an interpretation of the popular wide acanthus leaf.

Depth is introduced by working the bolder lines in broad satin stitch. The more delicate leaves within the motifs have their outlines in stem stitch and lighter veining in outline stitch which relieves any tendency to heaviness in the embroidering of sprays and tendrils.

The drawing is one unit of the whole design, and can be repeated as many times as necessary. The bold lines and registration marks indicate the start of adjacent units.

Crown copyright, Victoria and Albert Museum, London

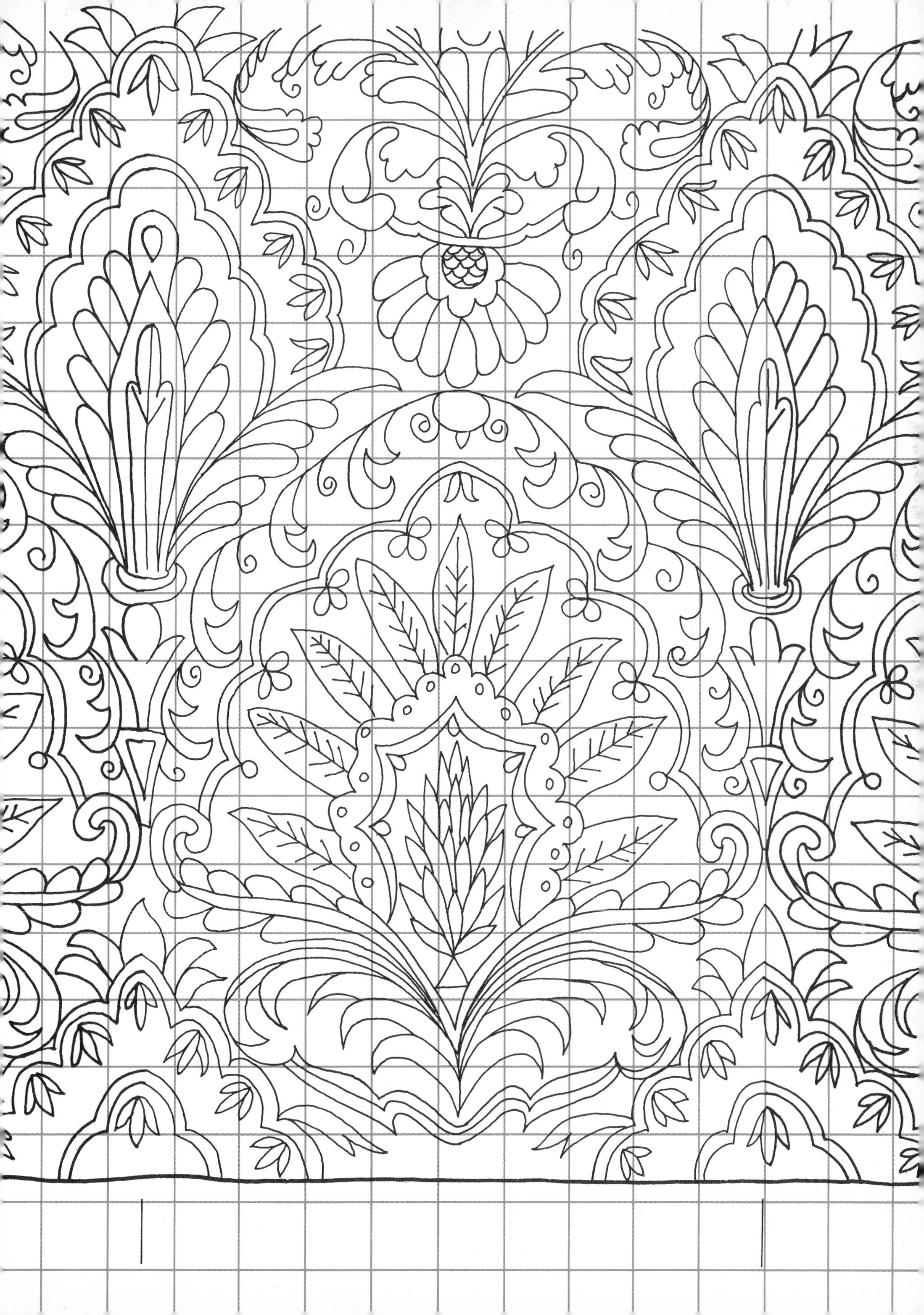

List of illustrations

(page numbers given)

9   Linen hanging, Egyptian, 4th to 5th century AD

10   Portion of the Bayeux tapestry, 11th to 12th century

25   Wall hanging, about 1675

28 29   Curtain border, detail from the bed furnishings (page 32)

32   (top and bottom) Bed furnishings for a four-poster, 1908–18

36 37   Panel called 'The Travellers', 20th century

38 39   Panel by May Morris, late 19th century

42   Elizabethan embroidery, 16th century

44   Part of a hanging, 18th century

46   Apron, 18th century

49   Detail from the floral spray (page 52)

51   Detail of floral motif from the bed furnishings (page 32)

52   Floral spray from the border of the bed curtain (page 54)

54   Detail from a bed curtain, late 17th to mid 18th century

56   Leaf motif, Jacobean design

58   Hanging, mid 17th century

62   Curtain, late 17th century

64   Foliate border, mid 17th century

68   Detail of woman's dress, late 17th century

72   Curtain, about 1696

76   Screen of the Four Elements, 1879

80   Stump-work panel, 17th century

82   Panel of St Francis of Assisi, 20th century

84   Panel of a medieval scene, 20th century

86   Floral spray and bird, 1910

89   Brown owl design, modern

91   Two parrots, details from the bed furnishings (page 32)

92   Part of an apron, Queen Anne period

94   External pocket for a woman, about 1720–60

96   (top) Floral panel, 20th century

96   (bottom) Cushion cover, 1902

100   Flowers in a vase or basket, about 1750

104   Bed curtains and valances by Abigail Pett, late 17th century

108   Detail of the Abigail Pett bed hanging (page 104)

110   Panel for a screen, about 1890

112   Girl's dress, 18th century

114   Bodice, late 17th century

116 117   Settee cover, 20th century

122   Curtain, late 17th century

126   Workbag, 1699

129   The Bocland hanging, 1825–50

131   Vase, details from the Bocland hanging (page 129)

134   Bird and butterfly, detail from the Bocland hanging (page 129)

136   Honeysuckle motif, detail from the Bocland hanging (page 129)

140   Tree of Life design (one of a pair), 20th century

142   Tree of Life design (one of a pair), 20th century

144   Cushion or chair cover, early 20th century

148   Border of evening dress, about 1825–28

150   Detail of dress, about 1816–18

152   Informal dress with floral pattern, 1790s

154   Curtain, late 17th century

Acknowledgements

The following photographers were commissioned for this book (photograph page numbers given):

C. Cannings   129, 131, 134, 136

Coe of Norwich   49, 52, 54

Dorchester Studios   82, 84, 140, 142

Michael R. Dudley, Oxford   42, 64, 86

Desmond Tripp Studios, Bristol   94, 126, 152

Grateful thanks are due to J. and P. Coats (UK) Limited of Glasgow for their kind permission to reproduce line drawings of stitches from the booklet *100 Embroidery Stitches*; these appear on pages 18–22.

Further reading

BERNER, I., *Embroidery Stitches, An Illustrated Guide*, New York 1968

CAVE, O., *English Folk Embroidery*, London 1965, New York 1966

DAVIS, M., *The Art of Crewel Embroidery*, London and New York 1962

DIGBY, G. F. W., *Elizabethan Embroidery*, London 1963

DONELLY, B. H., *The Crewel Needlepoint World*, New York 1973

EVANS, R., *Embroidery from Traditional English Patterns*, Massachusetts 1971

HUGHES, T., *English Domestic Needlework*, London 1961

JONES, M. E., *A History of Western Embroidery*, London 1969

JOURDAIN, M. A., *The History of English Secular Embroidery*, London 1910

KENDRIC, A. F., *English Embroidery*, London 1904

    English Needlework, rev. ed. by WARDLE, P., London 1967 (1st pub. 1933)

LEVEY, S. M., *Embroidery of the 19th Century*, New York 1971

MARSHALL, F. and H., *Old English Embroidery*, London 1894

MORRIS, B. J., *The History of English Embroidery*

    Victorian Embroidery, London 1962

NEVINSON, J. L., *Catalogue of English Domestic Embroidery*, London 1950

SCHUETTE, M. and MILLER, C. S., *Pictorial History of Embroidery*, New York 1964

SNOOK, B., *Embroidery Stitches*, London 1963

    English Historical Embroidery, London 1960

SWAIN, M., *Historical Needlework*, London and New York 1970

THOMAS, M., *Dictionary of Embroidery Stitches*, London 1974 (1st pub. 1934)

WILSON, E., *Craft of Crewel Embroidery*, New York 1971

    Crewel Embroidery, London 1964, New York 1962

100 Embroidery Stitches (J. & P. Coats), Glasgow 1967

Guide to English Embroidery (Victoria and Albert Museum), London 1970